MULTIPLE INTELLIGENCES

MULTIPLE INTELLIGENCES

New Horizons

HOWARD GARDNER

BASIC
BOOKS

A Member of the Perseus Books Group
New York

A catalog-in-publication record for this book is available from the Library of Congress.
ISBN 10: 0-465-04768-8
ISBN 13: 978-0-465-04768-0

21   20   19   18   17   16   15

CONTENTS

Contents

INTRODUCTION

My research in developmental and neuropsychology, which led to the theory of multiple intelligences (MI), began in the early 1970s. The main lines of the theory had been completed by 1980, and my book *Frames of Mind: The Theory of Multiple Intelligences* appeared in the fall of 1983. Though my editor and publisher had high expectations for the book, I don't think anyone anticipated the attention that these ideas would initially attract, particularly among educators, or the keen and continuing interest twenty-five years later in many regions of the world.

During the decade that followed, I became involved in a variety of educational projects that emanated, in one way or another, from MI theory. For the time being, I avoided an explicit compendium or revision of the theory. In 1993, I issued *Multiple Intelligences: The Theory in Practice*, a collection in which I reviewed the major points of the theory and reported on several educational experiments. Shortly thereafter, I began explicitly to address some of the misunderstandings and misuses of the theory. In *Intelligence Reframed* (1999), I provided a brief update of the theory; responded to many questions, conceptions, and criticisms; and explored the relationship of intelligence to other concepts that I had subsequently investigated, such as leadership, creativity, and morality.

In the middle of the first decade of the twenty-first century, twenty-five years after the idea of multiple intelligences first gelled, I determined to provide an up-to-date and comprehensive overview of MI theory. The result is the present volume.

Multiple Intelligences: New Horizons is divided into three parts. In part I, "The Theory," I provide both a summary of the original theory (chapter 1) and a discussion of major ways in which the theory has changed (chapter

2): the addition of intelligences, the distinction between domains and intelligences, and the differentiation among various conceptions of intellect. There follows a delineation of the relation between intelligence and other human cognitive capacities, such as creativity, expertise, and genius (chapter 3). I describe the way in which a psychological study evolved into a set of educational issues and recommendations (chapter 4). And I answer major questions and criticisms that have been raised in the past quarter century (chapter 5).

In part II, "Educational Perspectives," I focus on specific educational experiments. These range from efforts to nurture and assess the intelligences of preschoolers to attempts to inculcate in adolescents the major disciplinary ways of thinking, including those featured in the arts (chapters 6–9). Also included is a discussion of the major purpose of education (chapter 8) and a detailed proposal for new forms of assessment (chapter 10).

In part III, "New Vistas," I turn my attention to an emerging view of intelligence that takes into account the different social and cultural contexts in which young persons grow up (chapter 11). There follows a consideration of how ideas of multiple intelligences are being used and could be further implemented at the workplace (chapter 12). The final essay (chapter 13) looks toward the future: the direction of research on intelligence, new sources of information about the intelligences, the changing audiences for MI theory, and the place of the theory in a rapidly changing, increasingly globalized world.

Much of the material in this book is new; some of it was adapted from my 1993 book or from other writings. The essays have been ordered so that the book can be read from cover to cover. For the most part, I have replaced redundancies with references to earlier chapters; but on occasion, I permit a modest amount of repetition for ease of reading.

As will be apparent, MI theory and practice have taken on lives of their own. There are literally hundreds of books, hundreds of dissertations, and thousands of scholarly and popular articles on the theory. Hundreds, if not thousands, of schools all over the world claim to be implementing MI ideas. I do not even try to keep up with these works and enterprises, although I hope that the most important and most intriguing efforts will come to my attention. In an appendix to this book, I list some of the most important efforts and provide an up-to-date bibliography of my own writings on the topic.

From the beginning, my work on multiple intelligences could not have been pursued without an overwhelming amount of support, human as well as financial. Dozens of students and collaborators, both at Harvard and elsewhere, have helped to push forward the agenda of multiple intelligences and have contributed important ideas and practices. I have also benefited from many funders, both private foundations and generous individuals. It is not possible to thank everyone, but I do list the major funders in a separate acknowledgments section. At this time, I single out for special mention Seana Moran, an outstanding student who helped me with all facets of the preparation of this book and took the lead in drafting the chapter on MI at the workplace; my assistant Lindsay Pettingill who has worked deftly with Seana and me in the preparation of materials; my other assistant, Christian Hassold, who is always willing to lend one of his many skilled extra hands; my editor, Jo Ann Miller, Editorial Director of Basic Books; John J. Guardiano, my copy editor; Felicity Tucker, in charge of production; and, with great appreciation, my colleagues Mindy Kornhaber, Mara Krechevsky, and Joseph Walters, who allowed me to reprint materials that we coauthored.

MULTIPLE INTELLIGENCES

PART ONE
THE THEORY

Chapter 1

In a Nutshell

The original scene: Paris, 1900—La Belle Epoque. The city fathers approached a talented psychologist named Alfred Binet with an unusual request. Families were flocking to the capital city from the provinces, and a good many of their children were having trouble with their schoolwork. Could Binet devise some kind of a measure that would predict which youngsters would succeed and which would fail in the primary grades of Paris schools?

As almost everybody knows, Binet succeeded. In short order, his discovery came to be called the "intelligence test"; his measure, the IQ, for "intelligence quotient" (mental age divided by chronological age and multiplied by 100). Like other Parisian fashions, the IQ soon made its way to the United States, where it enjoyed a modest success until World War I, when it was used to test over one million American military recruits. With its use by the U.S. armed forces, and with America's victory in the conflict, Binet's invention had truly arrived. Ever since, the IQ test has looked like psychology's biggest success—a genuinely useful scientific tool.

What is the vision that led to the excitement about IQ? At least in the West, people had always relied on intuitive assessments of how smart other people were. Now intelligence seemed to be quantifiable. Just as you could measure someone's actual or potential height, now, it seemed, you could measure someone's actual or potential intelligence. We had one dimension of mental ability along which we could array everyone.

The search for the perfect measure of intelligence has proceeded apace. Here, for example, are some quotations from an advertisement for one such test:

Need an individual test which quickly provides a stable and reliable estimate of intelligence in four or five minutes per form? Has three forms? Does not depend on verbal production or subjective scoring? Can be used with the severely physically handicapped (even paralyzed) if they can signal yes or no? Handles two-year-olds and superior adults with the same short series of items and the same format? Only $16.00 complete.

Now, a single test that can do all that is quite a claim. American psychologist Arthur Jensen suggests that we could look at reaction time to assess intelligence: a set of lights go on; how quickly can the subject react? British psychologist Hans Eysenck recommends that investigators of intelligence look directly at brain waves. And with the advent of the gene chip, many look forward to the day when we can glance at the proper gene locus on the proper chromosome, read off someone's IQ, and confidently predict his or her life chances.

There are also, of course, more sophisticated versions of the IQ test. One of them is the SAT. Its name originally stood for Scholastic Aptitude Test, although with the passage of time, the meaning of the acronym has been changed—it became the Scholastic Assessment Test, and, more recently, it has been reduced to the plain old SAT—just the initials. The SAT purports to be a similar kind of measure, and if you add up a person's verbal and math scores, as is often done, you can rate him or her along a single intellectual dimension. (Recently, writing and reasoning components have been added.) Programs for the gifted, for example, often use that kind of measure; if your IQ is in excess of 130, you're admitted to the program—if it's 129, "Sorry, no room at the inn."

Along with this one-dimensional view of how to assess people's minds comes a corresponding view of school, which I will call the "uniform view." A uniform school features a core curriculum—a set of facts that everyone should know—and very few electives. The better students, perhaps those with higher IQs, are allowed to take courses that call on critical reading, calculation, and thinking skills. In the uniform school, there are regular assessments, using paper and pencil instruments, of the IQ or SAT variety. These assessments yield reliable rankings of people; the best and the brightest get into the better colleges, and perhaps—but only perhaps— they will also get better rankings in life. There is no question that this approach works well for certain people—schools such as Harvard and Stanford are eloquent testimony to that. Since this measurement and selection system is clearly meritocratic in certain respects, it has something to recommend it.

The uniform school sounds fair—after all, everyone is treated in the same way. But some years ago it occurred to me that this supposed rationale was completely unfair. The uniform school picks out and is addressed to a certain kind of mind—we might call it provisionally the IQ or SAT mind. I sometimes call it the mind of the future law professor. The more your mind resembles that of the legendary law professor Dr. Charles W. Kingsfield Jr., played on-screen by John Houseman in *The Paper Chase*, the better you will do in school and the more readily you will handle IQ-SAT-type measures. But to the extent that your mind works differently—and not that many of us are cut out to be law professors—school is certainly not fair to you.

I would like to present an alternative vision—one based on a radically different view of the mind, and one that yields a very different view of school. It is a pluralistic view of mind, recognizing many different and discrete facets of cognition, acknowledging that people have different cognitive strengths and contrasting cognitive styles. I introduce the concept of an individual-centered school that takes this multifaceted view of intelligence seriously. This model for a school is based in part on findings from sciences that did not even exist in Binet's time: cognitive science (the study of the mind) and neuroscience (the study of the brain). One such approach I have called the theory of multiple intelligences. Let me tell you something about its sources and claims to lay the groundwork for the discussions on education in the chapters that follow.

I introduce this new point of view by asking you to suspend for a moment the usual judgment of what constitutes intelligence, and let your thoughts run freely over the capabilities of human beings—perhaps those that would be picked out by the proverbial visitor from Mars. Your mind may turn to the brilliant chess player, the world-class violinist, and the champion athlete; certainly, such outstanding performers deserve special consideration. Are the chess player, violinist, and athlete "intelligent" in these pursuits? If they are, then why do our tests of "intelligence" fail to identify them? If they are not intelligent, what allows them to achieve such astounding feats? In general, why does the contemporary construct of intelligence fail to take into account large areas of human endeavor?

To approach these questions I introduced the theory of multiple intelligences (MI) in the early 1980s. As the name indicates, I believe that human cognitive competence is better described in terms of a set of abilities, talents, or mental skills, which I call *intelligences*. All normal individuals possess each of these skills to some extent; individuals differ in the degree of skill and in the nature of their combination. I believe this theory of intelligence may be more humane and more veridical than alternative views of intelligence and that it more adequately reflects the data of human "intelligent" behavior. Such a theory has important educational implications.

WHAT CONSTITUTES AN INTELLIGENCE?

The question of the optimal definition of intelligence looms large in my inquiry. And it is here that the theory of multiple intelligences begins to diverge from traditional points of view. In the classic psychometric view, intelligence is defined operationally as the ability to answer items on tests of intelligence. The inference from the test scores to some underlying ability is supported by statistical techniques. These techniques compare responses of subjects at different ages; the apparent correlation of these test scores across ages and across different tests corroborates the notion that the general faculty of intelligence, called g in short, does not change much with age, training, or experience. It is an inborn attribute or faculty of the individual.

Multiple intelligences theory, on the other hand, pluralizes the traditional concept. An intelligence is a computational capacity—a capacity to process a certain kind of information—that originates in human biology and human psychology. Humans have certain kinds of intelligences, whereas rats, birds, and computers foreground other kinds of computational capacities. An intelligence entails the ability to solve problems or fashion products that are of consequence in a particular cultural setting or community. The problem-solving skill allows one to approach a situation in which a goal is to be obtained and to locate the appropriate route to that goal. The creation of a cultural product allows one to capture and transmit knowledge or to express one's conclusions, beliefs, or feelings. The problems to be solved range from creating an end for a story to anticipating a mating move in chess to repairing a quilt. Products range from scientific theories to musical compositions to successful political campaigns.

MI theory is framed in light of the biological origins of each problem-solving skill. Only those skills that are universal to the human species are considered (again, we differ from rats, birds, or computers). Even so, the biological proclivity to participate in a particular form of problem solving must also be coupled with the cultural nurturing of that domain. For example, language, a universal skill, may manifest itself particularly as writing in one culture, as oratory in another culture, and as the secret language composed of anagrams or tongue twisters in a third.

Given the desideratum of selecting intelligences that are rooted in biology and that are valued in one or more cultural settings, how does one actually identify an intelligence? In coming up with the list, I reviewed evidence from various sources: knowledge about normal development and development in gifted individuals; information about the breakdown of cognitive skills under conditions of brain damage; studies of exceptional populations, including prodigies, savants, and autistic children; data about the evolution of cognition over the millennia; cross-cultural accounts of cognition; psychometric studies, including examinations of correlations among tests; and psychological training studies, particularly measures of transfer and generalization across tasks. Only those candidate intelligences that satisfied all or a healthy majority of the criteria were selected as bona fide intelligences. A more complete discussion of each of these criteria and of the intelligences that were initially identified may be found in *Frames of Mind* (1983b), especially chapter 4. In that foundational book I also consider how the theory might be disproved and compare it with competing theories of intelligence. An update of some of these discussions is presented in *Intelligence Reframed* (1999a), and in the chapters that follow.

In addition to satisfying the aforementioned criteria, each intelligence must have an identifiable core operation or set of operations. As a neurally based computational system, each intelligence is activated or triggered by certain kinds of internal or external information. For example, one core of musical intelligence is the sensitivity to pitch relations, and one core of linguistic intelligence is the sensitivity to the phonological features of a language.

An intelligence must also be susceptible to encoding in a symbol system—a culturally contrived system of meaning that captures and conveys important forms of information. Language, picturing, and mathematics are but three nearly worldwide symbol systems that are necessary for human survival and productivity. The relationship of an intelligence to a human symbol system is no accident. In fact, the existence of a core computational capacity anticipates the actual or potential creation of a symbol system that exploits that capacity. While it may be possible for an intelligence to develop without an accompanying symbol system, a primary characteristic of human intelligence may well be its gravitation toward such an embodiment.

THE ORIGINAL SET OF INTELLIGENCES

Having sketched the characteristics and criteria for an intelligence, I turn now to a brief consideration of each of the intelligences that were proposed in the early 1980s. I begin each sketch with a thumbnail biography of a person who demonstrates an unusual facility with that intelligence. (These biographies were developed chiefly by my longtime colleague Joseph Walters.) The biographies illustrate some of the abilities that are central to the fluent operation of a given intelligence. Although each biography illustrates a particular intelligence, I do not wish to imply that in adulthood intelligences operate in isolation. Indeed, except in abnormal individuals, intelligences always work in concert, and any sophisticated adult role will involve a melding of several of them. Following each biography is a survey of the various sources of data that support each candidate as an intelligence.

Musical Intelligence

When Yehudi Menuhin was three years old, his parents smuggled him into San Francisco Orchestra concerts. The sound of Louis Persinger's violin so entranced the young child that he insisted on a violin for his birthday and Louis Persinger as his teacher. He got both. By the time he was ten years old, Menuhin was an international performer (Menuhin, 1977).

Violinist Yehudi Menuhin's musical intelligence manifested itself even before he had touched a violin or received any musical training. His powerful reaction to that particular sound and his rapid progress on the instrument suggest that he was biologically prepared in some way for a life in music. Menuhin is one example of evidence from child prodigies that support the claim that there is a biological link to a particular intelligence. Other special populations, such as autistic children who can play a musical instrument beautifully but who cannot otherwise communicate, underscore the independence of musical intelligence.

A brief consideration of the evidence suggests that musical skill passes the other tests for an intelligence. For example, certain parts of the brain play important roles in the perception and production of music. These areas are characteristically located in the right hemisphere, although musical skill is not as clearly localized in the brain as natural language. Although the particular susceptibility of musical ability to brain damage depends on the degree of training and other individual characteristics, there is clear evidence that amusia, or a selective loss of musical ability, occurs.

Music apparently played an important unifying role in Stone Age (Paleolithic) societies. Birdsong provides a link to other species. Evidence from various cultures supports the notion that music is a universal faculty. Studies of infant development suggest that there is a "raw" computational ability in early childhood. Finally, musical notation provides an accessible and versatile symbol system. In short, evidence to support the interpretation of musical ability as an intelligence comes from many different sources. Even though musical skill is not typically considered an intellectual skill like mathematics, it qualifies under our criteria. By definition it deserves consideration; and in view of the data, its inclusion is empirically justified.

Bodily-Kinesthetic Intelligence

Fifteen-year-old Babe Ruth was playing catcher one game when his team was taking a "terrific beating." Ruth "burst out laughing" and criticized the pitcher loudly. Brother Mathias, the coach, called out, "All right, George, YOU pitch!" Ruth was stunned and nervous: "I never pitched in my life . . . I can't pitch." The moment was transformative, as Ruth recalls in his autobiography: "Yet, as I took the position, I felt a strange relationship between myself and that pitcher's mound. I felt, somehow, as if I had been born out there and that this was a kind of home for me." As sports history shows, he went on to become a great major league pitcher (and, of course, attained legendary status as a hitter) (Ruth, 1948, p. 17).

Like Menuhin, Babe Ruth was a prodigy who recognized his "instrument" immediately on his first exposure to it, before receiving any formal training.

Control of bodily movement is localized in the motor cortex, with each hemisphere dominant or controlling bodily movements on the contralateral side. In right-handers, the dominance for bodily movement is ordinarily found in the left hemisphere. The ability to perform movements when directed to do so can be impaired even in individuals who can perform the same movements reflexively or on a nonvoluntary basis. The existence of apraxia constitutes one line of evidence for a bodily-kinesthetic intelligence.

The evolution of specialized body movements is of obvious advantage to the species, and in human beings this adaptation is extended through the use of tools. Body movement undergoes a clearly defined developmental schedule in children; there is little question of its universality across cultures. Thus, it appears that bodily-kinesthetic "knowledge" satisfies many of the criteria for an intelligence.

The consideration of bodily-kinesthetic knowledge as "problem solving" may be less intuitive. Certainly carrying out a mime sequence or hitting a tennis ball is not solving a mathematical equation. And yet, the ability to use one's body to express an emotion (as in a dance), to play a game (as in a sport), or to create a new product (as in devising an invention) is evidence of the cognitive features of body usage. The specific computations required to solve a particular bodily-kinesthetic problem, hitting a tennis ball, are summarized by Tim Gallwey:

> In order to anticipate how and where to move the feet and whether to take the racket back on the forehand or backhand side, the brain must calculate within a fraction of a second the moment the ball leaves the server's racket approximately where it is going to land, and where the racket will intercept it. Into this calculation must be computed the initial velocity of the ball, combined with an input for the progressive decrease in velocity and the effect of wind and of spin, to say nothing of the complicated trajectories in-

volved. Then, each of these factors must be recalculated after the bounce of the ball to anticipate the point where contact will be made by the racket. Simultaneously, muscle orders must be given—not just once, but constantly refined on updated information. Finally, the muscles have to respond in cooperation with one another . . . Contact is made at a precise point that depends on whether the order was given to hit down the line or cross-court, an order not given until after a split-second analysis of the movement and balance of the opponent. . . . Even if you are returning the serve of an average player, you will have only about one second. Just to hit the ball is clearly a remarkable feat; to return it with consistency and accuracy is a mind-boggling achievement. Yet it is not uncommon. The truth is that everyone who inhabits a human body possesses a remarkable instrument (Gallwey, 1976, pp. 33–34).

Logical-Mathematical Intelligence

In 1983 Barbara McClintock won the Nobel Prize in Medicine or Physiology for her work in microbiology. Her intellectual powers of deduction and observation illustrate one form of logical-mathematical intelligence that is often labeled "scientific thinking." One incident is particularly illuminating. When she was a researcher at Cornell in the 1920s, McClintock was faced one day with a problem: while theory predicted 50 percent pollen sterility in corn, her research assistant (in the "field") was finding plants that were only 25 to 30 percent sterile. Disturbed by this discrepancy, McClintock left the cornfield and returned to her office where she sat for half an hour, thinking:

Suddenly I jumped up and ran back to the (corn) field. At the top of the field (the others were still at the bottom) I shouted, "Eureka, I have it! I know what the 30% sterility is!" . . . They asked me to prove it. I sat down with a paper bag and a pencil and I started from scratch, which I had not done at all in my laboratory. It had all been done so fast; the answer came and I ran. Now I worked it out step by step—it was an intricate series of steps—and I came out with [the same result]. [They] looked at the material and it was exactly as I'd said it was; it worked out

11

exactly as I had diagrammed it. Now, why did I know, without having done it on paper? Why was I so sure? (Keller, 1983, p. 104).

This anecdote illustrates two essential facts of the logical-mathematical intelligence. First, in the gifted individual, the process of problem solving is often remarkably rapid—the successful scientist copes with many variables at once and creates numerous hypotheses that are each evaluated and then accepted or rejected in turn. The anecdote also underscores the nonverbal nature of the intelligence. A solution to a problem can be constructed before it is articulated. In fact, the solution process may be totally invisible, even to the problem solver. This phenomenon need not imply, however, that discoveries of this sort—the familiar "aha!"—are mysterious, intuitive, or unpredictable. The fact that it happens frequently to some people (e.g., Nobel Prize winners) suggests the opposite. We interpret this phenomenon as the work of the logical-mathematical intelligence.

Along with the companion skill of language, logical-mathematical reasoning provides the principal basis for IQ tests. This form of intelligence has been thoroughly investigated by traditional psychologists, and it is the archetype of "raw intelligence" or the problem-solving faculty that purportedly cuts across domains. It is perhaps ironic, then, that the actual mechanism by which one arrives at a solution to a logical-mathematical problem is not as yet completely understood—and the processes involved in leaps like those described by McClintock remain mysterious.

Logical-mathematical intelligence is supported as well by empirical criteria. Certain areas of the brain are more prominent in mathematical calculation than others; indeed, recent evidence suggests that the linguistic areas in the frontotemporal lobes are more important for logical deduction, and the visuospatial areas in the parietofrontal lobes for numerical calculation (Houdé & Tzourio-Mazoyer, 2003). There are savants who perform great feats of calculation even though they are tragically deficient in most other areas. Child prodigies in mathematics abound. The development of this intelligence in children has been carefully documented by Jean Piaget and other psychologists.

Linguistic Intelligence

At the age of ten, T. S. Eliot created a magazine called *Fireside*, to which he was the sole contributor. In a three-day period during his winter vacation, he created eight complete issues. Each one included poems, adventure stories, a gossip column, and humor. Some of this material survives, and it displays the talent of the poet (see Soldo, 1982).

As with the logical intelligence, calling linguistic skill an intelligence is consistent with the stance of traditional psychology. Linguistic intelligence also passes our empirical tests. For instance, a specific area of the brain, called Broca's area, is responsible for the production of grammatical sentences. A person with damage to this area can understand words and sentences quite well but has difficulty putting words together in anything other than the simplest of sentences. Other thought processes may be entirely unaffected.

The gift of language is universal, and its rapid and unproblematic development in most children is strikingly constant across cultures. Even in deaf populations where a manual sign language is not explicitly taught, children will often invent their own manual language and use it surreptitiously. We thus see how an intelligence may operate independently of a specific input modality or output channel.

Spatial Intelligence

Navigation around the Caroline Islands in the South Seas is accomplished by native sailors without instruments. The position of the stars, as viewed from various islands, the weather patterns, and water color are the principal signposts. Each journey is broken into a series of segments, and the navigator learns the position of the stars within each of these segments. During the actual trip the navigator must mentally picture a reference island as it passes under a particular star. From that envisioning exercise, he computes the number of segments completed, the proportion of the trip remaining, and any corrections in heading that are required. The navigator cannot see the islands as he sails along; instead he maps their locations in his mental picture of the journey (see Gladwin, 1970).

Spatial problem solving is required for navigation and for the use of the notational system of maps. Other kinds of spatial problem solving are brought to bear in visualizing an object from different angles and in playing chess. The visual arts also employ this intelligence in the use of space.

Evidence from brain research is clear and persuasive. Just as the middle regions of the left cerebral cortex have, over the course of evolution, been selected as the site of linguistic processing in right-handed persons, the posterior regions of the right cerebral cortex prove most crucial for spatial processing. Damage to these regions causes impairment of the ability to find one's way around a site, to recognize faces or scenes, or to notice fine details.

Blind populations provide an illustration of the distinction between the spatial intelligence and visual perception. A blind person can recognize shapes by a nonvisual method: running a hand along the contours of an object translates into length of time of movement, which in turn is translated into the size and shape of the object. For the blind person, the perceptual system of the tactile modality parallels the visual modality in the seeing person. The analogy between the spatial reasoning of the blind and the linguistic reasoning of the deaf is notable.

There are few child prodigies among visual artists, but there are savants like Nadia (Selfe, 1977), a preschool child who, despite a condition of severe autism, made drawings of the most remarkable representational accuracy and finesse.

Interpersonal Intelligence

With little formal training in special education and nearly blind herself, Anne Sullivan began the formidable task of instructing a blind and deaf seven-year-old, Helen Keller. Sullivan's efforts at communication were complicated by the child's emotional struggle with the world around her. At their first meal together, this scene occurred:

> Annie did not allow Helen to put her hand into Annie's plate and take what she wanted, as she had been accustomed to do with her family. It became a test of wills—hand thrust into plate, hand firmly put aside. The family, much upset, left the dining room. Annie locked the door and proceeded to

eat her breakfast while Helen lay on the floor kicking and screaming, push-ing and pulling at Annie's chair. [After half an hour] Helen went around the table looking for her family. She discovered no one else was there and that bewildered her. Finally, she sat down and began to eat her breakfast, but with her hands. Annie gave her a spoon. Down on the floor it clattered, and the contest of wills began anew (Lash, 1980, p. 52).

Anne Sullivan sensitively responded to the child's behavior. She wrote home: "The greatest problem I shall have to solve is how to discipline and control her without breaking her spirit. I shall go rather slowly at first and try to win her love." In fact, the first "miracle" occurred two weeks later, well before the famous incident at the pump house. Annie had taken Helen to a small cottage near the family's house, where they could live alone. After seven days together, Helen's personality suddenly underwent a change—the therapy had worked: "My heart is singing with joy this morning. A mir-acle has happened! The wild little creature of two weeks ago has been transformed into a gentle child" (Lash, 1980, p. 54).

It was just two weeks after this that the first breakthrough in Helen's grasp of language occurred; and from that point on, she progressed with incredible speed. The key to the miracle of language was Anne Sullivan's insight into the person of Helen Keller.

Interpersonal intelligence builds on a core capacity to notice distinc-tions among others—in particular, contrasts in their moods, tempera-ments, motivations, and intentions. In more advanced forms, this intelligence permits a skilled adult to read the intentions and desires of others, even when they have been hidden. This skill appears in a highly so-phisticated form in religious or political leaders, salespersons, marketers, teachers, therapists, and parents. The Helen Keller–Anne Sullivan story suggests that this interpersonal intelligence does not depend on language. All indices in brain research suggest that the frontal lobes play a prominent role in interpersonal knowledge. Damage in this area can cause profound personality changes while leaving other forms of problem solving un-harmed—after such an injury, a person is often not the "same person."

Alzheimer's disease, a form of dementia, appears to attack posterior brain zones with a special ferocity, leaving spatial, logical, and linguistic computations severely impaired. Yet people with Alzheimer's often remain well groomed, socially proper, and continually apologetic for their errors. In contrast, Pick's disease, a variety of dementia that is localized in more frontal regions of the cortex, entails a rapid loss of social graces.

Biological evidence for interpersonal intelligence encompasses two additional factors often cited as unique to humans. One factor is the prolonged childhood of primates, including the close attachment to the mother. In cases where the mother (or a substitute figure) is not available and engaged, normal interpersonal development is in serious jeopardy. The second factor is the relative importance in humans of social interaction. Skills such as hunting, tracking, and killing in prehistoric societies required the participation and cooperation of large numbers of people. The need for group cohesion, leadership, organization, and solidarity follows naturally from this.

Intrapersonal Intelligence

In an essay called "A Sketch of the Past," written almost as a diary entry, Virginia Woolf discusses the "cotton wool of existence"—the various mundane events of life. She contrasts this cotton wool with three specific and poignant memories from her childhood: a fight with her brother, seeing a particular flower in the garden, and hearing of the suicide of a past visitor:

> These are three instances of exceptional moments. I often tell them over, or rather they come to the surface unexpectedly. But now for the first time I have written them down, and I realize something that I have never realized before. Two of these moments ended in a state of despair. The other ended, on the contrary, in a state of satisfaction. . . . The sense of horror [in hearing of the suicide] held me powerless. But in the case of the flower, I found a reason; and was thus able to deal with the sensation. I was not powerless. . . . Though I still have the peculiarity that I receive these sudden shocks, they are now always welcome; after the first surprise, I always feel instantly that they are particularly valuable. And so I go on to suppose that the shock-receiving capacity is what makes me a writer. I hazard the explanation that a shock is at once in my case followed by the desire to explain it. I feel that I have had a blow; but it is not, as I thought as a child, simply a blow from an enemy hidden behind the cotton wool of daily life;

it is or will become a revelation of some order; it is a token of some real thing behind appearances; and I make it real by putting it into words (Woolf, 1976, pp. 69–70).

This quotation vividly illustrates the intrapersonal intelligence—knowledge of the internal aspects of a person: access to one's own feeling life, one's range of emotions, the capacity to make discriminations among these emotions and eventually to label them and to draw on them as a means of understanding and guiding one's own behavior. A person with good intrapersonal intelligence has a viable and effective model of him- or herself—one consistent with a description constructed by careful observers who know that person intimately. Since this intelligence is the most private, evidence from language, music, or some other more expressive form of intelligence is required if the observer is to detect it at work. In the above quotation, for example, linguistic intelligence serves as a medium in which to observe intrapersonal knowledge in operation.

We see the familiar criteria at work in the intrapersonal intelligence. As with the interpersonal intelligence, the frontal lobes play a central role in personality change. Injury to the lower area of the frontal lobes is likely to produce irritability or euphoria, whereas injury to the higher regions is more likely to produce indifference, listlessness, slowness, and apathy—a kind of depressive personality. In persons with frontal lobe injury, the other cognitive functions often remain preserved. In contrast, among aphasics who have recovered sufficiently to describe their experiences, we find consistent testimony: while there may have been a diminution of general alertness and considerable depression about the condition, the individual in no way felt himself to be a different person. He recognized his own needs, wants, and desires and tried as best he could to achieve them.

The autistic child is a prototypical example of an individual with impaired intrapersonal intelligence; indeed, the child may not even be able to refer to himself. At the same time, such children may exhibit remarkable abilities in the musical, computational, spatial, mechanical, and other nonpersonal realms.

Evolutionary evidence for an intrapersonal faculty is more difficult to come by, but we might speculate that the capacity to transcend the satisfaction of instinctual drives is relevant. This potential becomes increasingly important in a species not perennially involved in the struggle for survival. The neural structures that permit consciousness probably form the basis on which self-consciousness is constructed.

In sum, then, both interpersonal and intrapersonal faculties pass the tests of an intelligence. They both feature problem-solving capacities that have significance for the individual and the species. Interpersonal intelligence allows one to understand and work with others. Intrapersonal intelligence allows one to understand and work with oneself. In the individual's sense of self, one encounters a melding of interpersonal and intrapersonal components. Indeed, the sense of self emerges as one of the most marvelous of human inventions—a symbol that represents all kinds of information about a person and that is at the same time an invention that all individuals construct for themselves.

NEWLY IDENTIFIED INTELLIGENCES

For the first ten years after I proposed the theory of multiple intelligences, I resisted any temptation to alter the theory. Many individuals proposed candidate intelligences—humor intelligence, cooking intelligence, sexual intelligence. One of my students quipped that I would never recognize those intelligences, because I lacked them myself.

Two factors led me to consider additional intelligences. Once I spoke about the theory to a group of historians of science. After my talk, a short, elderly man approached and said, "You will never explain Charles Darwin with the set of intelligences that you proposed." The commentator was none other than Ernst Mayr, probably the most important twentieth-century authority on evolution.

The other factor was the frequent assertion that there was a spiritual intelligence, and the occasional assertion that I had identified a spiritual intelligence. In fact, neither statement was true. But these experiences motivated me to consider whether there is evidence for either a naturalist or a spiritual intelligence.

This inquiry led to very different conclusions. In the first case, the evidence for the existence of a naturalist intelligence is surprisingly persuasive. Biologists like Charles Darwin and E. O. Wilson and ornithologists like John James Audubon and Roger Tory Peterson excel at identifying and distinguishing one species from another. Persons with a high degree of naturalist intelligence are keenly aware of how to distinguish the diverse plants, animals, mountains, or cloud configurations in their ecological niche. These capacities are not exclusively visual; the recognition of birdsong or whale calls entails auditory perception. The Dutch naturalist Geermat Vermij, who is blind, depends on his sense of touch.

On the eight criteria for an intelligence, the naturalist intelligence scores well. In this type of intelligence, there is the core capacity to recognize instances as members of a species. There is also the evolutionary history of survival often depending on recognizing conspecifics and on avoiding predators. Young children easily make distinctions in the naturalist world—indeed, some five-year-olds are better than their parents or grandparents at distinguishing among dinosaur species.

Examining the naturalist intelligence through the cultural or brain lenses brings some interesting phenomena into focus. Today few people in the developed world are directly dependent on naturalist intelligence. We simply go to the grocery store or order groceries on the phone or the Internet. And yet, I suggest, our entire consumer culture is based on the naturalist intelligence. It includes the capacities we deploy when we are drawn to one car rather than another, or when we select one pair of sneakers or gloves rather than another.

The study of brain damage provides intriguing evidence of individuals who are able to recognize and name inanimate objects but who lose the capacity to identify living things; less often, one encounters the opposite pattern, where individuals are able to recognize and name animate entities but fail with artificial (man-made) objects. These capacities probably entail different perceptual mechanisms (Euclidean geometry operates in the world of artifacts but not in the world of nature) and different experiential bases (we interact with inanimate objects and tools very differently than with living beings).

My review of the evidence on spirituality proved less straightforward. People have very strong views on religion and spirituality. For many (particularly in the contemporary United States), experiences of the spirit are the most important ones; and many assume that a spiritual intelligence not only exists but actually represents the highest achievement of human beings. Others, particularly those of a scientific bent, cannot take seriously any discussion of the spirit or the soul; it smacks of mysticism. And they may be deeply skeptical about God and religion—especially so in the academy. Asked why I had not endorsed a spiritual or religious intelligence, I once quipped, "If I did so, it would please my friends—but it would please my enemies even more!"

Quips are no substitute for scholarship. I devoted the better part of a year to reviewing the evidence for and against a spiritual intelligence. I concluded that at least two facets of spirituality were quite remote from my conception of an intelligence. First, I do not believe that an intelligence should be confounded with an individual's phenomenological experience. For most observers, spirituality entails a certain set of visceral reactions—for example, a feeling that one is in touch with a higher being or "at one" with the world. Such feelings may be fine, but I do not see them as valid indicators of an intelligence. A person with a high degree of mathematical intelligence may undergo feelings of "flow" in the course of solving a difficult problem, but the person is equally mathematically intelligent even if he or she has no such phenomenological reaction.

Second, for many individuals, spirituality is indissociable from a belief in religion and God generally, or even from allegiance to a particular faith or sect: "Only a real Jew/Catholic/Muslim/Protestant is a spiritual being" is the explicit or implicit message. This requirement makes me uncomfortable and takes us far from the initial set of criteria for an intelligence.

But although a spiritual intelligence does not qualify on my criteria, one facet of spirituality seems a promising candidate. I call it the existential intelligence—sometimes described as "the intelligence of big questions." This candidate intelligence is based on the human proclivity to ponder the most fundamental questions of existence. Why do we live? Why do we die? Where do we come from? What is going to happen to us? What is love? Why do we make war? I sometimes say that these are questions that transcend perception; they concern issues that are too big or too small to be perceived by our five principal sensory systems.

Somewhat surprisingly, the existential intelligence does reasonably well in terms of our criteria. Certainly, there are individuals—philosophers, religious leaders, the most impressive statesman—who come to mind as high-end embodiments of existential intelligence. Existential issues arise in every culture—in religion, philosophy, art, and the more mundane stories, gossip, and media presentations of everyday life. In any society where questioning is tolerated, children raise these existential questions from an early age—though they do not always listen closely to the answers. Moreover, the myths and fairy tales that they gobble up speak to their fascination with existential questions.

My hesitation in declaring a full-blown existential intelligence comes from the dearth, so far, of evidence that parts of the brain are concerned particularly with these deep issues of existence. It could be that there are regions—for example, in the inferotemporal lobe—that are particularly crucial for dealing with the Big Questions. However, it is also possible that existential questions are just part of a broader philosophical mind—or that they are simply the more emotionally laden of the questions that individuals routinely pose. In the latter instances, my conservative nature dictates caution in giving the ninth place of honor to existential intelligence. I do mention this candidate intelligence in passing, but, in homage to a famous film by Federico Fellini, I shall continue for the time being to speak of "8 ½ Intelligences."

The Unique Contributions of the Theory

As human beings, we all have a repertoire of skills for solving different kinds of problems. My investigation began, therefore, with a consideration of these problems, the contexts in which they are found, and the culturally significant products that are the outcome. I did not approach "intelligence" as a reified human faculty that is brought to bear in literally any problem setting; rather, I began with the problems that human beings solve and the products that they cherish. In a sense I then worked back to the intelligences that must be responsible.

Evidence from brain research, human development, evolution, and cross-cultural comparisons was brought to bear in the search for the relevant human intelligences: a candidate was included only if reasonable evidence to support its membership was found across these diverse fields. Again, this tack differs from the traditional one: since no candidate faculty is necessarily an intelligence, I could make an up-or-down decision on a motivated basis. In the traditional approach to intelligence, there is no opportunity for this type of empirical decision.

My belief is that these multiple human faculties, the intelligences, are to a significant extent independent of one another. Research with brain-damaged adults repeatedly demonstrates that particular faculties can be lost while others are spared. This independence of intelligences implies that a particularly high level of ability in one intelligence, say mathematics, does not require a similarly high level in another, like language or music. This independence of intelligences contrasts sharply with traditional measures of IQ that find high correlations among test scores. I speculate that the usual correlations among subtests of IQ tests come about because all of these tasks in fact measure the ability to respond rapidly to items of a logical-mathematical or linguistic sort; these correlations might be substantially reduced if one were to survey in a contextually appropriate way—what I call "intelligence-fair assessment"—the full range of human problem-solving skills.

Until now, my discussion may appear to suggest that adult roles depend largely on the flowering of a single intelligence. In fact, however, nearly every cultural role of any degree of sophistication requires a combination of intelligences. Thus, even an apparently straightforward role, like playing the violin, transcends a reliance on musical intelligence. To become a successful violinist requires bodily-kinesthetic dexterity and the interpersonal skills of relating to an audience and, in a different way, of choosing a manager; quite possibly it involves an intrapersonal intelligence as well. Dance requires skills in bodily-kinesthetic, musical, interpersonal, and spatial intelligences in varying degrees. Politics requires an interpersonal skill, a linguistic facility, and perhaps some logical aptitude.

Inasmuch as nearly every cultural role requires several intelligences, it becomes important to consider individuals as a collection of aptitudes rather than as having a singular problem-solving faculty that can be measured directly through pencil-and-paper tests. Even given a relatively small number of such intelligences, the diversity of human ability is created through the differences in these profiles. In fact, it may well be that the total is greater than the sum of the parts. An individual may not be particularly gifted in any intelligence, and yet, because of a particular combination or blend of skills, he or she may be able to fill some niche uniquely well. Thus, it is of paramount importance to assess the particular combination of skills that may earmark an individual for a certain vocational or avocational niche.

In brief, MI theory leads to three conclusions:

1. All of us have the full range of intelligences; that is what makes us human beings, cognitively speaking.
2. No two individuals—not even identical twins—have exactly the same intellectual profile because, even when the genetic material is identical, individuals have different experiences (and identical twins are often highly motivated to distinguish themselves from one another).
3. Having a strong intelligence does not mean that one necessarily acts intelligently. A person with high mathematical intelligence might use her abilities to carry out important experiments in physics or create powerful new geometric proofs; but she might waste these abilities in playing the lottery all day or multiplying ten-digit numbers in her head.

All of these statements are about the psychology of human intelligence—to which MI theory seeks to make a contribution. But of course they raise powerful educational, political, and cultural questions. Those questions will engage us in later parts of the book.

CONCLUSION

I believe that in our society we suffer from three biases, which I have nicknamed "Westist," "Testist," and "Bestist." "Westist" involves putting certain Western cultural values, which date back to Socrates, on a pedestal. Logical thinking, for example, is important; rationality is important; but they are not the only virtues. "Testist" suggests a bias towards focusing on those human abilities or approaches that are readily testable. If it can't be tested, it sometimes seems, it is not worth paying attention to. My feeling is that assessment can be much broader, much more humane than it is now and that psychologists should spend less time ranking people and more time trying to help them.

"Bestist" is a thinly veiled reference to David Halberstam's 1972 book *The Best and the Brightest*. Halberstam's title referred ironically to the figures, among them Harvard faculty members, who were brought to Washington to help President John F. Kennedy and in the process launched the Vietnam War. I think any belief that all the answers to a given problem lie in one certain approach, such as logical-mathematical thinking, can be very dangerous. Current views of intellect need to be leavened with other, more comprehensive points of view.

It is of the utmost importance that we recognize and nurture all of the varied human intelligences and all of the combinations of intelligences. We are all so different largely because we have different combinations of intelligences. If we recognize this, I think we will have at least a better chance of dealing appropriately with the many problems that we face in the world. If we can mobilize the spectrum of human abilities, not only will people feel better about themselves and more competent; it is even possible that they will also feel more engaged and better able to join the rest of the world community in working for the broader good. Perhaps if we can mobilize the full range of human intelligences and ally them to an ethical sense, we can help increase the likelihood of our survival on this planet, and perhaps even contribute to our thriving.

Chapter 2

THE VIEW AFTER
TWENTY-FIVE YEARS

As the individual responsible for the theory of multiple intelligences, I can assert that I never expected the fame the theory would attain, nor its staying power. I had written books before *Frames of Mind* (1983b), and they had received reasonable reviews and produced reasonable sales figures. But within months after *Frames* was published, I realized things were different. The book received many reviews. While they were not all favorable, they were prominently featured, thereby suggesting that the book was important. I received many invitations to speak, including from venues that were new to me. When I entered the room, there was a buzz that I had not heard before. Within a year or two, publishers approached me about other books; test makers approached me about creating a test—or, more often, seven tests, one for each intelligence. Speaking requests and inquiries about translating my works came from abroad. In Andy Warhol's too-often quoted phrase, I enjoyed my fifteen minutes of fame.

Even when attention is paid to a book, the theory it contains, and its author, such attention is typically short-lived. As Warhol understood, audiences have short interest spans. This is particularly true with respect to "educational fashion" and particularly true in the United States. This truism has been controverted by the contemporary theory of multiple intelligences. Every year, I discover new interest in the theory—from countries that have never contacted me before; from sectors of society that have not expressed an interest before; from students of disciplines that I have never heard of. I am flattered—and humbled—by this continuing interest. Sometimes my visits to a country are front-page news. And the theory has received the oddest kind of societal affirmation—it appears in jokes, on television shows, in crossword puzzles, and in standardized tests. Happily, the attention falls primarily on the theory and not on me. As I often say, "I love when people discuss my ideas; but I would rather not be recognized in the airport."

What has surprised me as much as the continuing attention has been the fact that the theory has taken on a life of its own. In large part that is because scholars and practitioners have taken it in directions that I could never have anticipated. Scholars have raised questions that I would never have considered and carried out studies that I could never have envisioned. For example, neuroscientist Antonio Battro devoted a whole book to the possibility of a digital intelligence, and legal scholars Peggy Davis and Lani Guinier drew on the theory to reconceptualize admission to law schools and the teaching of law. Educators, for their part, have also come up with wonderful innovations. In Indianapolis twenty years ago, teacher Patricia Bolanos created the first school in the world dedicated to multiple intelligences: the Key Learning Community thrives today. In the Philippines, educator Mary Jo Abaquin gave awards to eight national figures who exemplified each intelligence and were also recognized as being good workers.

I have gained considerable satisfaction from the fact that the theory has also disclosed a depth and richness that I never suspected in my early work. One of the reasons the theory has initial appeal is that it can be summarized in a brisk sentence or two: "Most people think that there is but a single intelligence; MI theory holds that we each have eight or more intelligences, and we can use them to carry out all kinds of tasks." No one is more surprised than I am to discover that, after twenty-five years, the theory continues to raise new questions and to transport me (and many others) in new directions.

In this chapter, I review the principal new directions in which my own thinking has proceeded in the two and a half decades since *Frames of Mind* was completed. I begin by elaborating on some of the distinctions introduced in the opening chapter. I then focus on three more recent elaborations on the theory: the distinction between intelligences and domains; the three distinct meanings of the term intelligence; and the nature and form of different intellectual profiles. Other new twists, particularly those of an educational or broader cultural nature, are introduced as appropriate throughout the rest of the volume.

ADDITIONAL INTELLIGENCES

As I noted in the previous chapter, almost all individuals who delve into the theory are curious about the possibility of additional intelligences. I have been extremely conservative about adding intelligences. My conservatism stems chiefly from the criteria I established for an intelligence. While it is easy to meet one or two of the criteria, it is not so easy to meet the ensemble of eight features. I think of the intelligences as a mental chemistry set; it is desirable to explain as many human capacities as possible through a combination of the existing elements rather than through the creation of a new one. Thus, for example, while it is tempting to talk about a technological or tool intelligence, I prefer to think of such capacities as involving a combination of logical, spatial, and bodily intelligences. By the same token, a philosophical capacity—including the existential dimension—might be adequately explained through a combination of language and logical capacities directed toward one or another content.

With the exception of existential or spiritual intelligence, I have thought the most about two candidates: humor intelligence and moral intelligence. For different reasons, I think that neither candidate qualifies. When it comes to humor, I believe that it is simply a revision—or light-hearted perversion—of our logical capacity. In humor, the normal state of affairs is altered in some logical way. If we think something is funny, our own logical and intrapersonal intelligences are involved. If we are able to amuse someone else, it is because we have used logic to engage their interpersonal intelligence. It does not matter if *we* think something is funny; what matters is whether we understand our audience—whether it is one person or a thousand—well enough to evoke a mirth response.

There is a great deal of interest nowadays in human moral capacities—and for good reason. Indeed, the GoodWork Project, in which I have been engaged for well over a decade, probes human moral capacities and attempts to create conditions in which moral excellence will be forthcoming.

Many individuals believe that human beings have a moral capacity that is present from birth and that morality follows a predictable trajectory through maturity.

Why, then, not invoke a moral intelligence? My short answer is that intelligences are presented in a descriptive and not a normative way. An intelligence is simply a computational capacity; individuals with a high intelligence with language, say, are able readily to compute linguistic information—more able than those with less linguistic intelligence. How one chooses to use one's linguistic intelligence is a question of values and norms—and hence it falls outside the descriptive realm. Both the poet Goethe and the propagandist Goebbels had considerable intelligence in the German language; Goethe used it to write great works of art, Goebbels to engender hatred.

A somewhat longer answer can be given to the question of why neither humor nor morality qualify as intelligences, in my view. This answer grows out of my conception of the human sciences. Some human capacities are clearly hardwired in the brain; historical and cultural forces have little or no effect. How we hear the difference between p and b is determined by the nature of our auditory system. Whether we can see stereoscopically—and why, for example, I cannot—is also a function of our perceptual system. To be sure, both auditory discrimination and depth perception have experiential components; but the experiential range is sharply fixed in time and in the nature of the relevant sensory input.

Other human capacities, on the other hand, vary far more from one culture to another. While the ability to laugh is clearly a specieswide capacity, what we laugh at and why is strongly determined by the culture(s) in which we happen to reside. A person slipping on a banana peel is hilarious in one setting, mildly amusing in a second, and an object of sympathy in a third. By the same token, while the capacity to make a moral judgment is equally part of the human condition, the judgments that we make about many moral questions are also heavily colored by the culture in which we live. One person's terrorist is another person's freedom fighter. To say that human beings are capable of moral judgments is a truism; to say that we share basic moral precepts and values is hyperbole. The same point obtains with respect to humor. For these reasons, I consider both morality and humor to be "culture-dependent" capacities and hence must remove them from consideration as basic human intellectual faculties.

THE SCIENTIFIC BASIS OF MI THEORY

While intelligences are determined by a range of criteria drawn deliberately from several disciplines, there is little question that certain criteria have loomed larger in my mind than others. As a developmental psychologist, I have been interested in the evidence for core human capacities in infancy and the extent to which their developmental trajectories can be monitored. As a sometime neuroscientist, I have searched for evidence that a particular candidate capacity seems to require its own specific neural bases.

It is scarcely an exaggeration to say the following: As much new knowledge about the nervous system has been accumulated in the last 25 years as in the preceding 500 years. This change in pace is due in part to the introduction of powerful new technologies that allow us to probe the operation of the brain *in vivo*. It is also due to the massive growth of the neuroscience community; while there were a few hundred neuroscientists at midcentury, there are now tens of thousands. And it is due to the emergence of better questions and the geometric nature with which knowledge accumulates.

The explosion of new knowledge is so great that no one can keep up. A distinguished biologist told me a few years ago that if he stopped reading journals for just three months, he would fall so far behind that he could never catch up. While I conducted neuropsychological research for two decades, I am at present neither a neuroscientist nor a geneticist; so my own continuing education in those fields remains at the level of an engaged amateur.

Given this state of affairs, it is quite possible that the picture of multiple intelligences could have been radically altered by scientific findings in the last few decades. It is my considered judgment that this is not the case. I would go further. The accumulating scientific knowledge makes the claims of MI theory more, and not less, likely.

The thrust in cognitive-developmental psychology has moved sharply away from the Piagetian belief in a core logical capacity that underlies all other human capacities and from broad developmental stages that encompass all domains of knowledge. Instead, the research topography involves increasingly detailed studies of specific human intellectual spheres: linguistic cognition, musical cognition, spatial cognition, and the like. A sizable cottage industry has developed around the study of how individuals understand others (theory of other minds) and how they understand themselves (self knowledge). Within these spheres, psychologists identify "core capacities"—some of them unchanging from birth and some more alterable with experience and development, some of them shared with other primates and others more specific to humans. In all, the research terrain in the development of human cognition has an MI flavor, although MI theory is rarely mentioned explicitly.

The same general picture emerges in the study of the brain. There is relatively little interest at present in exploring the bases of general intellectual capacities, should such capacities exist. Instead students of the brain, like their psychologist colleagues (with whom they often collaborate), are identifying the very specific structures that are involved in processing diverse forms of information—again, information about language, space, music, and the personal realm. Where neuroscience goes further is in the specificity of the capacities that are delineated. There may be no general spatial capacity, but rather specific capacities that deal with large-scale space, more local kinds of space, the space within which the body operates, or the space that is being captured in a map or in a sculpture. There may be no general logical-mathematical capacity, but rather far more specific capacities that deal with the processing of small numbers, the processing of large numbers, the logic of daily experience, the logic involved in abstract propositions, and so on. Were MI theory to be refashioned in terms of the most up-to-date neuroscience, we would have to recognize several dozen more focused skills. Translation to educators would remain a separate challenge.

Probably the biggest revision in our thinking in the future will come about as a result of research in genetics. With the completion of the Human Genome Project, a great many of our previous assumptions have been challenged. We have learned, for example, that humans have 20,000–30,000 genes, one fifth of early estimates. We have learned that our genetic heritage is virtually identical to that of the great apes, quite similar to that of mice, and not even very far from that of corn! There may well be a small number of genes that are responsible for mental retardation; and, though less likely, a small number of genes may determine high IQ. But, as with psychology and neuroscience, the energy motivating genetic studies of capacities related to the intelligences is directed toward the identification of genes, or gene clusters, involved in more specific disorders—for example, impairments in oral or written language and impairments in the understanding of other persons, as seems to be associated with autism and Asperger's syndrome.

It is actuarially unlikely that I will be able, a quarter century from now, to survey once again the scientific evidence in favor of the idea of multiple intelligences and the identification of specific intelligences. I hope that someone else will be motivated to undertake that task.

Intelligences and Domains

One of the most important clarifications in MI theory resulted from my own confusion on a matter. This confusion is easy to state but merits some unpacking. When I first wrote about multiple intelligences, I was insensitive to the distinction between an intelligence, on the one hand, and a domain, discipline, or craft, on the other. This confusion caused me to ignore certain points and, to my regret, contributed to some ill-considered implementations of the theory.

On to definitions. An *intelligence* is a computational capacity. For example, an individual with high musical intelligence finds it easy to remember melodies, to recreate rhythms, to trace the changes that take place in a theme over the course of a composition. A *domain* (shorthand for domain, discipline, or craft) is any kind of organized activity within a society, in which one can readily array individuals in terms of expertise. A quick glimpse of the range of domains in a society can be gathered from any list of principal occupations (such as one might find in the yellow pages of a phone book), or, within an educational context, a catalog of course offerings.

The confusion arises because intelligences and domains may share the same name. There is musical intelligence and the domain of music; there is logical-mathematical intelligence and the domains of logic, mathematics, and science. It might seem, then, that a one-to-one mapping obtains between intelligences and domains. Not so. A domain such as music—or, to cite a more specific example, musical performance—can involve any number of intelligences. Indeed, I once analyzed a master class in piano and uncovered six of the initial seven intelligences in operation. By the same token, a particular intelligence—like linguistic intelligence—can be seen at work in professions ranging from orator to journalist to poet. In the first half of the twentieth century, the profession of linguist was populated by individuals whose talent lay in learning languages. After the cognitive-linguistic revolution was ushered in by the work of Noam Chomsky, skill with languages became much less important; logical-mathematical skills, of the sort associated with logicians, were at a premium.

In short, an intelligence is a biopsychological construct; a domain (or discipline or craft) is a sociological construct. No doubt there are interesting connections between the kinds of intelligences human beings possess, the kinds of domains that we develop, and how those intelligences and domains map onto one another, but it is analytically confusing to mix these two kinds of entities. And it is lamentable when educators are unaware of this distinction. It leads to situations where teachers say, "Johnny can't learn geometry because he does not have spatial intelligence." To be sure, spatial intelligence is helpful for learning geometry, but there is more than one way to master geometry; and the challenge facing every geometry teacher is to figure out how to teach students to carry out and understand proofs, whether or not their spatial intelligence is up to snuff.

THE THREE MEANINGS OF INTELLIGENCE

In recent years, I have come to appreciate that there are three distinct meanings or connotations of the term *intelligence*. Each has its own sphere and utility; it is unfortunate when these three senses are confused. I suggest, further, that the issue of training or enhancing intelligence differs across these three types, and educators should respect these differences.

Consider these three sentences and their respective labels:

1. *Intelligence as a species characteristic.* In view of the close resemblance between chimpanzee and human genetic material, it is challenging to delineate the defining characteristics of human *intelligence*.

2. *Intelligence as individual difference.* On most dimensions of interest, Susan simply displays more *intelligence* than John.
3. *Intelligence as fit execution of an assignment.* What distinguishes Alfred Brendel's piano playing is not his technique per se but the
sheer *intelligence* of his interpretations.

Each of these sentences fulfills the requirements of both English syntax
and semantics. None would be flagged by linguists as impermissible. Moreover, each of these sentences is reasonably intelligible; I doubt that many
readers will find them confusing. And yet, each reflects a distinctive psychological approach, and each harbors distinct educational implications.

When invoking the first meaning of intelligence, we attempt *a general
characterization of human (or nonhuman) capacities.* We might, for example, speak of human intelligence as the capacity to solve complex problems,
or to anticipate the future, or to analyze patterns, or to synthesize disparate
pieces of information. A major disciplinary tradition, begun with Charles
Darwin's studies of the "descent of man" and continuing with Jean Piaget's
investigation of children's minds, seeks to capture what is unique and
generic about intelligence.

The second meaning of intelligence is the one that has been most widely
employed by psychologists. Those in the psychometric tradition—whether
unitarians or pluralists—assume that intelligence is a trait, like height or
extroversion. Individuals can be usefully compared with one another on
the extent to which they exhibit this trait or ensemble of traits. I term this
tack *the examination of individual differences on a trait of interest.* Much of
my own work on multiple intelligences has entailed descriptions of the differing profiles of intelligence across individuals.

The third meaning of intelligence has been the least explored, although it
may be the most intriguing. As suggested in the Brendel example, the focus
here falls on *the manner in which a task is executed.* We often speak in this
way: we talk about whether a decision was wise or ill advised, whether the
manner in which the decision was reached was clever or foolish, whether a
leadership transition was handled intelligently or ineptly, whether a new
concept was introduced intelligently into a lecture, and so forth.

What distinguishes this third connotation of intelligence? We cannot
characterize an act or decision as intelligent without some sense of the goal

or purpose at issue, the choices involved in a genre, and the particular value system of the participants. Brendel's playing may not be technically more accurate on some objective index. Rather, in view of his own goals, the choices available in piano performance, and the values of the listener, one can validly speak of his interpretations as intelligent or wanting in intelligence. Moreover, I could dislike Brendel's interpretations and still concur that they were intelligent, if you could convince me of what he was trying to achieve and why it made sense in his terms. Or, perhaps in turn, I could convince you that Glenn Gould's performance of the same piece was intelligent, whether or not you personally liked it. There do not exist example-independent criteria for what constitutes a wise or foolish decision, planning process, leadership transition, introduction of a topic in a class, and so on. Yet, armed with information about goals, genres, and values, we can make assessments about whether these tasks have been performed intelligently—even as we can agree to disagree about the conclusions reached.

How does the third sense of intelligence relate to multiple intelligences? I speculate that different tasks call on different intelligences or combinations of intelligences. To perform music intelligently involves a different set of intelligences than preparing a meal, planning an academic course, or resolving a quarrel.

So, one might ask, what is achieved by this exercise in the "semantics of intelligence"? Let me suggest three possible dividends. The first is indeed lexical. It is useful and important to distinguish the three distinct definitions of intelligence; otherwise we risk speaking past one another, with a Piagetian needlessly clashing with a psychometrician, or a critic believing that she is engaged in the same kind of endeavor as a school psychologist.

The second dividend concerns research. There is little question that scholars and researchers will continue to examine the nature of intelligence. We can expect to read about new tests of intelligence, new forms of artificially intelligent machinery, and even candidate genes for intelligence. Some researchers will be quite clear about what they mean in using the term "intelligence," but we can expect there to be considerable confusion as well, unless scholars take care to indicate which aspect of intelligence they are studying and how (or whether) it relates to the other ones.

Finally, and most important for me, are implications for education. When educators speak about intelligence in the first sense, they are referring to a capacity that can be assumed to exist in all human beings. Perhaps it is manifested more quickly or dramatically in one person than in another, but ultimately we are dealing with part of the human birthright: no special measures are needed to ensure that a particular intelligence becomes manifest. In contrast, intelligence in the "individual difference" sense involves judgment about the potential of individuals and how each might be taught in the most effective manner. If (following Richard Herrnstein and Charles Murray, 1994) one assumes that Sally has little intellectual potential in general, or (following the theory of multiple intelligences) one assumes that Sally has little potential for the development of spatial intelligence, one is faced with clear-cut educational choices. These can range from giving up to working much harder to searching for alternative ways to deliver instruction, be the topic geometry, ancient history, or classical music.

And what of doing something intelligently or stupidly? The greatest educational progress could be achieved here. All too often, those of us involved in education ignore goals, genres, or values, or we assume that they are apparent and we do not bother to highlight them. Yet teachers' judgments about whether an exercise—a paper, a project, an essay response on an examination—has been done intelligently or stupidly are often difficult for students to fathom. And since these evaluations are not well understood, few if any lessons can be drawn from them. Laying out the criteria by which judgments of quality are made may not suffice in itself to improve quality; but in the absence of such clarification, we have little reason to expect our students to go about their work intelligently.

PROFILES OF INTELLIGENCES

On a logical basis, all kinds of profiles of intelligence may exist. From the point of view of the classical theory of intelligence, we would expect profiles to be relatively flat. That is, a gifted person of high psychometric intelligence should be good in everything; a retarded person of low psychometric intelligence should be poor in everything. And most of the rest of us should bear a strong resemblance to the average person—a flat profile hovering around the 100 point zone on the IQ scale. Alternatively, one could think of profiles as being completely random, with each person's intellectual strengths being drawn, as it were, from eight or nine separate bins. And of course there could be various combinations. Perhaps strength in musical intelligence goes hand in hand with strength in mathematical intelligence. Or perhaps strength in mathematical intelligence predicts mediocre personal intelligences.

Whether and to what extent intelligences correlate with one another is an empirical matter. Defenders of standard psychometric data point to the "positive manifold" that obtains between almost any pair of tests. Those who have studied specific intelligences—spatial and emotional come to mind—go to pains to indicate that these intelligences can and should be measured apart from general IQ. In the case of my own research, a principal source of evidence of MI theory is the dissociability among intellectual strengths in brain-damaged patients as well as in talented (or cognitively impaired) young persons.

We will not know the degree of independence of separate intelligences until we have devised much better measures for each intelligence and until we have explored the neural and genetic bases for whichever factors emerge. Nor can we look at the results in only one cultural context. The spread or overlap among intelligences may well differ among cultures and even historical eras.

Having voiced these reservations, I should mention an intriguing contrast that has recently emerged: the contrast between "laser" and "searchlight" intellectual profiles. Individuals with laser profiles, as the name implies, have a sharp spike in their profile. The spike is likely to involve one or possibly two intelligences. Mozart had a laser profile emphasizing musical intelligence; Einstein had a laser profile with spikes in logical-mathematical and spatial intelligences. Individuals with laser profiles draw heavily on a single or a pair of intelligences, usually choose to work in a domain in which the strong intelligences are privileged, and generally spend decades probing ever more deeply into the relevant domains. Mozart and Einstein were likely to devote most of their waking, cognizant hours to the pursuit, respectively, of musical and scientific concerns.

The searchlight profile, by contrast, is characteristic of individuals who have roughly equivalent strengths in three or more spheres but do not exhibit a single, markedly pronounced intellectual strength. While the laser profile is found chiefly among artists, scientists, scholars, and inventors, the searchlight profile is common among people involved in politics and business. A politician or businessperson is not expected to be the world's expert in a particular topic—if specific expertise is needed, someone with a laser profile can be located and hired. Rather, the person with a searchlight profile is expected to have a wide radar screen, to monitor it regularly, and to make sure that nothing vital is completely missed. The particular intelligences involved in searchlight-supportive positions vary: a football coach might draw on bodily, spatial, logical, linguistic, and personal intelligences, whereas a politician running for public office would be more dependent on linguistic, interpersonal, and intrapersonal intelligences.

It would not distort my meaning greatly to translate this distinction into one of generalists and specialists—and indeed, psychometricians speak of "general" and "specific" intellectual factors. But I mean to add a stylistic dimension to the computational analysis of intelligences. The style of the laser profile is to focus deeply and regularly on a particular domain and to make ever deeper inroads into that domain. The style of the searchlight profile is constantly to survey the terrain, to monitor many different elements, to make sure that no corner is altogether neglected, and to try to piece together a big picture.

My contrast also suggests an intriguing psychopathological aspect. Presumably most of us have some choice in whether to mobilize our intellectual profile in a laser or a searchlight manner. But perhaps some individuals do not. I suggest that autistic individuals and, to a lesser degree, persons suffering from Asperger's syndrome possess involuntary laser minds. In contrast, individuals who have attention-deficit disorders may have involuntary searchlight minds. They do not simply avoid long-term focus; they are unable to do so. In these cases, the challenges to educators and parents are clear.

As Michael Connell, Kim Sheridan, and I (2003) have suggested, the laser/searchlight distinction may go deeper than simply a distinction among domains. Within politics, there can be laser-supportive roles—for example, monitoring polls or writing speeches—as well as the more searchlight role of the public official or the campaign manager. The dedicated pollster may have more in common with the circuit designer in engineering, whereas the senator's role is more like that of the general electrical contractor or the CEO of an electronics firm.

We should avoid the trap of thinking that the searchlight profile—and the g (general intelligence) often associated with it—may be more important than the laser profile with its more limited special faculties. Of course, we should equally avoid the academic snobbishness that highlights expertise in a narrow topic over the ability to manage an organization. Any complex society needs both kinds of skills. Perhaps, at any given moment, the searchlight mind is more needed to keep the society functioning, while, in the long run, it is the achievements of the laser mind that we most value.

CONCLUDING NOTE

These, then, are some of the major changes in focus and direction that have taken place with respect to the theory of multiple intelligences that I first proposed in the early 1980s. It remains to be said that a far greater number of individuals have been involved in the application of the theory, particularly in the educational sphere. Although primarily a scholar rather than a practitioner, I too have devoted more time to the applied side of multiple intelligences. But that is another story, to be related in later chapters.

Chapter 3

BEYOND INTELLIGENCE:
OTHER VALUED HUMAN CAPACITIES

During the celebrations in 1991 commemorating the 200th anniversary of the death of Wolfgang Amadeus Mozart, this master musician was cited in the service of many different enterprises. Such exploitation is not surprising—the works of Mozart have spoken to so many individuals over so many years in so many powerful ways. Mozart has also been spoken of in many ways: as a genius, a prodigy, an expert, an individual who was talented, creative, intelligent, and gifted. I hope it will be seen as a token of respect, rather than as a mark of further exploitation, if I draw on the case of Mozart for yet two further purposes: (1) to clarify the nature of the terminology that we use in talking about exceptional individuals; and (2) to introduce a particular perspective that I have brought to bear in the area of human talents or gifts.

Mozart evokes a plethora of positive characterizations. He is our prototype of a prodigy, as precocious as Pablo Picasso or John Stuart Mill, as preternaturally talented as his fellow musicians Felix Mendelssohn or Camille Saint-Saëns. He is seen as infinitely creative and as unmistakably individualistic as Igor Stravinsky or Richard Wagner. At the same time, however, his ingenuity was evolutionary rather than revolutionary in character. He was as productive as his prolific contemporaries, Antonio Salieri or Karl Ditters von Dittersdorf. And he is granted a deep intelligence, an insight into the human condition that is as profound in its way as that associated with Goethe, Rembrandt, or George Eliot.

Students of Mozart and, for that matter, students of psychology might well leave this situation just as it is. Terminology has a tendency to proliferate;

ordinarily, little harm is done by a cornucopia of terms. Yet at times it can be valuable to step back and consider how one might apply this terminology in a consistent way. And if its application is based on a coherent theoretical framework, it can sometimes aid in discussion, research, and understanding. Hence, in what follows I introduce a general framework for the consideration of what I term the *giftedness matrix*, in the process presenting a set of distinctions that I hope prove useful.

A FRAMEWORK FOR ANALYSIS

Every cognitive act involves an agent who carries out an action or set of actions in some task or domain. Even when the agent is operating in a solitary fashion, his or her acts can potentially be evaluated by someone competent in that particular task or domain space (Csikszentmihalyi, 1988a). Whether one is dealing with the most remarkable acts of genius or the meanest accomplishment of the average citizen, this analytic perspective proves applicable. In the social sciences, this analytic framework has been decomposed as follows (Gardner, 1988b).

The *biopsychological* perspective examines the agent and his or her capacities, inclinations, values, and goals. Included are a consideration of the genetic and neurological substrates of behavior, as well as the analysis of the individual in terms of cognitive powers, traits, and temperamental disposition.

The *domains* or *tasks* perspective examines a task or activity as it has been realized within a societal domain or discipline. Traditionally, tasks have been analyzed by philosophers or by individuals expert in a domain; since the advent of computer science, experts in the field of artificial intelligence have analyzed the structural and processing properties of tasks.

Finally, evaluations or judgments of actions (or works) performed in a domain are put forth by individuals knowledgeable in that domain—members of the *field*, in Csikszentmihalyi's term (1988a). Absent a judgment by individuals or groups who are knowledgeable, it is simply not possible to tell whether a task has been executed satisfactorily, intelligently, or in an exemplary fashion. It is not that in the absence of such judgment a task or work is necessarily inadequate; rather, one simply is unable to render a judgment one way or another. The disciplines of sociology and social psychology can clarify the operation of the field.

The Framework and the Words

Using this analytic framework as a point of departure, I return to the lexicon of the giftedness matrix and offer some provisional definitions.

As I noted in the opening chapter, *intelligence* is a biopsychological potential. Whether and in what respects an individual may be deemed intelligent is a product of his genetic heritage and his psychological properties, ranging from his cognitive powers to his personality dispositions. Recent advances in cognitive studies suggest how best to conceptualize intelligence.

Giftedness is a sign of precocious biopsychological potential in particular domains that exist in a culture. An individual who advances quickly, who is "at promise" in an available task area or domain, earns the epithet "gifted." Individuals can be gifted in any area that is recognized as involving intelligence.

Prodigiousness is an extreme form of giftedness. Mozart qualified as prodigious because his extraordinary musical gifts were manifest early in his life. By and large, prodigiousness is specific to a domain: the giftedness of the youthful mathematician Carl Gauss is quite different from the precociousness of the English painter John Everett Millais or the prodigiousness of the chess player Samuel Reshevsky. Similarly, Mozart differed from other gifted youngsters, including his sister Nannerl. On occasion, however, there may be universal or omnibus prodigies—perhaps Leonardo da Vinci was one.

The terms *expertise* and *expert* are appropriately invoked only after an individual has worked for a decade or so within a domain. By this time, the individual will have mastered the skills and lore that are requisite to performance at the highest levels of the domain. However, there is no implication of originality, dedication, or passion in such a performance; expertise is better conceived as a kind of technical excellence. Colleagues of Mozart (long since forgotten) who could produce on demand a set of concerti or symphonies may have attained expertise without evincing originality.

Creativity is a characterization reserved to those whose products are initially seen to be novel within a domain but are ultimately recognized as acceptable within an appropriate community. Judgments of originality or creativity can be made only by knowledgeable members of the field, though that field can be ancient or newly constituted. There is a tension between creativity and expertise: certainly one may be expert without being creative; and creativity may be manifest before someone has attained the level of a master.

It is with some trepidation that I introduce a final term into the discussion: that of *genius*. I reserve this honorific label for those persons who not only are expert and creative but whose works also assume a universal or quasi-universal significance. Within the scientific domains, it is individuals of genius, such as Isaac Newton and Charles Darwin, who discover principles of universal significance. And within the artistic domains, it is individuals of genius who create works that speak to individuals from diverse cultures and eras. I would speculate that those works endure because they capture some kind of truth about the human condition, often not in words. We are comfortable applying the epithet genius to Shakespeare, Goethe, Rembrandt, and Mozart because their works have transcended their own era. Presumably individuals from other cultures and eras also merit the term genius, but that determination must be left to those with the requisite knowledge and judgment.

Traditional Psychological
Approaches to the Giftedness Matrix

In most traditional approaches, the focus has been on the individual agent. As a result of this bias, there has been too little consideration of the specific tasks or domains in question: it has been assumed that abilities will emerge irrespective of the particular domains that happen to be available in one's culture. Also as a result of this bias, there has been little consideration of the processes by which judgments of quality are made; at least among psychologists, the field has been as little visible as the domain.

The most influential approach to the giftedness matrix has been a direct descendant of work in the area of intelligence and intelligence testing. In the Binet-Spearman tradition, intelligence is a trait of the isolated individual, who can be assessed alone; there is typically the additional assumption that individuals are born with a certain amount of intelligence, which can be measured early in life and which proves relatively insensitive to environment or training. Even when there have been efforts to pluralize intelligence, as in the work of L. L. Thurstone, intelligence is still seen as a relatively fixed trait, one that is readily elicited through the administration of paper-and-pencil instruments.

Given this traditional (and, to my mind, outmoded) view of intelligence, an ensemble of moves can be made with respect to the giftedness matrix. The *gifted* are those with high IQs; the *precocious* are those with even higher IQs ascertainable at an even younger age. *Genius* can be applied to either a youngster or an adult, so long as his or her IQ is high enough—perhaps over the level of 150. On some definitions, *creativity* and intelligence are viewed as related, while other investigators have stressed the relative independence of the two. Recently an informal consensus has emerged that in persons whose IQ is over 120, creativity is not connected to psychometric intelligence. Yet from my point of view, the measures of creativity growing out of the psychometric tradition are even more impoverished than the measures of intelligence. Such measures focus almost exclusively on the most mundane instances of creativity, the type associated with clever repartee at cocktail parties, rather than with human accomplishments of scope and depth. Finally, the word *expert* seems somewhat anomalous in the context of intelligence testing because it refers to specific areas of competence, while intelligence is styled as the most general property of an individual's cognitive capacity. Certainly some members of Mensa are expert in virtually nothing—except in taking tests of intelligence.

A Contemporary View of Intelligence and Related Matters

Countering the notion of a single intelligence has been the view, which has recurred from time to time, that intellect is better conceived of as pluralistic in nature. Typically, as noted earlier, this conclusion has been reached as the result of factor analytic studies of test scores; as such, it is limited by the nature of the instruments used to assess various competences.

In my own work, I have approached issues of intelligence from a quite different perspective. Some years ago I set myself the following task: given the wide range of competences, of "end states" that are valued around the world, what is the nature of the mind that can give rise to a plethora of possibilities? Posing the question in this way was heterodox: it made no use of standardized tests; it focused on meaningful roles in a society rather than on abstract competences; and it harbored a culturally relative perspective. So long as a capacity is valued in a culture, its expression can count as an intelligence; but in the absence of such a cultural or "field" endorsement, a capacity would not be considered an intelligence. It was from this perspective that I developed my theory of multiple intelligences (see chapters 1 and 2).

Building on this concept of intelligence, it proves possible to come up with a new and consistent way of speaking about the giftedness matrix. An individual is *gifted* if he or she is "at promise" in any domain where intelligences figure; and the term *prodigy* would be applied to an individual of unusual precocity. An *expert* is a person who has achieved a high level of competence within a domain, irrespective of whether any of his or her approaches are novel or experimental in any way. Conversely, an individual is considered *creative* if he or she regularly solves problems or fashions products in a domain in a way that is initially seen as novel but that ultimately is recognized as appropriate for the domain. No definition of genius flows directly from this work. But I would propose that an individual merits the term *genius* to the extent that his or her creative work in a domain exerts a significant effect on the definition and delineation of the domain—in the future, individuals who work in that domain will have to engage with the contributions made by the creative genius. The more universal the contribution, the more it travels across cultures and eras, the greater the genius. That is why young English and German writers traditionally shudder when confronted, respectively, with the examples of Shakespeare and Goethe; these titanic individuals have cast formidable shadows over the future dimensions and possibilities of the literary domain.

In the preceding discussion, I introduced an innovative way of conceiving intelligence; I then went on to suggest how the remainder of the giftedness matrix can be conceptualized with reference to this view of

TABLE 3.1   THE GIFTEDNESS MATRIX

Term	Sphere	Age Focus	Domain/ Field Status	Relevant Issues
Intelligence	bio- psychological	all	—	—
Giftedness	bio- psychological	youth	predomain/ prefield	crystallizing experience
Prodigiousness	bio- psychological	youth	current domain/field	wide resources sought and exploited
Expertise	current domain/field	post- adolescence	accept domain/field	cumulative knowledge/ skills
Creativity	future domain/field	post- adolescence	clash with domain/field	fruitful asynchrony
Genius	broad domain/ wide field	mature person	universal	link to childhood

intelligence. The effectiveness of such an analysis can be determined in part on the basis of its internal coherence; but for a behavioral scientist, a more important test is the extent to which the analysis is consistent with what is known about human behavior and the extent to which the analysis can lead to increased understanding.

Accordingly, in what follows, I carry out a developmental analysis. I examine four different points in the developmental trajectory of individuals, with special reference to the valued human capacities being treated here. Major notions are recorded in the accompanying table 3.1. Then, in conclusion, I touch on a few educational implications of this perspective.

The Five-Year-Old:
Indifferent to Domain and Field

In the first years of life, young children the world over develop powerful theories and conceptions of how the world works—the physical world and the world of other people. They also develop at least a first-draft level of competence with the basic human symbol systems—language, number, music, two-dimensional depiction, and the like. What is striking about these acquisitions is that they do not depend on explicit tutelage. Children develop these symbolic skills and theoretical conceptions largely by dint of their own spontaneous interactions with the world in which they live. This is not to deny that specific cultures exert specific effects, but rather to assert that the kinds of capacities that evolve would be difficult to thwart, given any reasonably rich and supportive environment.

With respect to most youngsters, then, one can speak of early development as being "pre-domain" and "pre-field." That is, youngsters develop with only dim alertness to the domains that exist in their culture and with even less sensitivity to the existence of fields that judge. At young ages, children are sometimes attracted to specific domains—what have elsewhere been termed crystallizing experiences (Walters & Gardner, 1986). However, for the most part, those who are attracted are more interested than they are proficient.

There are exceptions: Mozart was certainly one. There is the occasional prodigy who early on discovers an affinity to a culturally approved domain, and who begins immediately to master that domain. In such instances, the child has a jump-start on the attainment of expertise, and, perhaps, creativity.

The issue of childhood creativity is a vexing one. In many ways, I have argued, all young children partake of the elixir of creativity. They are willing to transcend boundaries of which they are at least peripherally aware; they throw themselves into their play and work with great passion; they create products that often strike "the field" as more impressive than works of much older youngsters. And yet, I think it is fair to say that such creativity occurs outside of the field. Even though the field may be impressed by works of young children—and legitimately so—the young child proceeds in sublime indifference to the operations of the field.

THE TEN-YEAR-OLD: MASTERING THE RULES OF THE DOMAIN

Shortly after the age at which school begins, youngsters gradually assume a quite different stance toward the opportunities in their culture. Whether or not this trend is abetted by school, it seems evident that youngsters want to know the rules of domains and the conventions of culture, and that they seek to master these as rapidly and expeditiously as possible. In the arts we encounter a period of literalness—students averting metaphor and striving to produce works of art that are as accurate as possible in terms of representational fidelity. But the same trends occur in every domain—the students want to know the rules of the game.

And so one might say that the existence of the domain and a sensitivity to the field arise with a vengeance. To the extent that students choose (or are chosen) to work in a specific domain, they attempt to gain expertise as quickly as possible. And even with reference to the wider society, students attempt to become acculturated as fully as possible.

This period then functions as an apprenticeship—an apprenticeship en route to expertise in specific domains as well to expertise in the ways of one culture. Those who advance most rapidly may be seen as gifted or prodigious, but reference to creativity or genius seems inappropriate here. The free-ranging explorations of the young child have ceased, while informed exploration of the boundaries of the domain cannot yet be undertaken.

If creative work is not yet forthcoming, the conditions for a creative (or noncreative) life may already be falling into place: creativity depends heavily on dispositional and personality traits and on the accidents of demography (Gardner, 1993; Perkins, 1981; Sternberg, 1988a). Those youngsters who are (and who feel) marginal within their culture, those who are ambitious and stubborn, those who can ignore criticism and stick to their guns are "at risk" for a creative life. On the other hand, those who feel comfortably a part of the group and who advance in their domain with little feeling of pressure or asynchrony are probably headed for (or consigned to) the life of the expert.

The Adolescent: At the Crossroads

The period between the ages of fifteen and twenty-five represents a moment of truth in the development of the entries on the giftedness matrix. The possibility for prodigiousness is already at an end—and genius lurks in the distant future. The crucial issue surrounds expertise. Individuals who devote themselves for a decade to a domain are likely to attain the level of the expert and have the option of continuing to make at least modest contributions to the domain for the foreseeable future. They may also become members in good standing of the dominant field. Their intelligences are being deployed in the service of the normal, productive functioning of their current society. Here the intelligences work comfortably within the tastes of the current field.

But at least some individuals do not remain simply at the level of expertise. At some point they make a decisive turn—a turn toward greater risk taking, increased testing of orthodoxy, and determined iconoclasm. No longer do they wish simply to follow in the steps of their mentors; instead, they address challenges and seek to go beyond what has come before. This heightened tension may result in a so-called midlife crisis, and, indeed, some adolescents cease their creativity altogether, either temporarily or permanently (Bamberger, 1982a; Csikszentmihalyi, Rathunde, & Whalen 1993). Others directly challenge the field, with unpredictable and varying degrees of success. In any event, if this period of crisis is successfully navigated, then the opportunities for sustained creative achievement remain alive.

The Mature Practitioner:
Ensconced Somewhere on the
Matrix of Giftedness

Speed forward another decade or so to the age of thirty to thirty-five, and one encounters an individual whose ultimate location on the giftedness matrix is likely to have been determined. On an actuarial basis, most individuals committed to a domain will either be contented experts, discontented experts, or individuals who sought to transcend expertise but failed. Of special interest, however, is the individual who, for whatever reason, transcends "mere" intelligence, giftedness, or expertise and seeks a creative life. We have long known some of the characteristics of such individuals: ambitious, self-confident, mildly neurotic, adventurous (Albert & Runco, 1986; Barron, 1969; MacKinnon, 1961). My own studies confirm that highly creative individuals, whatever their domain differences, have quite consistent personalities, and that they are typically demanding, self-centered individuals with whom it is difficult to remain on good terms.

But I have also sought to understand what it is like to be operating on the edge of current knowledge and expertise (Gardner, 1993). It is a bracing but frightening prospect to consider ideas and practices that have never, to one's knowledge, been attempted before. Such individuals, no matter how solitary, seem to need both cognitive and affective support at times of vulnerability. And in a way that approaches the uncanny, these individuals are reminiscent of the mother who is teaching a first language and introducing an initial culture to her child. To confirm that she is not mad, the creator needs to be able to convince at least one other person that she has invented a language, a way of seeing things, that makes sense. Absent an unusual set of intellectual, social, affective, and personality traits, such dedication to the enterprise of creativity is difficult to fathom.

My studies have suggested a certain pattern to the enterprise of the highly creative individual. After the first decade of expertise, the individual goes on to make a quite radical statement, one that shakes up the domain and field in which the person is working. A more synthetic statement is likely to emerge a decade or so later. In some domains, such as mathematics, physical science, or lyric poetry, the prospect of continuing breakthroughs is quite modest. But in others, it is possible to make new breakthroughs for several more decades. This is why artists such as Pablo Picasso, Igor Stravinsky, and Martha Graham could continue to lead highly creative lives and why some scientists, such as Sigmund Freud and Charles Darwin, found a lode that they could mine for the remainder of their active lives. And there are certain fields—for example, traditional philosophy and psychoanalysis—where important contributions are typically made in the middle or later decades of life.

Understanding creativity is difficult enough; to shed light on genius borders on the impossible. Let me simply propose that the genius is a creative individual who is able to arrive at insights that are novel and yet strike a deeply responsive chord across the world's diverse cultures. It is no easy task to make an advance within a domain; but to make an advance that can reverberate loudly across intellectual and geographical borders on the miraculous. Perhaps it is not fanciful to consider Mozart or Confucius or Shakespeare as miraculous—the incredible coinciding of a human being with the secrets of the universe.

With the genius, the developmental path comes full circle. The young child creates without respect to the domain and the field. The expert accepts the domain and the field. The would-be creator challenges the domain and the field. It is the special province of the genius to challenge the domain and the field, yet to arrive at a product or a solution that once again constitutes a new, more comprehensive domain—yielding an insight of broad human significance.

In speaking of genius, one moves rather far from the province of behavioral science—invoking a term that smacks more of the literary or artistic pages than of the volumes of a scientific journal. Yet, even if we cannot explain genius, we are wrong to pretend that it does not exist. Whether or not he can inspire insights in social scientists, Mozart is at least a vivid reminder of the heights to which a human being can occasionally rise.

EDUCATIONAL IMPLICATIONS

A developmental scheme designed to describe giftedness and its corollaries leads naturally to the question: What can be done to foster or educate facets of giftedness? It has sometimes been quipped, more in sorrow than in joy, that it is easier to thwart gifted and creative youngsters than it is to encourage their flowering. And, indeed, precisely because we know so little about these precious phenomena, it is most important that parents and teachers "do no harm."

Nonetheless, I believe that the foregoing discussion yields at least a few modest implications. To begin with, the very delineation of the varying forms that constitute giftedness, expertise, creativity, and the like can be of aid to educators in that it raises the question: What kind of extraordinary performances or achievements are wanted? To seek to develop an individual who is creative is a far different challenge than to nurture an individual who will be prodigious or to train an individual who will become an expert. What is deemed a gift in China may seem a frill or even a burden in Chicago, or vice versa. Disaggregating these "end states" and deciding which are desired and which are not desirable seems a useful step for any educator.

A second implication is entailed in the adoption of a developmental approach. Once one recognizes that children of different ages or stages have different needs, attend to different forms of cultural information, and assimilate content to different motivational and cognitive structures, then the kinds of educational regimens that we design ought to take into account these developmental factors. It is as inappropriate to subject a five-year-old to the critique of the field as it is to withhold such a critique from a committed apprentice or an aspiring master.

A third point concerns the kinds of educational models that are provided to children. Children glean quite different messages depending on whether the adults or masters with whom they come into contact embody expertise, thwarted creativity, realized creativity, or even some form of genius, and which sorts of early intimations of these end-states are encouraged or discouraged by these role models. The simple decision about which teachers or mentors to include in a giftedness program carries powerful signals about the direction children should ultimately pursue.

Overlaying the decision about specific individuals is the broader question of the messages about giftedness that are conveyed in the wider society. As I showed in a study of arts education in China and the United States (Gardner, 1989), two societies can convey contrasting messages about the uses to which talents can be put and the ways in which those talents can be developed within a culture. Within our own society, as well, there can be contrasting and even contradictory models of what counts as a gift—and what *should* count in the future.

Perhaps inevitably, discussions of giftedness and education in our current cultural context highlight the importance of the individual child. Yet, the above discussion reminds us that gifts of all sorts can never be properly conceptualized as existing solely within the head or body of individuals (see also chapters 11 and 13). By calling attention to the domain and field characteristics that surround any kind of activity, and particularly any kind of extraordinary activity, I hope to remind educators that they too should remain alert to the extrapersonal factors that play a vast role in the development (or thwarting) of talent.

A discussion of values may seem out of place in a contribution that purports to be scientific. Yet, if there is any societal realm in which issues of value are prominent, it is the terrain that must wrestle with the questions of what constitutes gifts and how they should be identified, fostered, and mobilized within a community. For example, equity and excellence need not be in direct conflict, but there is undeniably a tension between them, and particularly so in times of limited resources. Those of us who elect to devote our energies to the exploration of the fascinating matrix of human gifts have a special obligation to keep these issues of value in mind and, when possible, help make the value considerations and choices clear to colleagues, educators, and the wider public.

Chapter 4

THE BRIDGE TO EDUCATION

THE RORSCHACH TEST

Ever since I chose a career in scholarship, I have thought of myself primarily as a psychologist. My book *Frames of Mind* was written by a psychologist who thought he was addressing his fellow psychologists. In this book of some 400 pages, I included just a few paragraphs about the educational implications of the theory—and for the most part, these were ancillary thoughts.

For reasons that I do not fully understand, the theory of multiple intelligences spoke immediately to educators—loudly and quite clearly. Many educators saw an evident relation between the theory, as they understood it, and educational practices that they embraced. In a sense, I had presented educators with a Rorschach inkblot, and they were trying to decipher it.

I read or heard about schools that had created seven or eight learning centers or even classrooms, one for each intelligence; schools that had decided to focus on one of the neglected intelligences; schools that taught subjects in seven or eight ways; schools that introduced new ways to assess the intelligences; schools that put together all the students who were strong in one intelligence; schools that grouped students who were challenged in a particular intelligence; and schools that believed the best education occurred when children representing different intellectual profiles were placed together in a classroom.

None of these approaches was described or advocated in my book. I had not written as an educator: I did not know enough to be able to make cogent educational recommendations. Educators were projecting their "projects" onto my uninterpreted inkblot tests; whatever they thought, they were not divining what I had *really* meant, nor what the theory had *really* meant.

For roughly a decade, this state of affairs was fine with me. I was a psychologist, author, creator of ideas who had unleashed a powerful new "meme"—a unit of meaning—into the world that came to have a life of its own. The creator of the meme has no obligation to shepherd it through various milieus; and even if he did, there is no reason to think that he would be successful in doing so. Far better for me to move on to other concerns, and let the meme fend for itself.

First Actions

A number of events changed my mind. I began to visit classrooms and schools that were using ideas derived from the concept of multiple intelligences; inevitably, these ideas affected me positively or not so positively. Chief among these schools were the Key School in Indianapolis (now renamed the Key Learning Community), with which I have worked closely since the middle 1980s, and the New City School in St. Louis, with which I began to work around 1990. I learned a great deal from my interactions with colleagues at these fine schools.

In collaboration with other colleagues, I also began to carry out a number of educational interventions related—some related closely, some less so—to MI theory. I was finally getting my feet wet in the educational landscape. Needless to say, one thinks about educational issues differently when one is in an elementary school classroom each day than when one sits in an ivory tower.

But probably the key factor that influenced me was an incident that I have often retold. In the early 1990s, I received a communication from a colleague in Australia who said, roughly, "Your ideas are being used in an Australian state, and you won't like how they are being used." Uncertain what the colleague meant, I asked for details. This exchange occurred in the days before e-mail and attachments, and so the colleague sent me a stack of written materials a foot high. My colleague was right. The more I looked through these materials, the less I liked them. Eventually, I encountered the "smoking gun"—a list of various ethnic and racial groups coupled with the intelligences that each purportedly possessed and the intelligences that each purportedly lacked.

I reached a boiling point—and a tipping point. These materials were a perversion of my own emerging educational philosophy. With little hesitation, I accepted an invitation to appear on Australian television. Along with other educators and scientists, I denounced the program as "pseudoscience." As a result of the clamor that followed, the state canceled the program, much to my relief.

Because of this and other experiences, I changed my mind about the relationship between the creation of ideas and the uses to which they are put. I concluded that although I could not—and should not—serve as the chief of the MI police, I had an obligation to speak out about what I liked and, more particularly, what I felt was an improper use of my ideas.

My next public act was to publish a paper on various myths about multiple intelligences (Gardner, 1995b). The purpose of the paper was to guide friends and critics toward a more accurate understanding of the claims of the theory and its proper implications. The myths I addressed ranged from ones that had to do with the theory itself (e.g., the notion that an intelligence is the same as a domain or discipline—see chapter 2) to ones related to educational applications of the theory (e.g., that there is an "official" MI approach to education). I have not reprinted the paper here, because the important points have been incorporated into this text (notably in chapter 5).

Since then, I have not hesitated to speak out—on paper, in talks, and in videos—on how MI ideas should be used. I have emphasized the positive examples rather than berating those whose uses I deplore. But I have also made it clear that these are just one person's parsing. While I can legitimately claim credit for having introduced MI theory to the world, I hold no monopoly on how the theory should or should not be implemented; and, like anyone else, I can be wrong.

Another point I should mention parenthetically here is that my shift in attitude toward MI theory was part of a larger shift in the focus of my scholarly work. Since the mid-1990s, my major scholarly activity has been the study of professional ethics—what we have termed the GoodWork Project. This project focuses on the ways in which professionals can and should attend to the ethical implications of their work. I doubt that I would have become involved in the GoodWork Project had it not been for the ethical issues raised by the applications and the misapplications of MI theory.

THREE KEY EDUCATIONAL IMPLICATIONS

Of the various educational themes in the MI world, three stand out in my own mind. They concern the individualization of teaching and assessment, the need to articulate educational goals, and the advantages of multiple representations of key concepts. I discuss each in turn.

Individual Centered Education

Most schools throughout history have been uniform schools: students are taught the same things in the same way and are assessed in equally similar manner. This approach is seen as fair—after all, everyone is being treated equal. Yet, as I have pointed out, this approach is fundamentally unfair. It privileges those who have strong linguistic and logical-mathematical intelligences, whereas it makes school difficult for the many among us who exhibit somewhat different intellectual profiles.

An individual-centered education is not one that is self-centered or narcissistic. Rather, it is an education that takes the differences among individuals very seriously. Educators attempt to learn as much as they can about the learning strengths and proclivities of each student. As far as possible, educators make use of this information to craft the optimal education for each child.

I have suggested three roles that could be used in individualized education. The job of the assessment specialist is to acquire as much information as possible about each child and present it to teachers, parents, and the child in ways that are readily grasped. There is no imperative to assess each child, however; when the child is thriving educationally, one should say a prayer of thanks and move on to the next order of business. But when a child is having learning difficulties, it is important to understand his or her cognitive modes as accurately as possible.

The other two roles are brokering ones. The student-curriculum broker should match students with curricula (and, when possible, with appropriate assessments). When there are options—and I certainly favor some electives—the broker should recommend electives that might suit the child's intellectual profile. When there is a required curriculum—and I certainly favor some required courses—the broker should help the student find the best presentation of the curriculum. Everyone should study history and mathematics, but these topics need not be taught and assessed in a single way to all students.

The school community broker plays an analogous role outside the walls of the school. It is his or her job to expose the student (and the parents) to various vocational and avocational options in the community that might appeal to a student with a given intellectual profile. Not everyone wants to be a law professor; and, indeed, not everyone can occupy any particular occupational niche. The chance for a child to explore options that might be congenial to his or her strengths and interests can spell the difference between a frustrating educational experience and one that has purpose.

Of course, most schools will not be in a position to hire individuals to fill these positions. That is why I refer to "roles" rather than "positions." It is up to teachers, parents, peers, and the broader community to see that these needs are met when it is not possible to hire people who are expert in these roles.

Now, Howard Gardner could write about individualized education for decades and it might have little impact. (That might not keep Howard Gardner from trying—he is a persistent fellow!) What *will* bring individualized education to the fore are powerful computer programs. Once it has been demonstrated that algebra can be taught three or even thirty ways, it will be malpractice to declare "Johnny could not learn algebra my way— bring me another child." With the patience and versatility of tomorrow's computers, many facets of these three roles will be within the grasp of educators everywhere.

The Priority of Educational Goals

When I travel, I am frequently greeted with the words, "I have an MI classroom," or "We work in an MI school." I am flattered by these words; wishing to be polite, I respond by smiling and saying, "That's great. Thank you." But what I am really thinking is something different.

MI theory is certainly relevant to education, but it is not in itself an educational rationale or goal. As I have noted earlier, the assertion that we as a species have a number of intelligences, and that individuals differ in their particular profiles, could lead to any number of educational practices, some of them actually contradicting others. A fact or a hypothesis about the human condition can never in itself dictate what to do on Monday morning or next year.

This point was brought home to me vividly in a conversation I had with Richard Herrnstein, senior author of *The Bell Curve* (1994), shortly before his death. We were discussing the implications of the claim in that book that psychometric IQ is difficult to change. Were that true, Herrnstein and I agreed, one could draw two diametrically opposed conclusions:

1. IQ is difficult to change, and so we should not bother.
2. IQ is difficult to change, and so we should devote all of our efforts to changing it. We might prove successful. Indeed, we might even discover a way to change it much more readily than anyone had anticipated.

It is no secret that Herrnstein and his coauthor Charles Murray were more sympathetic to the first conclusion and I to the second. But the important point is that we agreed that both inferences were possible. Indeed, in the late 1970s and early 1980s, Herrnstein himself joined a project called Project Intelligence, whose declared aim was to raise the intelligence of the entire Venezuelan population. Paradoxically, in that particular instance, Herrnstein was the enthusiast and I was the skeptic.

The general point is this: One can never go from a scientific finding to an educational practice. Any finding has a multitude of implications, not all of them consistent with one another.

Instead, I argue, we need to proceed by stating as clearly as possible, what our educational goals are. There are many goals from which we could choose: critical thinking, creative thinking, civil individuals in a civil society, an orientation toward service, knowing the major facts and ideas in several disciplines, thinking well within disciplines, interdisciplinary thinking, mastering technology, immersion in the arts and humanities, cultivating the right questions, building on the strengths of each individual, and the like. Once we go beyond vapid generalities—to use our minds well, to be culturally literate—realistic and attainable goals are not easy to articulate, as I have frequently discovered. It is easier and more tempting to argue about practice. Should we track? Should we have bilingual classes? Should we have eighty-minute rather than forty-minute periods?

Alas, too many schools claim that they are achieving all of the goals I listed above. That omnibus claim cannot be true. One has to prioritize, one has to make tough choices. Just as one should find out what a school wants to achieve, one should ask the tougher question: "What is *not* a priority? What are you *not* trying to achieve?" If one seeks to be all things to all persons, the chances are high that one will not serve anyone well.

Returning to the phenomenon of MI classes and schools, I much prefer an exchange where an educator says to me, "My educational goal is X. I will know that I have achieved it when my students can Y. And here is how I propose to use the concept/theory/hypothesis/claim of multiple intelligences to help achieve that goal."

Multiple Representations of Key Concepts

In chapter 8, I discuss the educational goal that I most prize today: the ability of students to exhibit genuine understanding in a number of key disciplines. Far more important than the attainment of cultural literacy or factual mastery, I crave evidence that the student can think of and critique a scientific experiment; that the student is able to analyze a current event in terms of historical precedents and non- or pseudo-precedents; that the student can confront a work of art and illuminate its power and its modes of operation.

Even when the goal of disciplinary understanding is given high priority, it is difficult to achieve; and no doubt there are many ways to approach this goal. My own belief is that disciplinary understanding is most likely to be realized if educators focus on a manageable number of key concepts and explore them in some depth. Only under those conditions are the concepts likely to be understood. And in the process of deeply understanding gravity in physics, or revolution in history, or the transformation of a theme in a classical fugue, the student gains an invaluable asset—significant exposure to the ways in which experts in that discipline think.

Here is where the idea of multiple intelligences can be of genuine benefit to educators oriented toward the goal of disciplinary understanding. Mastery of a concept or theory requires repeated exposure to that material: one almost never achieves instant understanding. But it is a mistake to present the same content in the same way. Understanding is far more likely to be achieved if the student encounters the material in a variety of guises and contexts. And the best way to bring this about is to draw on all of the intelligences that are relevant to that topic in as many legitimate ways as possible.

In chapter 8, I focus on the attainment of disciplinary understanding of a few key concepts. At this point, it suffices to make three points. First, approaching topics in numerous legitimate ways ensures that one will reach more students. Some students will learn from linguistic entry points, others from artistic or personal or logical entry points; indeed, some will learn one subject best via one entry point, another subject via another entry point. Second, these multiple approaches to a topic convey to students what it is like to be a disciplinary expert—indeed, any kind of an expert. An expert is distinguished by the fact that he or she can think of his or her topic or skill in a variety of ways. Finally, through these multiple approaches, one activates different clusters of neural networks. To the extent that numerous neural networks are activated, and eventually connected, one obtains a solid and enduring mental representation of the topic in question.

WHERE MI APPEALS AND WHERE IT DOES NOT

The reaction to my embracing of the disciplined mind has been puzzling and instructive. I had thought that this traditional goal would reassure individuals who feared that an MI approach to education is a license for "doing your own thing" and that it would help advocates of MI use these ideas in ways that should satisfy conservative critics. In fact, at least so far, my pursuit of a disciplined mind has satisfied neither side of the political spectrum. Traditionalists suspect that my allegiance still remains with educational adventurers; they would prefer a curriculum that focuses on facts and information rather than one that pursues the elusive goal of "understanding." Progressives fear that I may have deserted the cause of individual-centered education and placed faith in the designers of curriculum rather than in students and teachers themselves. What I perceived as an elegant middle ground—a traditional educational goal with flexible means to achieve it—seems to have satisfied neither party in the educational wars.

In fact, there are few regions of the world where MI ideas would triumph in an up-or-down plebiscite. Most individuals—including policymakers and parents—are comfortable with traditional means as well as traditional ends. I have found equally fervent defenders of the status quo among individuals who thrived in school ("It was good enough for me, and it is good enough for my kids") and individuals who hated school and did poorly in it ("My kids had better just put their noses to the grindstone and do a better job than I did"). I've found mathematicians to be particularly leery of MI views; as far as they are concerned, there is but one intelligence. The chief thing that moves the minds of mathematicians is to have a child who does not learn in the conventional way. There is where I have seen converts.

But even if MI theory is unlikely to be embraced as an educational tool—let alone panacea—around the world, I have discovered a reassuring corollary. Everywhere I go, I encounter a minority of individuals—it could be 5 percent, it could be 25 percent—who believe that MI theory has important educational contributions to make. Sometimes these areas are ones open to progressive ideas—for example, northern Italy and large parts of Scandinavia. Sometimes there are individuals or groups or schools that want to be effective with students from diverse cultures, value the arts, care about children with learning difficulties, and seek to involve parents and communities in education. Other indices of MI readiness are described by Mindy Kornhaber and her colleagues in the COMPAS analysis (Kornhaber, Fierros, & Veenema, 2004). These researchers find receptivity to MI ideas in schools that value diversity, the arts, cooperation among teachers, willingness to reflect on practice, and an experimental attitude.

One day in late 2004, I was awakened by a phone call from the BBC. "Test scores have gone up," I was told, "and this success is being attributed to MI theory. Can you appear on our broadcast later during the day?" I was startled by the timing and the content of this message. A little digging revealed that David Milliband, the minister in charge of schools, had indeed mentioned recognition of MI ideas as a contributing factor to an improvement in test scores.

When I appeared on the broadcast, I quipped, "I am happy to take credit for the rise in scores, but I refuse to take blame if the scores go down." Speaking more seriously, I indicated that it is extremely difficult to identify factors that contribute to changes in test scores. Also, I pointed out that if one wanted to raise test scores, the most reliable way would be to practice taking tests every day throughout the school year. In defense of MI theory, I indicated that recognition of children's intellectual strengths and scope is probably a wise practice in itself. Moreover, to the extent that teachers present important ideas in many ways and give students many ways and opportunities to indicate what they have learned, these educational practices are likely to have benign effects—and perhaps even contribute to a rise in the (alas) all-important scores on standardized tests.

Clearly, much has happened between the publication of my psychological tract in 1983 and the offhand comments of a powerful schools minister two decades later. MI ideas now belong to the world of education and are talked and argued about around much of the world. We are now observing the theory in practice. In the chapters in part II, I take a closer look at some of the specific experiments in which others and I have been involved as we have explored the educational implications of MI theory.

Chapter 5

Frequently Asked Questions About Theory and Practice

Almost every day, I receive questions about multiple intelligences theory. Some of the questions concern the theory itself, although many more deal with recommended practices or with questionable applications. The questions come from professors, teachers, parents, college students, high school students, and elementary school students. They come from many states and many countries. The questions used to reach me primarily by letter and phone; now, of course, they arrive as well by fax and by e-mail. And whenever I speak publicly about MI theory, whether in person or on radio or television, a set of questions greets me on my return to the office.

Initially, I sought to answer each question individually; there were not that many, and I learned from and enjoyed the process. But after a while, the questions became repetitive, and there were too many of them. I began to use generic letters to answer the most frequent questions. For example: "Is there a test for multiple intelligences?" (Answer: "Not one that I endorse"). "Are there multiple intelligence high schools?" (Answer: "Many, but each has been developed by a group of practitioners, not by me"). When an interesting and novel question arises, I sometimes write an answer of some length and then include it in a future publication.

In the pages that follow, I respond to questions raised frequently by people interested in the theory. Some of these answers were initially developed in conjunction with Joseph Walters and Margaux Wexberg, to whom I give thanks.

Terminology

Q. I am confused by terminology. Is intelligence a product, a process, a content, a style, or all of the above?

A. I wish that this were a simple matter. Fundamentally, an intelligence refers to a biopsychological potential of our species to process certain kinds of information in certain kinds of ways. As such, it clearly involves processes that are carried out by dedicated neural networks. No doubt each of the intelligences has its characteristic neural processes. Most of these neural processes are quite similar across all human beings, but some might prove to be customized to a group or even an individual.

The intelligence itself is not a content, but it is geared to specific contents. That is, the linguistic intelligence is activated when individuals encounter the sounds of language or when they wish to communicate something verbally to another person. However, the linguistic intelligence is not dedicated only to sound. It can be mobilized as well by visual information when an individual decodes written text. In deaf persons, linguistic intelligence is mobilized by signs (including syntactically arranged sets of signs) that are seen or felt.

From an evolutionary point of view, it seems probable that each intelligence evolved to deal with certain kinds of contents in a predictable world. However, once such a capacity has emerged, there is nothing that mandates that it must remain tied to the original inspiring content. As the term has it, the capacity can be *exapted* for other purposes. I assume, for example, that mechanisms related to the recognition of species in nature are now regularly used in recognizing commercial products—that is, the so-called naturalist intelligence is used in the cultural world. Also, some of the most powerful human systems—like written language—came about not directly through evolution but through the yoking of capacities—for example, spatial and linguistic capacities that had presumably evolved for different purposes.

Speaking more loosely, we can describe certain products—for example, maps, drawings, architectural plans—as involving a particular intelligence: in this case, of course, spatial intelligence. However, we must be aware that this characterization entails an inference on the part of the observer. It might be that an individual could create architectural plans or fashion a sculpture using intelligences other than spatial. Until such time as we can actually designate neural circuitry as representing one or another intelligence "in action," we cannot know for sure which intelligence or intelligences are actually being invoked on a specific occasion.

Educators are prone to collapsing the terms *intelligence* and *style*. For informal matters, that is no great sin. However, style and intelligence are really fundamentally different psychological constructs. Style refers to the customary way in which an individual approaches a range of materials—for example, a playful or a planful style. Intelligence refers to the computational power of a mental system: for example, a person whose linguistic intelligence is strong is able readily to compute information that involves language. Speak of styles, speak of intelligences, but don't conflate the two if you can help it. For further discussion of this point, see myth 3 in *Intelligence Reframed* (1999a, pp. 83–85).

Q. You use the word "domain" a lot. What is a domain, and how does it relate to an intelligence?

A. I am glad you asked this question. A domain is a new construct developed by my colleague David Feldman (1980). It refers to any organized activity in society in which individuals can be ranked in terms of expertise. Any occupation, art, craft, or sport is a domain. The domains in a society can be thought of as the kinds of roles listed in the Yellow Pages of a phone book—anything from Accounting to Zoology.

As I use it, the term *intelligence* refers to a set of human computational capacities. As humans, we have the ability to "compute" language, number, social relations, spatial relations, etc. We cannot directly see the intelligences. We observe them at work by observing individuals carrying out various kinds of behaviors and tasks. When a person sings, we assume that she is using at least her musical intelligence. When she dances, we assume that she is using at least her bodily-kinesthetic and spatial intelligences.

You can see, then, that we really only observe individuals working in domains. We infer the intelligences on the basis of our best guess about the intelligences that are characteristically involved. But we cannot know for sure. The aforementioned dancer might well be relying heavily on her linguistic or intrapersonal intelligences along with, or instead of, her bodily or spatial intelligences.

Through psychological and neurological research, it is possible to gather more compelling evidence about which intelligences are being used in a behavior or task. More casual observation has to be tentative. For more on domains and disciplines, see myth 2 in *Intelligence Reframed* (1999a, pp. 82–83).

Q. Isn't it odd to speak of skill in gym or on the playing field as an intelligence? And wouldn't this mean that individuals with physical defects are mentally retarded?

A. I don't find it odd to speak of the bodily skill used by, say, an athlete, a dancer, or a surgeon as embodying intelligence. The performances of these individuals are valued in many societies, and they involve an enormous amount of computation, practice, and expertise. Snobbishness about use of the body reflects the Cartesian split between mind and body and a concomitant degradation of processes that seem less mental or not mental; contemporary neuroscience, however, has sought to bridge this split and to document the cognition involved in planful action (and, for that matter, in emotional anticipations and reactions).

As for the issue of retardation, it is true that the loss of a certain physical capacity could cause an individual to have problems in bodily-kinesthetic capacity, just as loss of hearing or sight could cause problems with, respectively, linguistic or spatial capacities. As in those cases, therapists are challenged to substitute other systems, be they other bodily mechanisms or prostheses. There is a big difference between losing a sensory system or a motor system, on the one hand, and losing the actual intelligence on the other. Indeed, computer scientists have already created robots that carry out physical actions as well as other kinds of prostheses that can substitute for impaired sensory or motor capacities. In the future, people with such impairments will be able to use these devices to carry out the same actions that unimpaired people execute with their bodies. The once notable gap between physically impaired and unimpaired may disappear.

Should one still use the term *intelligence* in such cases? It depends on the role the individual plays. If the prosthetic device simply substitutes for the individual, then it is the device, rather than the individual, that is displaying intelligence. But if the individual is programming the device or making consequential decisions about its deployment, then the individual is exercising a particular intelligence. The computer is a tool in his or her hands. Indeed, the same line of reasoning can be invoked with respect to music. Composition used to presuppose instrumental and notational skills on the part of the composer. Now computers can substitute for both. The analyst must locate the *source* of the intelligence: does it inhere in the programmer, the program, or the user of the program?

Q. How does intelligence relate to creativity?

A. Having studied intelligence and proposed a pluralistic view of intelligence, I turned my attention to creativity (see chapter 3). Not surprisingly, I ascertain that there are many forms of creativity. Domains involving characteristic combinations of intelligences also exhibit characteristic forms of creativity. So, for example, creativity in physics turns out to be quite different from creativity in poetry or politics or psychology. Generalizations about creativity are destined to be weak; the devil lies in the details about the creator and the creative domain in question.

A few more comments about creativity. First, one cannot be creative unless one has mastered a domain—that process can take up to ten years. Second, creativity probably has more to do with personality than with sheer intellectual power. People who enjoy taking risks, who are not afraid of failure, who are attracted by the unknown, or who are uncomfortable with the status quo are those likely to make creative discoveries. Finally, as stressed by my colleague Mihaly Csikszentmihalyi (1996), creativity should not be viewed simply as a characteristic of an individual. Rather, creativity emerges from the interaction of three entities: (1) the individual with his given talents, personality, and motivation; (2) the domain—the discipline or craft in which the individual is working; and (3) the field—the set of individuals and social institutions that render judgments about quality and originality.

I have written a good deal about creativity. See my books *Creating Minds* (1993), *Extraordinary Minds* (1997), *Changing Minds* (2004b), and chapter 8 of *Intelligence Reframed* (1999a).

THE THEORY

Q. Is the idea of multiple intelligences really a scientific theory? Could it be confirmed or disconfirmed by experiment?

A. The term *theory* oscillates between two quite different meanings. Among physical scientists, the term is reserved for an explicit set of conceptually linked propositions whose individual and joint validity can be assessed through systematic experimentation. Among lay persons, the term is used promiscuously to refer to any set of ideas put forth orally or in writing—asked about the rise of the stock markets, the man on the corner says, "I've got a theory about that."

Multiple intelligences theory falls somewhere between these two uses. There is no systematic set of propositions that could be voted on by a board of scientists. On the other hand, the theory is not simply a set of notions that I dreamed up one day. Rather, I offer a definition, a set of criteria for what counts as an intelligence, data that speak to the plausibility of each individual intelligence, and methods for revising the formulation. The criteria are laid out in chapter 1 of this book and more fully in chapter 4 of *Frames of Mind* (1983b).

In many sciences, theories occupy this intermediary status. Certainly, theories in the social sciences attempt to be as systematic as possible, yet they are rarely proved or disproved in a decisive way. And broad theories in the natural sciences, like evolution or plate tectonics, are similarly immune from a single, simple test. Rather, they gain or lose plausibility on the basis of an accumulation of many findings over a long period of time.

This is how I think about MI theory. I have put forth a candidate set of intelligences that are said to have their own characteristic processes and to be reasonably independent of one another. Over time the particular intelligences nominated and their degree of dependence on or independence from one another will be more firmly established by empirical evidence.

Individuals in search of a decisive thumbs-up or thumbs-down vote on the validity of any theory of intelligence are naive. Still, it is important to indicate what kinds of considerations would lend greater or lesser plausibility to the theory. Suppose it was discovered that a certain region of the brain in fact subserved more than one intelligence; or that individuals who were strong in one intelligence were invariably impaired in another intelligence; or that symbol systems that were ostensibly associated with one intelligence actually drew on the same cognitive processes as another intelligence. Each of these lines of evidence would cast doubt on the validity of the overall theory, although with appropriate revisions, the theory might retain some validity. We do not reject Piaget's overall theory of cognitive development just because some of its specific claims have been undermined by subsequent research.

Q. How does MI theory relate to the psychometricians' notion of *g* or general intelligence?

A. MI theory questions not the existence but the province and explanatory power of *g*. This construct is a statistical outcome, and its strength varies to some extent depending on the assumptions that are built into the factorial model being employed on the population being assessed. We do not really understand what is measured in *g*—it could be anything from sheer intellect to motivation to skill in following instructions to the ability to shift facilely from one kind of problem to another.

I am uncomfortable with the assumption inherent in *g* that an individual who has a high *g* could be equally accomplished in any intellectual area. MI theory is an extended argument against this all-purpose view of intellect. For additional discussion, see myth 5 in *Intelligence Reframed* (1999a, pp. 87–88).

ASSESSMENT

Q. Could one construct a test or a set of tests for each of the intelligences?

A. At one time, I thought it would be possible to create a test for each intelligence—an intelligence-fair version, to be sure—and then simply to determine the correlation between the scores on the several tests. I now believe that this feat would be extremely difficult to accomplish. Indeed, I think it could be accomplished only if one were to develop *several* measures for each intelligence, and then make sure that people were comfortable in dealing with the materials and methods through which each intelligence was being measured. Thus, for example, the measure of spatial intelligence would be a product of one's performances in such activities as finding one's way around an unfamiliar terrain, playing chess (or some other spatially demanding game), reading blueprints, and remembering the arrangement of objects in a recently visited room.

Were such a measurement of intelligence to be done, the findings would be of scientific interest. However, one reason why I have moved away from attempting to create such measures is that they may lead to new forms of labeling and stigmatization. As I argue in later chapters, the intelligences should be mobilized to help people learn important content and not used as a way of categorizing them. To use the language of one of my critics, I do not want to inspire the creation of a new set of "losers."

Q. Speaking of science, does the brain evidence from neuroscience research continue to support your theory?

A. In neuroscience, a decade is a long time, and the theory of multiple intelligences was developed more than two decades ago. We now know much more about the functioning and development of the nervous system. I find the neurological evidence to be amazingly supportive of the general thrust of MI theory. The evidence supports the particular intelligences that I described and provides elegant evidence of the finer structure of such capacities as linguistic, mathematical, and musical processing. For example, the French cognitive neuroscientist Olivier Houdé has provided convincing evidence that logical and numerical capacities are cognitively and neurologically distinct and might properly be considered separate intelligences (Houdé, 2004).

It is sometimes said that the brain is a very flexible organ subject to the events of early experience and that this feature calls into question the theory of multiple intelligences. This remark is not pertinent. The fact of "neural plasticity" is independent of the issue of distinct intelligences. Multiple intelligences theory holds that linguistic processing occurs through a different set of neural mechanisms than does spatial or interpersonal processing. The fact that the processing may occur in somewhat different regions of the brain across individuals as a result of their differing early experiences is interesting but not relevant to the identification of intelligences per se.

Indeed, suppose that in one person musical processing occurred in region A and spatial processing in region B, and that in another person these representations were reversed. MI theory would not thereby be affected. Even if musical intelligence were represented in regions A, B, and C in one person and regions D, E, and F in a second person, that still would not affect the theory. If, however, musical and spatial processing were identically represented in a population of persons, that fact would suggest that we are dealing with one intelligence and not two separate intelligences.

Q. What do other scholars think of MI theory?

A. As one might expect, there is a wide spectrum of opinion both within psychology and across the biological and behavioral sciences. Those involved in standard psychometrics are almost always critical of the theory. Among psychologists who are not psychometricians, there is more openness to the expansion of the concept and measurement of intelligence. Still, psychologists like to have neat measures of their constructs, and many are frustrated that the "new" intelligences are not as readily measured as the standard one. Also, psychologists generally continue to think of intelligence as "scholastic capacity," whereas MI theory attempts to expand the notion of intelligence to extend to all manner of human cognitive capacities. The same individuals who are skeptical of MI theory are also reluctant to embrace Daniel Goleman's notion of emotional intelligence or Robert Sternberg's concept of successful intelligence.

Scholars are not known for responding generously to new theories, and so I have not been surprised at the considerable criticism leveled at MI theory. One index of its reception is the extent and tenor of citations of the theory in scholarly articles and textbooks. Over the years, MI theory has been mentioned in innumerable articles and in most texts that touch on issues of intelligence. These references are generally respectful.

Most gratifying has been the response by scholars in the "harder" sciences (such as biology) on the one hand, and in more distant fields (such as the arts and humanities) on the other. The idea of multiple intelligences has considerable appeal across the disciplines, and my particular choice of intelligences is often endorsed. If one wanted to deploy such endorsements to critique the theory, one could point out that these people are not expert in the psychology of intelligence. If one wanted to use them to praise the theory, one could point out that these scholars have no ax to grind. Some trenchant criticisms of my work and my responses to those critiques appear in *Gardner Under Fire* (Schaler, 2006).

Q. Is a rapprochement possible between MI and competing theories of intellect?

A. Certainly, to some extent. Aspects of the theory are compatible with propositions put forth by other theorists. I am comfortable with the biocultural approach defended by Stephen Ceci, the emphasis on media and symbol systems adopted by David Olson, the cultural sensitivity emphasized by Patricia Greenfield, and the multifactorial stance of earlier scholars, such as L. L. Thurstone. More broadly speaking, the modular approach put forth by psychologists like Steven Pinker, Leda Cosmides, and John Tooby, linguists like Noam Chomsky, and anthropologists like Stephen Mithen is quite consonant with the recognition of distinct intelligences.

Recently, the most widely discussed approach to intelligence is the triarchic model put forth by Robert Sternberg (1985). Sternberg and I agree more on our criticism of standard intelligence theory than on the directions that new theoretical work should take. That is, we reject the focus on a single scholastic intelligence that is measured by a certain kind of short answer test. Sternberg proposes three different facets of intelligence, which he labels the componential, the experiential, and the contextual, and he has devised various measures for each.

Along with most other theorists in this area, Sternberg does not attend to the particular contents with which intelligence operates. That is, it is immaterial to his theory whether a person is processing words or pictures or bodily information or material from the personal or natural world. Rather, more sympathetic to a "horizontal" view of mind, he assumes that the same components will operate irrespective of the kind of material being processed. Here our intuitions and claims differ fundamentally.

I applaud Sternberg's effort to develop new measures of intelligence. Such measures cannot but help broaden our notions of human capacities. I wish, however, that his new measures were more adventurous. In my view, Sternberg adheres too closely to the kinds of linguistic and logical items that have traditionally dominated intelligence testing; I predict that his new measures will end up correlating quite highly with standard tests and with one another.

In the emphases of his model, Sternberg reveals that he is much more of a psychologist and a psychometrician than I am. This may explain why his work has been of greater interest to psychologists, whereas mine has captured the interest of educators and the lay public (see Kornhaber, 2004).

THE STRUCTURE OF INTELLIGENCES AND THEIR COMBINATION

Q. Need the intelligences be entirely independent of one another?

A. The theory is simpler, both conceptually and biologically, with the various intelligences conceived of as totally independent of one another. However, such independence is by no means theoretically necessary. It may turn out empirically that certain intelligences are more closely tied together than others, at least in particular cultural settings.

The independence of intelligences makes a good working hypothesis. It can be tested only by using appropriate measures in different cultural settings (see the questions on assessment above). Otherwise, we might prematurely conclude that two intelligences are tied together, when in fact the apparent correlation is an artifact of a particular measure in a particular culture that features particular activities.

The reason for underscoring independence is to alert people to the possibility that strength in one area does not necessarily signal strength in other areas. The same, of course, goes for weaknesses. At a practical level, some individuals will show groupings of strengths (say, linguistic and bodily intelligences) as well as groupings of weaknesses (say, spatial and intrapersonal intelligences). Life is interesting, however, because these couplings are no more predictable than the romantic attraction or aversion between two individuals.

Q. How do you know that the intelligences represent the right-sized unit of analysis? Can't each of the intelligences be broken down indefinitely?

A. I question the notion that there is a single, uniquely correct unit of analysis for constructs as complex as intelligence. For certain purposes— for example, determining whether a retarded person is capable of benefiting from schooling—a single measure like IQ *might* suffice. On the other hand, if one wants to model what is involved in particular musical tasks, such as performing or composing, it is evident that a single construct of musical intelligence is far too gross.

In writing about multiple intelligences, I have always noted that each intelligence is itself composed of constituent units. There are several musical, linguistic, and spatial subintelligences; for certain analytic or training purposes, it may be important to dissect intelligence at this further level of fineness.

I justify my small set of intelligences on the basis of parsimony and usefulness. If I were to write about dozens of subintelligences, I might well be more accurate in a scientific sense, but doing so would make the construct unwieldy for practical purposes, such as educational uses. Moreover, there is evidence to suggest that the subintelligences often work together and support one another; for this reason, too, it makes sense to speak of eight or nine intelligences, rather than of one or a hundred.

Q. What about the often noted connection between mathematical and musical intelligences?

A. There is no doubt that individuals who are mathematically talented often show an interest in music. I think that this linkage occurs because mathematicians are interested in patterns, and music offers itself as a gold mine of harmonic, metric, and compositional patterns. Interest, however, is not the same as skill or talent; a mathematician's interest in music does not predict that he or she will play well or be an acute critic of the performances of others.

Of equal importance, the imputed link rarely works the other way. We do not expect of randomly chosen musicians that they will be interested, let alone skilled, in mathematics. There may also be a bias in the kind of music at issue. Those involved in classical music are far more likely to be oriented toward science and mathematics than those involved in jazz, rock, rap, and other popular forms.

These observed correlations and lack of correlations suggest another factor at work. In certain families and perhaps also certain ethnic groups, a strong emphasis is placed on scholastic and artistic accomplishment. Youngsters are expected to do well in school and to perform creditably on a musical instrument. These twin goals yield a population of youngsters who stand out in math and music. There may be other common underlying factors, such as a willingness to drill regularly, an inclination toward precision in dealing with marks on a piece of paper, and a desire to attain high standards. One would have to sample a wide variety of skills—from being punctual to writing cogent essays to following instructions in a drill—before jumping to the conclusion that a privileged connection exists between musical and mathematical intelligences.

Q. What about capacities that cut across the different intelligences, such as memory?

A. I am skeptical about the existence of horizontal faculties—faculties like memory or attention or perception that are alleged to operate equivalently across all kinds of content. In my view one of the most important discoveries in the cognitive and brain sciences is that the mind is better viewed in a *vertical* way—as a set of faculties geared to particular contents found in the external world and in human experience.

Looking more specifically at memory, considerable neuropsychological evidence documents different kinds of memory: immediate memory, short-term memory, long-term memory, semantic (or generic) memory, episodic memory (memory for particular events), procedural memory (knowing how), and propositional memory (knowing that). These memories reflect different psychological processes and are served by different neural centers. There is convincing neuropsychological evidence that memory for language can be separated from memory for music, shapes, faces, bodily movements, and so on. On close inspection, the notion of a single, unitary memory falls apart.

It is instructive to consider what we ordinarily mean when we say a person has a good memory. Usually we mean that the person has a good linguistic memory—she can remember names, dates, definitions. We generally do not have a clue about whether she is equally facile at remembering visual patterns, musical patterns, bodily movements, or the way she or other persons felt at a recent social event. Each of these skills may have its own mnemonic process, unrelated to the others.

Q. How can diverse and independent intelligences function effectively without a leader or executive?

A. A theory that does not posit an executive function has certain advantages over one that does. Such a theory is simpler; it also avoids the specter of infinite regression—the question of who or what is in charge of the executive. Nor does effective work necessarily require an executive. Many groups—be they artistic or athletic—perform well without designated leaders; and an increasing number of work teams are organized heterarchically rather than hierarchically. Complexity theory documents how well-organized entities can arise naturally, without the need for a "master plan."

The question of an executive—what I have sometimes called a "central intelligence agency"—needs to be considered on the theoretical and practical planes. On the theoretical plane, the question is whether behavior is better modeled as the result of some kind of executive function. That executive function could be "smart"—intentionally making well-motivated decisions—or "dumb"—simply a traffic cop that ensures that two processes are not going off simultaneously. Considerable evidence suggests that such executive functions are handled by structures in the frontal lobe. The "modeler" must then decide whether to consider this executive function a separate intelligence or emergent from other intelligences, such as the intrapersonal intelligence. At present, I lean toward the latter (see Moran & Gardner, 2007).

At a practical level, we need to ask how individuals can best organize their activities and their lives. Here there are vast and revealing individual differences. Some individuals are quite reflective and metacognitive: they are immersed in self-conscious planning, and this planning can be of considerable aid in accomplishing goals. Other individuals are more intuitive: they know what they want to do, and they just accomplish their business when they find themselves in the appropriate context. It has been said that Dante and Shakespeare had minds so fine that they were never violated by a thought. If this statement has meaning, it suggests that neither craftsman devoted much time to obsessing about what to do, when to do it, and how to do it; he just waited until he was prepared to commence his creations, then did his job as well as he could.

Ultimately, I have no objection if individuals find it useful to invoke some kind of an executive function. For modeling purposes, I find it useful to see whether one can explain human behavior in the absence of such hierarchical considerations, or whether the hierarchy can emerge naturally as part of everyday functioning rather than by invoking a separate executive intelligence (with the regression problems that entails—who or what is in charge of the executive?).

Q. What of a general capacity called *critical thinking*? Isn't it important in today's society? Shouldn't we have courses that help young people develop such a faculty?

A. As with executive function, I am not irredeemably opposed to the notion of critical thinking. Indeed, I would like myself, my children, my students, and my friends to think critically, and anything that can aid in that process should be encouraged.

I doubt, however, that there is a particular species of thinking called "critical thinking." As I've suggested with reference to memory and other putative "across-the-board" capacities, closer analysis calls their existence into question. Particular domains seem to entail their own idiosyncratic forms of thinking and critique. Musicians, historians, taxonomic biologists, choreographers, computer programmers, and literary critics all value critical thinking. But the *kind* of thinking required to analyze a fugue is simply of a different order from that involved in observing and categorizing different species, or editing a poem, or debugging a program, or creating and revising a new dance. There is little reason to think that training to think critically in one of these domains is the same as in another domain; nor would I expect appreciable "savings" or "transfer" when a new domain is broached. That is because each of these domains exhibits its own particular objects, moves, and logic of implications.

To be sure, certain habits of thought may prove useful across domains. One can get purchase from so-called weak moves such as taking one's time, considering alternatives, brainstorming, eliciting critical feedback from sympathetic peers, putting work aside for when one hits a snag, planning backwards from an end product, and so forth. Such habits of mind ought to be cultivated early and widely. But even these habits must be practiced explicitly in every domain in which they are applicable; indeed, they are called "weak" precisely because they do not in themselves get you very far. It is unrealistic to expect that the individual who takes her time in, say, investing in the stock market will necessarily do so when completing her homework, eating lunch, or falling in love.

For these reasons, I do not place much stock in courses that feature critical thinking per se. I much prefer that critical thinking be featured in each and every course or activity where it could prove valuable. Courses that help people draw on these lessons can be useful; courses that are expected to substitute for, or render unnecessary, the modeling of critical thinking in particular domains strike me as a waste of time. Ultimately, the surest road to critical thought "across the board" is a regimen where critical thinking is inculcated in one discipline and domain after another.

I often encounter the greatest resistance to this perspective when I speak to mathematicians or logicians. To these individuals, thinking *is* critical thinking wherever you encounter it; if one knows how to be logical, one should be able to apply logic everywhere. (And if you don't, life is hopeless!) No doubt mathematics and logic merit our admiration precisely because those domains strive for the greatest generality for the propositions and patterns that they feature. However, neither in their practice nor in their person do mathematicians and logicians epitomize what they believe. Often these individuals prove to be quite impractical or illogical in their own personal lives. Or, equally suspect, they seek to apply logical approaches in areas where they are manifestly inappropriate, such as when pursuing a love relation; dealing with a difficult student, child, or colleague; or, as we have seen with reference to both Vietnam and the Middle East, foreign policy following Rand Corporation–style algorithms. Psycho-logic turns out to be quite a different affair from mathematical logic.

Q. Is there an artistic intelligence?

A. Strictly speaking, there is no artistic intelligence. Rather, intelligences function artistically—or not artistically—to the extent that they exploit certain properties of a relevant symbol system. When one uses language in an ordinary expository way, as I am doing here, one is not using the linguistic intelligence in an aesthetic way. If, however, language is used metaphorically, expressively, or in such a way as to call attention to its formal or sound properties, then it is being used artistically. By the same token, spatial intelligence can be exploited aesthetically by a sculptor or a painter, but routinely by a geometer or a surgeon. Even musical intelligence can function nonaesthetically, as when bugle calls are used in the armed services to signal meal times or the raising or lowering of the flag. Conversely, patterns designed by mathematicians for mathematical purposes have ended up on display in art galleries.

Whether an intelligence is deployed for aesthetic purposes represents a decision made by the individual and/or the culture. An individual can decide to use linguistic intelligence in the manner of a lawyer, a salesperson, a poet, or an orator. However, cultures also highlight or thwart artistic uses of intelligences. In some cultures, almost everyone writes poetry, dances, sings on key, or plays an instrument. In contrast, Plato would have eliminated poetry from his Republic, and Stalin scrutinized every poem issued by certain hands as if it were a diplomatic note.

Of course, informally, it is perfectly all right to speak of artistic intelligences. I do this myself, particularly as a shorthand for those intelligences that are frequently mobilized for artistic ends. In this context, it is worth remembering that ideas based on the concept of multiple intelligences have grown comfortably in schools that highlight the arts, and such ideas seem an uncomfortable stretch in schools where the arts have been eliminated or marginalized.

GROUP DIFFERENCES

Q. Are intelligences the same in quality or quantity across groups? For instance, do men exhibit profiles of intelligences that differ from women? What about different racial or ethnic groups?

A. This question is potentially explosive. I suspect that if intelligence-fair tests were developed, they would elicit differences across genders and other readily identifiable groups. Even should such differences be found, it is unclear how to interpret them. Women might perform worse than men on spatial tasks in the West; but if there existed an environment in which spatial orientation were important for survival, then such differences might disappear or be reversed. Apparently, this erasure of gender differences happens among the Eskimos. By the same token, the gender difference regularly found in mathematics scores on standardized tests in the West is less marked in Asian populations, where, indeed, Asian women often score better than Western men.

Additionally, there exists the intriguing question of whether men and women use their intelligences in identical ways. In lower mammals, there is evidence that spatial orientation is mediated by landmarks for females and by body position for males; a similar difference may be found in human beings. Also, there is the question of whether men and women prioritize intelligences in the same way. Carol Gilligan's (1982) pioneering work on moral judgments suggests that women place a higher premium on interpersonal considerations, whereas men are more likely to draw on logical-mathematical thinking.

In my own work, I have elected not to pursue the question of group differences. So often, apparent group differences have been exploited for politically dubious ends—as happened in the Australian case that I mentioned in chapter 4. I prefer not to provide additional ammunition for such efforts. In any event, should investigations demonstrate replicable differences among groups, I would regard these differences as starting points for imaginative efforts at remediation rather than as proof of inherent limitations within a group.

Q. Does the theory of multiple intelligences apply to other species and to artificial intelligence?

A. This is an intriguing subject. I've suggested that my list of intelligences is one way of characterizing human intellect. However, it also offers a set of categories that can be applied to other entities that might be deemed intelligent.

One could conduct an inventory of intelligences and then apply it to other organisms. Such an inventory might reveal that rodents have considerable spatial intelligence, that primates have superior bodily-kinesthetic intelligence, and that birds exhibit musical intelligence. Perhaps some species—like bats and dolphins—exhibit intelligences that are unknown or not developed in human beings. And certain intelligences—like intrapersonal or existential—may be the exclusive purview of human beings. In *A Year at the Races* (2004) novelist Jane Smiley applied MI theory to an analysis of the intelligences of horses; psychologist Stanley Coren did a similar thing with dogs some years before (1994).

We already know that highly intelligent computer programs have been created. There are programs that compose music, carry out complex calculations, and defeat chess champions in mind-to-mind combat. Whether computers can also develop personal intelligences is a subject of considerable dispute. Many experts in artificial intelligence believe that it is just a matter of time before computers exhibit intelligence about human entities. I personally feel that this assertion is a category error. An entity cannot have conceptions of persons in the absence of membership in a community with certain values and under certain vulnerabilities; it seems to me an undue stretch to attribute such a status to computers. However, in a few years, both human beings and computers may chuckle at my naïveté.

INTELLIGENCE AND THE LIFE COURSE

Q. What happens to multiple intelligences during later life?

A. In many ways, multiple intelligences seem a particular gift of childhood. When we observe children, we can readily see them making use of their several intelligences. Indeed, one of the reasons for my enthusiasm about children's museums is their evident cultivation of a plethora of intelligences. Nowadays, the children's museum simply has a better fit with the minds of children than does the average school. I have similar enthusiasm for the preschools of Reggio Emilia, which cultivate "the hundred languages of children" (Guidici, Rinaldi, & Krechevsky, 2001).

It could be that some of the multiple intelligences decline with age in importance as well as in visibility. But I believe that quite the opposite is true. As individuals become older, our intelligences simply become internalized. We continue to think in multiple ways—indeed, differences in modes of mental representation are likely to increase throughout active life. These differences are simply less manifest to outside observers.

Consider, for example, what happens in the average high school or college classroom. The teacher lectures, the students remain in their seats either taking notes or looking vaguely bored. One might easily infer that no processing is going on or that all the process is linguistic in nature. However, when it comes to representing disciplinary skills or contents outside this setting, those students are free to make use of whatever representational capacities they have at their disposal. A lecture on physics might be represented in language, logical propositions, graphic form, some kind of kinesthetic imagery (which is how Einstein thought about physics), or some kind of musical format (for example, the Greeks stressed the parallels between musical and mathematical forms). Students also may take all kinds of notes in class and use disparate aids for study and recall.

The recesses of our minds remain private. No one can tell the mind exactly what to do. As I see it, the challenge to the mind is somehow to make sense of experience, be it on the street or in the classroom. The mind makes maximal use of the resources at its disposal—and those resources consist of our several intelligences. Perhaps someday we will actually be able to peer into the brain and observe which of our intelligences are at work as we listen to a lecture or create a new song.

Q. I've heard it said that there is no proof that MI schools work. What's the evidence?

A. In terms of claims, "soft" data, and "hard" data, there is much evidence that schools influenced by multiple intelligences theory are effective. Testimonials from satisfied administrators, parents, students, and teachers are legion. Many of the classes and schools claim that students are more likely to come to school, to like school, to complete school, and to do well in various assessments.

But there are problems with this evidence. It is almost entirely based on self-reports. We would not expect individuals who did not like MI approaches to spend much time reporting their failures. We would expect individuals who like MI approaches to chronicle their positive effects.

Even if these claims could be independently substantiated, we would not know for sure just which effects are due to MI theory. Schools are highly complex institutions located in highly complex environments. When quantitative measures (e.g., test scores, dropout rates) go up or down, it is easy to attribute these highs or lows to one's favorite hero or villain. But absent the kind of controlled studies that are almost impossible to mount outside of agricultural or medical settings, it is simply not possible to *prove* that it was MI approaches that did the trick.

For these reasons, I have been reluctant to claim that applied MI theory is a proven enhancer of schools. I had thought that I might be admired for this reticence; but instead my silence has been perceived in many quarters as a sign that MI approaches do not work or that I disapprove of what is being done in MI schools.

Recently, however, we have an important new resource. Mindy Kornhaber and her colleagues undertook the SUMIT project (Schools Using Multiple Intelligences Theory). The research team studied a set of forty-two schools that had been using MI theory for at least three years. The results from these schools were very encouraging. Seventy-eight percent of the schools reported improved standardized test scores, and five-eighths of these attributed the improvement to practices inspired by MI theory. Seventy-eight percent of the schools reported improved classroom performances by students with learning difficulties. Eighty percent of the schools reported improvement in parent participation, and three-quarters of these attributed the increase to MI theory. Finally, 81 percent of the schools reported improvement in student discipline, and two-thirds of these attributed the improvement to MI theory. Even if these figures show a positive spin, they are based on hard data; it is not possible for an impartial party to dismiss these results. I strongly recommend the book *Multiple Intelligences* by Mindy Kornhaber, Edward Fierros, and Shirley Veenema (2004).

ADDITIONAL TOPICS

Q. How might your multiple intelligences theory have a positive impact on public schools in the United States and elsewhere?

A. Briefly, my theory can reinforce the idea that individuals have many talents that can be of use to society; that a single measure (like a high-stakes test) is inappropriate for determining whether a student graduates, has access to college, and the like; and that important materials can be taught in many ways, thereby activating a range of intelligences and consolidating the learning. MI ideas can be used to help those involved in special education as well as those who work with U.S. populations for whom English is a second language.

Q. Can you recommend techniques for identifying students' strengths?

A. If you want to get to know your students' intelligences during the first weeks of school, here are two suggestions:

1. Take them on outings to a children's museum or to some other setting that provides a rich experience, like a playground with many kinds of games, and watch them carefully (see the description of the Explorama in chapter 13). This perspective will complement what you observe in class.
2. Give a short questionnaire about their strengths to the students *and* their parents *and,* if possible, their teachers from the previous year. To the extent that all three report the same strengths and weaknesses, you are on pretty safe ground. I don't trust self-reports unless they are corroborated.

Q. Are the origins of our variations in intelligence biological or cultural? Do particular cultures tend to evince particular strengths?

A. The extent to which intelligences develop is a joint product of biological or genetic potential, the emphasis a culture places on an activity, the excellence of the instruction, and the motivation of the individual. Any person can strengthen an intelligence if he or she is well motivated, if the ambient culture values that intelligence, and if there are human and artifactual resources (e.g., texts, computer programs, and study groups) on which the person can draw.

Q. How can I teach multiple intelligences theory in an innovative way to a group of new teachers?

A. See the writings of Tom Hoerr (2000), principal of the New City School in St. Louis.

Q. What role does MI theory play in promoting the implementation of the American curriculum standards?

A. Curriculum standards in several states have no close link to MI theory. Of course, I regret this. But the people who are charged with implementing the curriculum standards sometimes embrace MI ideas. They then try to teach important disciplinary understandings and concepts by drawing on several of the intelligences (see chapters 7 through 9 of my book *The Disciplined Mind*, 1999b, for examples). They also try to build on students' individual strengths, using those strengths either as a privileged way to teach to the standards or as a way of building up the students' confidence and sense of efficacy so they are more willing to take on difficult materials.

Q. Can MI approaches aid in the teaching of foreign languages?

A. Initially I was skeptical that MI approaches could be much help in learning foreign languages. I saw mastery of languages as a function either of the opportunity to live in a setting in which the student is compelled to use the language, or of extensive drill and practice in a language laboratory.

But all over the world, teachers of foreign languages (including English as a second language) tell me that foreign language instruction is enhanced by MI theory. To mention just a few ways: linguistic structures present in one language but not in another (for example, cases in Romance languages) can be conveyed in several ways, drawing on several intelligences; vocabulary and appropriate syntax are most readily learned when students engage in activities (like dancing, sketching, or debating) that draw on their favored intelligences; students learn best when they converse on topics about which they are knowledgeable, and those topics often are ones that use a characteristic blend of intelligences. Even drill-and-practice can be more effective if the various intelligences are drawn on (for example, in singing, dancing, creating different kinds of lists).

One place to read more about this topic is in the January 2004 special issue of *Teachers College Record* on multiple intelligences, notably the article by Marjorie Hall Haley as well as the references she cites (Haley, 2004).

FURTHER RESOURCES

For an update on frequently asked questions about multiple intelligences theory, please visit www.howardgardner.com.

For information about progress, oral ethics, and the Interdisciplinarity Project, see the papers listed at www.goodworkproject.com.

For information about Project Zero, please visit www.pzweb.harvard.edu.

For information about the Harvard Graduate School of Education, please visit www.gse.harvard.edu.

PART TWO

EDUCATIONAL
PERSPECTIVES

Chapter 6

Nurturing Intelligences in Early Childhood

Coauthored with Mara Krechevsky

Standardized tests of intelligence have been used to identify unusual talents, and such instruments are certainly capable of revealing prodigies. But consider the individuals who do not perform well on such assessments. How can we assess their strengths, and what would it mean to do so?

Jacob is a four-year-old boy who was asked to participate in two forms of assessment at the start of the school year: the Stanford-Binet Intelligence Scale (4th ed.) and a new approach to assessment called Project Spectrum. Jacob refused to be tested on the Stanford-Binet. Three subtests were attempted and partially completed, after which Jacob ran out of the testing room, left the building, and climbed a tree.

Consider Jacob's contrasting reaction to the Spectrum battery, which includes fifteen different tasks spanning a wide range of domains. Jacob participated in most of the activities, and he demonstrated outstanding strength in the areas of visual arts and numbers. He revealed a consuming love of different materials and worked with every possible medium in the art area. On other activities, even when he resisted engaging in the task at hand, he always expressed interest in the materials from which the games were made—for example, the small figures on a storytelling board and the metal of the bells for the music activity. This passion for the physicality of materials extended to almost every area: Jacob's exploration of the discovery or natural science area focused at one point on an examination of bones and how they fit together and led to a remarkably accurate sculpture of a bone fashioned from clay.

Of all the activities in the Spectrum battery, Jacob was least interested in movement and music. At first he also resisted participating in a numbers task embedded in a bus game. However, when he at last became engaged, he seemed to take special delight in figuring out the correct number of people boarding and leaving the bus. Tapping Jacob's understanding of numbers in a context that was meaningful and familiar to him seemed to help elicit abilities that might otherwise have remained hidden.

While the Spectrum and Stanford-Binet assessments can reveal similar qualities, there are distinct advantages to an assessment conducted over time with rich materials in the child's own environment. The example of Jacob indicates four ways in which the Spectrum assessment system might benefit children. First, Spectrum engages children through games that are meaningful and contextualized. Second, Spectrum blurs the line between curriculum and assessment, thereby integrating assessment more effectively into the regular educational program. Third, the Spectrum approach to assessment makes the measures "intelligence-fair" by using instruments that look directly at the intelligence in operation, instead of through an intermediating linguistic or logical-mathematical lens. Fourth, Spectrum suggests how a child's strength may provide access to more challenging areas in which the child shows less promise.

In this chapter we consider the possibility that children's exceptional talents can be identified at an early age and that the profile of abilities exhibited by preschoolers can be clearly distinguished from one another. We also consider some of the educational implications of an approach that focuses on the early identification of areas of strength and weakness. After a brief introduction to the theoretical background and framework of the Spectrum approach to assessment, we discuss some of the research findings and offer some preliminary conclusions.

The Spectrum Approach to Assessment

Project Spectrum is an innovative attempt to measure the profile of intelligences and working styles of young children. It has been undertaken by several researchers at Harvard Project Zero with our colleague David Feldman, at Tufts University (see Chen & Gardner, 2005; Feldman & Gardner, 1989; Malkus, Feldman, & Gardner, 1988; Ramos-Ford, Feldman, & Gardner, 1988). Spectrum began with the assumption that every child has the potential to develop strength in one or more areas. The project's focus on preschool children has both a scientific and a practical thrust. On the scientific side, we address the question of how early individual differences can be reliably detected as well as the predictive value of such early identification. On the practical side, parents and teachers are likely to benefit most from information about their children's cognitive competences during this stage of childhood, when the young child's brain is relatively plastic, when schools are likely to be less rigid, and when a free-choice component is typically built into most curricula.

Although Spectrum started out with a search for the early indices of the intelligences, it soon became apparent that many more competences warranted examination. To be sure, we identified a number of core capacities in each intelligence. But rather than attempting to look at intelligences in pure form, we looked at the domains of accomplishment of the culture through which those forms are taken up by children (Feldman, 1986). For example, we address both production and perception in music; invented and descriptive narrative in language; and expressive and athletic movement in the bodily-kinesthetic realm. We also used the notion of adult end-states to help us focus on the skills and abilities that are relevant to achieving significant and rewarding adult roles in our society, rather than just on those skills that are useful in the school context. Thus, instead of looking at logical-mathematical skills in the abstract, we examined competences that may culminate in scientific inventiveness; instead of examining competence at repeating a series of sentences, we look at the child's ability to tell a story or provide a descriptive account of an experience.

In order to capture fully a child's approach to a task, we found it important to look at cognitive or working styles as well as sheer intellectual capacities. Working style describes the way a child interacts with the materials of a content area, such as ability to plan an activity and to reflect on a task, and level of persistence. Whereas some individuals exhibit working styles that determine their approach to any task, no matter what the content area, others have styles that prove much more domain-specific. Such information may be particularly important for fashioning an effective educational intervention for a child. We addressed fifteen areas of cognitive ability and eighteen stylistic features (see tables 6.1 and 6.2).

IMPLEMENTATION OF THE SPECTRUM APPROACH

In a Spectrum classroom, children are surrounded each day by rich and engaging materials that evoke the use of a range of intelligences. We do not attempt to stimulate intelligences directly, with materials that are labeled "spatial" or "logical-mathematical." Rather, we use materials that embody valued societal roles or end-states and that draw on relevant combinations of intelligences. So, for example, there is a naturalist's corner, where various biological specimens are brought in for students to examine and compare with other materials; this area draws on sensory capacities as well as naturalistic and logical intelligences. There is a storytelling area, where students create imaginative tales using an evocative set of props and designing their own storyboards; this area evokes linguistic, dramatic, and imaginative faculties. There is a building corner, where students can construct a model of their classroom and manipulate small-scale photographs of the students and teachers in the room; this area draws on spatial, bodily-kinesthetic, and personal intelligences. Numerous other intelligences, and combinations of intelligences, are tapped in the remaining dozen areas and activities in a Spectrum classroom.

It is highly desirable for children to observe competent adults or older peers at work or at play in these areas. With such observation, youngsters readily come to appreciate the reasons for the materials as well as the nature of the skills that enable a master to interact with the materials in a meaningful way. Because it is not always feasible to provide such an apprentice-master setting, learning centers have been constructed in which children can develop some facility from regular interactions with the materials by themselves or with only other novice-level peers. In this sense, our entry-level environment is a self-sustaining one that harbors the potential for cognitive and personal growth.

Over the course of a year or more spent in this nourishing environment, children have ample opportunity to explore the various learning areas, each featuring its respective materials and its unique set of elicited skills and intelligences. Reflecting the resourcefulness and curiosity of the mind of the five-year-old, most children readily explore the majority of these areas. Children who do not cast their nets widely are encouraged to try out alternative materials or approaches. For the most part, the teacher can readily observe a child's interests and talents over the course of the year, and no special assessments are needed. For each domain or craft, however, we also devised specific games or activities that allow a more precise determination of a child's intelligences in that area.

At the end of the year, the information gathered about each child is summarized by the research team in a brief essay called a Spectrum Report. This document describes the child's individual profile of strengths and weaknesses and offers specific recommendations about what might be done at home, in school, or in the wider community to build on strengths as well as to bolster areas of relative weakness. Such informal recommendations are important. In our view, psychologists have traditionally been far too concerned with norming or ranking. Instead, efforts comparable to the Spectrum Report made throughout the school years should help students and their families make informed decisions about their future course, based on a survey of their capacities and options.

What of the actual measures that we devised? In order not to confound competences, we tried as much as possible not to rely exclusively on logical and linguistic measures. Instead we used measures that were "intelligence fair"—measures that tap the intelligence directly and in a holistic manner (see chapter 10). We also tried to avoid hypothetical situations and abstract formulations; we provided children with something concrete to manipulate no matter which domain was being assessed. For example, the classroom model described above provides children with small figures of their peers and teachers, offering a tangible structure through which to consider children's knowledge of friends, social roles, and classroom dynamics. The music perception task provides children with Montessori bells with which they can play a pitch matching game or create their own melody.

As table 6.1 indicates, Spectrum measures range from relatively structured and targeted tasks (for example, in the number and music domains) to relatively unstructured measures and natural observations (in the science and social domains). These measures are implemented throughout the course of a year—the classroom is equipped with engaging materials, games, puzzles, and learning areas. Documentation takes a variety of

TABLE 6.1.
AREAS OF COGNITIVE ABILITY EXAMINED IN PROJECT SPECTRUM

NUMBERS

Dinosaur game: designed as a measure of a child's understanding of number concepts, counting skills, ability to adhere to rules, and use of strategy.

Bus game: assesses a child's ability to create a useful notation system, perform mental calculations, and organize number information for one or more variables.

SCIENCE

Assembly activity: designed to measure a child's mechanical ability. Successful completion of the activity depends on fine-motor skills and visual-spatial, observational, and problem-solving abilities.

Treasure hunt game: assesses a child's ability to make logical inferences. The child is asked to organize information to discover the rule governing the placement of various treasures.

Water activity: used to assess a child's ability to generate hypotheses based on observations and to conduct simple experiments.

Discovery area: includes year-round activities that elicit a child's observations, appreciation, and understanding of natural phenomena.

MUSIC

Music production activity: designed to assess a child's ability to maintain accurate pitch and rhythm while singing, and to recall a song's musical properties.

Music perception activity: assesses a child's ability to discriminate pitch. The activity consists of song recognition, error recognition, and pitch discrimination.

LANGUAGE

Storyboard activity: measures a range of language skills, including complexity of vocabulary and sentence structure, use of connectors, use of descriptive language and dialogue, and ability to pursue a story line.

Reporting activity: assesses a child's ability to describe an event with regard to the following criteria: ability to report content accurately, level of detail, sentence structure, and vocabulary.

VISUAL ARTS

Art portfolios: reviewed twice a year and assessed on criteria that include use of lines and shapes, color, space, detail, and representation and design. Children also participate in three structured drawing activities. The drawings are assessed on criteria similar to those used in the portfolio assessment.

MOVEMENT

Creative movement: the ongoing movement curriculum focuses on children's abilities in five areas of dance and creative movement: sensitivity to rhythm, expressiveness, body control, generation of movement ideas, and responsiveness to music.

Athletic movement: an obstacle course focuses on the types of skills found in many different sports, such as coordination, timing, balance, and power.

SOCIAL

Classroom model: assesses a child's ability to observe and analyze social events and experiences in the classroom.

Peer interaction checklist: a behavioral checklist is used to assess the behaviors in which children engage when interacting with peers. Different patterns of behavior yield distinctive social roles such as facilitator and leader.

---

forms, from score sheets and observation checklists to portfolios and tape-recordings. Although most teachers do not find it practical to administer formally all fifteen measures to each child, we have used such a procedure for research purposes.

In addition to the Spectrum Report, parents are provided a Parent Activities Manual with suggestions for activities in the different domains addressed by Spectrum. Most of the activities use readily accessible and affordable materials. A cautionary note to parents is included regarding the premature streaming or fast-tracking of a child. The idea is not to make each child a prodigy in his or her area of greatest strength. Rather, Project Spectrum stresses the notion that every child is unique: parents and teachers deserve to have a description faithful to the child as well as suggestions for the kinds of experiences appropriate to the child's particular configuration of strengths and weaknesses.

INITIAL RESULTS

We now turn to a discussion of the results of our initial research. We posed three questions:

1. Do young children have domain-specific as well as more general strengths?
2. Is there any correlation between performances in different activities?
3. Does a child's strength in one domain facilitate or hinder performance in other domains?

Below we report on each question in turn.

1. The Spectrum battery was administered in two preschool classrooms at the Eliot-Pearson Children's School at Tufts University in Medford, Massachusetts. We restricted our analyses to twenty-three four-year-olds.

We looked at each child's strengths and weaknesses, both in relation to the group and to the self. Children who scored one standard deviation or more above the mean on the Spectrum measures in a domain were considered to have a strength in that domain, whereas children who scored one standard deviation or more below the mean were considered to demonstrate a weakness. The majority of the children revealed a strength in at least one domain and a weakness in at least one domain. A few children exhibited one or more strengths across Spectrum activities and no weaknesses, and a few children exhibited no strengths and one or more weaknesses. Finally, every child exhibited at least one strength and one weakness relative to him- or herself.

2. To determine the degree of correlation between performances on the different activities, we created a matrix of the correlations between pairs of the ten activities. The results indicated very little correlation between the activities, reinforcing the notion that the Spectrum measures identify a range of nonoverlapping capabilities in different content areas. Only one pair was significant at the $p < 0.01$ level: the two number activities—the dinosaur game and the bus game ($r = 0.78$). In contrast, the two music and the two science activities were not significantly correlated ($r = -0.07$ and $r = 0.08$, respectively).

3. There was also some evidence that a child's strength in one area might facilitate performance in another. For example, one child exhibited a keen sensitivity to color and demonstrated both interest and ability in the area of visual arts. While playing the treasure hunt game, which focuses on log-

ical inference skills, this child's attentiveness to colors apparently helped her identify the rule governing the placement of treasures under color-coded flags. Another child, who was identified as having a strength in music production (singing), found it easier in the creative movement sessions to synchronize his movements to the underlying rhythm of a piece of music if he sang while he moved. His musical talents also characterized his performance on the invented narrative task: he created both a theme song and a death march for the characters in his story.

A third child, who exhibited outstanding ability in storytelling, yet remained motionless in the creative movement sessions, moved with uncharacteristic expressiveness when storyboard props were used as a catalyst in one of the exercises. She also transformed tasks in visual arts, social analysis, and mathematics into occasions for further storytelling (see Renninger, 1988, on the effect of children's interests on their attention and memory for tasks and types of play). Her drawings in art often served to illustrate accompanying narratives. Her mother reported that she often made puppets and dolls at home, modeling them on characters from the books she was "reading." She also used the classroom model as a reality-based storyboard, creating vignettes with the figures of her classmates. On the bus game, however, she became so involved in the motivations for the different figures boarding and leaving the bus that she was distracted from recording the correct numerical information.

It seems that strength in one area can also interfere with a child's performance. One child exhibited outstanding strength in visual arts, demonstrating an unusual sensitivity to line, color, and composition. However, his sensitivity to visual cues led him to misinterpret directional signs when using dice that had a + and − on their sides. He interpreted the crossing lines (+) to mean that the player could move in two directions and the single horizontal line (−) to mean that the player could proceed in only one direction.

WORKING STYLES

As noted earlier, in addition to recording a child's performance, we also recorded *working style* or the way in which the child approached each activity (see table 6.2). We were primarily interested in two issues:

TABLE 6.2.
STYLISTIC FEATURES EXAMINED IN PROJECT SPECTRUM

The child is:

easily engaged/reluctant to engage in activity
confident/tentative
playful/serious
focused/distractible
persistent/frustrated by task
reflects on own work/impulsive
apt to work slowly/apt to work quickly

The child:

responds to visual (auditory, kinesthetic) cues
demonstrates methodical approach
brings personal agenda (strength) to task
finds humor in content area
uses materials in unexpected ways
shows pride in accomplishment
shows attention to detail (is observant)
is curious about materials
shows concern over "correct" answer
focuses on interaction with adult
transforms task (material)

1. Do children utilize distinctive working styles when solving problems from different domains? If so, what is the nature of the differences in a child's areas of strength and weakness?
2. Are some working styles more effective than others in particular domains?

It seemed that for the majority of children, while one or two working styles usually obtained across domains, other working styles depended more on the content of the area being explored. Approximately three-quarters of the children in the sample exhibited general working styles that, in specific instances, combined with one or two others to yield domain-specific configurations. For example, one girl displayed attention to detail only on the classroom model activity, her one area of strength, and was impulsive only in the music perception activity, her area of weakness. Another child was easily engaged and confident, even in areas of weakness, as long as the task involved a performance aspect.

Not surprisingly, performances in an area of strength were typically characterized by "easy to engage," "confident," and "focused" working styles. In contrast, weak performances were characterized by "distractible," "impulsive," and "reluctant to engage" working styles. "Playfulness" characterized both strengths and weaknesses. Also, a number of children showed reflectiveness and attention to detail in their area of strength. Three of the five children who exhibited no strengths relative to their peers never reflected on their own work, and eight children reflected only on their work in areas of strength.

Five of the children demonstrated working styles that were highly domain specific. Jacob, the boy described at the beginning of this chapter, exhibited confidence, attention to detail, seriousness, planning skills, and reflectiveness *only* in the visual arts and numbers domains—his areas of strength. Another child found it very difficult to remain focused on most of the Spectrum and classroom activities. However, when she was presented with the materials for the assembly activity, she worked in a focused and persistent manner until she had completely taken apart and reassembled the objects. This result gave the teacher valuable information about how she might use this child's strength to engage her in focused work in the classroom.

With regard to the second question, some of the children who exhibited a consistent working style were clearly helped by their content-neutral style, whereas others were probably hindered by it. One child worked in a serious and focused manner across domains; this tack helped him complete activities in which he experienced difficulty as well as those in which he exhibited competence. Every child exhibited confidence in at least one activity. One girl who revealed no strengths relative to her peers, nonetheless demonstrated pride in accomplishment on more tasks than any other child, perhaps indicating a resilience that augurs well for her scholastic prospects. Ironically, it may be that too pervasive a confidence inhibits successful performance across tasks. The child who was identified as having the most weaknesses of the five children and no strengths relative to her peers never showed any tentativeness, whereas all but three of the rest *were* tentative in their approach at least once.

One child brought his own agenda to every Spectrum activity. Although his ideas were often compelling, his unwillingness to attend to the task caused him to perform poorly on many of the activities. On the music perception activity, for example, he was most interested in how the metal bells, which all looked exactly the same, could produce different sounds. To explore this phenomenon, he examined the differences in their vibrations after hitting them with the mallet. He also invented new rules for the dinosaur game, and he tried to fashion tools out of the parts of the two food grinders in the assembly activity. Because he was so interested in exploring his own ideas, he often resisted exploring the ideas of others. When he experienced difficulty with an activity, he would become frustrated and rely on his sense of humor to distract the adult from the task at hand.

It also appeared that the structure of the tasks (or sometimes their lack of structure) served to inhibit the performances of some children. In the less structured environment of the Spectrum classroom, the boy just described demonstrated great experimental ability and constantly formulated and tested hypotheses to find out more about the world around him. Jacob was another child who required very little structure, so immersed in the materials did he become. Unfortunately, his intense focus on materials, to the exclusion of other people—whether child or adult—may present problems for his future scholastic performance.

A COMPARISON OF VIEWS: PARENTS, TEACHERS, AND SPECTRUM

While the Spectrum measures clearly identified domain-specific strengths in the children, it also seemed important to determine whether we were uncovering abilities hitherto unrecognized by teachers and parents. To address this question, we asked parents and teachers to fill out a questionnaire indicating the level of ability shown by each child in a number of different areas. We also sent response forms to parents to solicit their reactions to the Spectrum profiles.

Seventeen of the twenty sets of parents returned a completed questionnaire. In general, parents were quite generous in identifying their child as demonstrating outstanding ability in an area. The average number of areas checked by parents for their child was eight out of thirty. On the other hand, the teachers rarely scored a child as exhibiting outstanding ability in any area, identifying on average one out of thirty. This discrepancy between parent and teacher ratings presumably reflects the broader frame of reference available to teachers, who see children in the context of their peer group. While parents may understandably be biased, they also have fewer opportunities to view the strengths of a large number of children. These factors should be kept in mind in the comparison.

A child was considered by Spectrum to have an outstanding strength only if the score in a given domain activity was at least one standard deviation above the mean. Spectrum identified outstanding strengths that had not otherwise been identified in eight of the seventeen children—twelve strengths in all, in the domains of science, visual arts, music, and social understanding. Seven children were identified by parents and teachers as exhibiting outstanding strengths, but not by Spectrum. In most of these cases, although Spectrum identified relative strengths, they were not considered outstanding in relation to the group. For a number of other children, strengths scoring close to but less than one standard deviation above the mean were identified by Spectrum, but not by parents or teachers. Finally, parents, teachers, and Spectrum identified the same areas of outstanding ability in nine of the seventeen children in the comparison.

It appears that some areas, such as language and numbers, can be relatively easily identified regardless of whether the child is at home or at school, but other areas, such as music perception, mechanical skills, and social analysis, are not so easily noticed. In fact, Spectrum never identified language or numbers as outstanding strengths where they were not already identified by parents or the teacher. However, even in a commonly recognized area of ability like language, Spectrum provides a breakdown of the area into component skills (vocabulary, sentence structure, use of descriptive language, and so on) employed in the service of a meaningful endeavor (storytelling).

Of course, many competent preschool teachers simply cannot provide experiences in all areas, especially areas with which they may be relatively unfamiliar, such as music perception and logical inference tasks. The assembly activity in particular helps break down gender preconceptions by providing girls with the same opportunity as boys to reveal a strength and become engaged in an area traditionally considered masculine. The profile response forms also revealed that the areas in which parents were most surprised to learn of strengths included music perception, mechanical ability, and creative movement. Because the information in the profiles is generated from contextualized tasks, it may be easier for parents to translate it into meaningful follow-up activities.

A COMPARISON OF SPECTRUM RESULTS WITH THE STANFORD-BINET INTELLIGENCE SCALE

A trained diagnostician administered the Stanford-Binet Intelligence Scale (4th ed.) to nineteen of the twenty children in one class. Two of the nineteen children did not complete the measure and are therefore not included in the analysis. The results from this sample, while useful for providing a very general sense of how the two measures compare, should be read with several caveats in mind.

First, Spectrum addresses seven domains of ability through fifteen activities, ten of which are included in the analysis, whereas the Stanford-Binet focuses on four areas or factors (verbal reasoning, abstract/visual reasoning, quantitative reasoning, and short-term memory) through eight subtests. Second, the battery of Spectrum activities is administered in a series over the course of a year, whereas the Stanford-Binet is administered in a one- to two-hour session. Finally, the Stanford-Binet is a standardized measure and Spectrum is not.

The seventeen children in the sample who completed the Stanford-Binet assessment scored in the range of low-average to very superior, with composite scores ranging from 86 to 133. The average score was 113. As with the preceding analysis, a child was considered to demonstrate a strength or weakness on a Spectrum activity only if he or she scored one standard deviation or more above or below the mean of the group.

To determine whether Stanford-Binet composite scores were predictive of performance on some or all Spectrum activities, we ranked the composite scores of the children to see how the top five children (with composite scores from 125 to 133) and the bottom five children (with scores from 86 to 105—the low-average to average range) performed on the Spectrum battery. Of the five children with the highest Stanford-Binet composite scores, one demonstrated a strength on three of the ten Spectrum activities in the analysis, three displayed strengths in two activities, and one child exhibited one strength. The areas Spectrum identified as strengths for these children were as follows: two in narrative language, four in music perception and production, two in the visual arts, one in social understanding, and one in science (logical inference).

The movement, numbers, and mechanical component of the science domains were not identified as strengths for any of the children, and, in fact, movement and numbers were identified as areas of weakness for two of them. Moreover, only one of the three children who displayed three or more strengths on the Spectrum measures was among the top five scorers on the Stanford-Binet. One of the top three Spectrum scorers was also the top scorer on the combined Spectrum numbers activities.

It seems that the Stanford-Binet Intelligence Scale did not predict successful performance either across Spectrum activities or on a consistent subset of them. One qualification to be made in that regard is the possibility of a connection between the Stanford-Binet composite scores and performance on the Spectrum music tasks. Four of the five strengths in music identified by the Spectrum measures were displayed by the children who received the highest Stanford-Binet composite scores. However, in general, no correlation was found between Stanford-Binet subscores and the individual Spectrum activities. Of course, without a much larger sample, no firm conclusions can be drawn.

The Stanford-Binet also did not seem to predict lack of success across Spectrum tasks, although it did identify three of the lowest-scoring children (children with no strengths and zero to five weaknesses on the Spectrum activities). Of the five children with the lowest Stanford-Binet composite scores, one exhibited one strength (social understanding) and one weakness (music perception), and another exhibited no weaknesses and three strengths (mechanical ability, language, and music perception). The remaining three children displayed no strengths on the Spectrum activities and zero to five weaknesses.

The child who received the lowest composite score in the group (86) was also identified by the Spectrum battery as the lowest-scoring child across tasks: she exhibited no strengths and five weaknesses on the Spectrum activities (two more weaknesses than any other child). However, Spectrum did identify two relative strengths displayed by this child in the domains of social understanding and creative movement. The Stanford-Binet sub-tests also revealed some scatter (the verbal reasoning skills and memory for sentences subscores were in the 53rd and 49th percentiles, respectively, while bead memory and pattern analysis scores fell into the 39th and 40th percentiles).

These data suggest that whereas the Stanford-Binet Intelligence Scale yielded a range of factor scores and subtest variability within factors, the Spectrum measures produced more jagged profiles. Part of this difference can be attributed to the number of domains addressed by each measure: eight tasks in four content areas for Stanford-Binet versus fifteen tasks (ten in our analysis) in seven areas for Spectrum. But Spectrum does more than simply expand the areas addressed by the Stanford-Binet. All of the Stan-ford-Binet subtests can be considered either good or fair measures of g, the general intelligence factor (see Sattler, 1988, for a full discussion). The Spectrum model, however, does not postulate g as a general intelligence factor that is present in a wide range of mental abilities and that accounts for children's performances in different content areas. Rather, the Spec-trum model suggests that the jagged profiles represent domain-specific abilities that reflect real-world problem solving in the context of meaning-ful activities—for example, analysis of one's own social environment, as-sembling a mechanical object, telling a story, and so on. The information gained from the Spectrum inventory may therefore be potentially more useful in designing appropriate educational interventions for children.

SOME LIMITATIONS AND LONG-TERM
IMPLICATIONS OF PROJECT SPECTRUM

At this point, it may be worthwhile to raise several issues that may well be on the reader's mind. Clearly, this study has limitations. Because of the small sample that received the Spectrum battery, the study should be re-garded as useful for generating hypotheses rather than providing any con-clusive findings. However, we can identify some of the potential benefits of Spectrum in comparison with other assessment approaches, such as the Stanford-Binet. First, Spectrum provides an opportunity to involve children more actively in the assessment, giving them a chance to reflect on their experience and their own sense of their interests and strengths. Children also become actively involved in helping collect and document their work in the Spectrum model—for example, saving their work for the art portfolios, taping stories and songs, and bringing in items for the discovery or natural science area. Such involvement conveys to children the sense that their products are being taken seriously, and it includes them in the process of monitoring their own growth.

For children who are unusually sensitive about performance issues, Spectrum may have information to offer that a one-session, decontextualized, heavily verbal measure does not (see chapter 10). For example, as part of the intrapersonal component of the social analytic activity, children are shown pictures of the different Spectrum activities and asked which activities they consider their favorite, their best, and the hardest. One boy who had remained unengaged in either Spectrum activities or the Stanford-Binet subtests (the Stanford-Binet testing had to be discontinued because of his great anxiety about his performance) showed a surprising degree of interest in answering questions about his reactions to the different activities. He seemed to have an accurate sense about his areas of relative interest and strength. He identified the storyboard as his best activity and, indeed, it was the only one of the eight tasks he completed for which his score was above the group mean. He selected the water activity as his favorite, and although he was reluctant to try out his ideas for sinking and floating experiments during the task, he became so excited about a discovery he made at one point that he called his teacher over to the area in an uncharacteristic display of enthusiasm.

Of course, the Stanford-Binet Intelligence Scale has advantages as well. It is a standardized measure with excellent internal consistency and high reliability. The measure is easily and efficiently administered, and the areas examined map readily onto the standard school curriculum. While we do not yet know whether a Spectrum assessment can predict scholastic success with the reliability of standardized forms of assessment, the Spectrum measures do identify distinctive areas of strength, with immediate implications for further avenues to explore, both inside and outside school. The Spectrum battery also allows teachers and parents to perceive individual differences in areas traditionally considered important only with regard to passage through universal stages of development (Feldman, 1980) or as a reflection of general intelligence.

However, the Spectrum approach contains its own risks. The danger of premature streaming of children must be weighed against the benefits of giving every child a chance to do well. There is also the potential for achievement-oriented parents to push their children to excel not just in the traditional academic areas but in all domains, increasing an already power-ful pressure on children to achieve. Moreover, families outside the main-stream culture may quite properly be less concerned with performance in elective domains like visual arts and music, and more concerned with those areas that continue to be valued most by the society—language and logic.

Clearly, family environment will determine in part both the use and the usefulness of the information contained in the Spectrum profile. As one parent reported, because the family members were either not interested in music or were simply not musical, her child's musical capabilities might never have surfaced without Spectrum, and even if they had, they would not have been recognized as talent. This result can be contrasted with the case of a mother who considered music to be an important part of her son's life and greatly encouraged his interest in it. During follow-up a year later, she reported that he loved watching musical and operatic perform-ances, and would sit through them attentively, without talking or moving. While no one really knows the exact relationship between early talents and later achievements, the identification of strengths early on may become a self-fulfilling prophecy.

Could a Spectrum perspective lead to a reasonable curriculum for the primary years? Our data suggest the potential influence of the structure of the environment the particular qualities that can be discerned in children. They emphasize the importance of continuing to provide a rich set of stimulating materials across diverse curricular areas. Creative movement and mechanical skills are unlikely to be recognized in a kindergarten that does not offer these areas in the curriculum. Also, starting in first grade, many children are taught subjects such as art, music, movement, and sci-ence by specialists once or twice a week. Unless these specialists communi-cate with the classroom teachers, the latter may be unaware of a child's abilities in a particular area. At a minimum, teachers may find it easier to be good teachers in the Spectrum framework, both in terms of document-ing their observations and individualizing their curriculum.

The emphasis on end-states may also provide a more direct link be-tween identification of a strength and a decision on what to do once it has been identified. An apprenticeship model emerges as a particularly attrac-tive alternative educational approach. Once an end-state has been defined, the possibility arises for staking out an educational regimen toward its re-alization. Apprenticeships embed the learning of skills in a social and func-tional context, with well-defined stages of mastery. In our view, the apprenticeship model, where students receive frequent and informal feed-back on their progress in highly contextualized settings, holds much prom-ise educationally. Thus, in the case of a child like Jacob, we would recommend that if he continues to exhibit interest in a chosen domain, he could well benefit from the guidance of an expert in a variety of rich, hands-on learning situations.

Finally, although Spectrum reflects in part a value system of pluralism associated with the middle class, it may also have something to offer chil-dren from less privileged backgrounds. The Spectrum assessment system has the potential to reveal unsuspected areas of strength and bring about enhanced self-esteem, particularly for children who do not excel in the standard school curriculum.

A Preliminary Look at Follow-Up Data

A second year of participation in the Spectrum program plus interviews with parents and teachers showed that strengths identified during the first year continued to develop, and working styles became more ingrained. Whether a strength would resurface depended on several conditions: fam-ily beliefs about the ability's value, the student's relative standing among peers, and the match between the student's interests and strengths.

Teachers and parents carry considerable sway over the developmental trajectory of an ability. For example, one domain where teachers', parents', and Spectrum evaluations differed was the social domain. Teachers tended to give low ratings to their students' social skills, whereas Spectrum and parents had identified them as strengths. The social domain is one in which judgments about ability seem particularly influenced by *how* such ability is used. Parental responses revealed that they most encouraged drama and pretense. This activity seems to have been considered effective for combining ability in the storytelling and social domains with the performance aspect of the movement domain.

Sometimes, the particular configuration of a child's working style and areas of strength determined whether or not a strength would resurface. For example, one girl who "liked to shine," according to her teacher, was not the most able in her group at the writing table or book area. Consequently, she frequented the art and construction areas where she would be more likely to stand out. Given the context of her relative standing within the group, there was less chance that her previously identified ability in language would reemerge and develop during the year.

Furthermore, if a child's interests did not match his or her strengths, or if an individual chose to focus on the same set of materials or to explore new skill areas, opportunities to observe ability in other domains would be correspondingly reduced. One girl who had demonstrated both interest and ability in art became much more interested in learning how to read in kindergarten. Perhaps that change in interest explains why she avoided the art area.

EXTENSIONS OF THE PROJECT SPECTRUM APPROACH

Until this point, we have focused on the original Project Spectrum, which was developed for use in a middle-class American preschool setting. Both the tasks described and the data analyzed reflect this history and particular milieu.

The question naturally arises about the extent to which Spectrum could be extended to other settings. Our first effort to do this involved the utilization of Spectrum in several preschool, kindergarten, and first grade classes in Somerville, Massachusetts, a working-class suburb of Boston with high rates of social and economic problems. Allaying our doubts about transportability, the children found the Spectrum materials most attractive, and they looked forward eagerly to their time in a Spectrum environment. Indeed, it turned out to be parents and teachers who had concerns about Spectrum, either because they feared that the students would not be comfortable with such open-ended tasks or because they themselves had a different, far more regulated view of what school should be like.

In such a setting Spectrum has shown particular power in identifying talents and inclinations that are typically missed in the regular school. Donnie, a six-year-old from a single-parent home with more than its share of violence and substance abuse, was at high risk of school failure. He was having such difficulty in the tasks of first grade that by the second month, his teacher had reluctantly concluded that he would have to be retained.

In Project Spectrum, however, Donnie excelled at the assembly tasks. He had greater success in taking apart and putting together common objects, such as a food grinder and a doorknob, than any other student his age. (Indeed, most teachers and researchers failed to match Donnie's skilled and seemingly effortless achievements in these mechanical tasks.) We videotaped Donnie's impressive performance and showed it to his teacher. A thoughtful and dedicated person, she was overwhelmed. She had difficulty believing that this youngster, who experienced such trouble with school-related tasks, could do as well as many adults on this real-world endeavor. She told us afterward that she could not sleep for three nights; she was distraught by her premature dismissal of Donnie and was correspondingly eager to find ways to reach him. Donnie subsequently improved in his school performances, possibly because he had seen that there were areas in which he could excel and that he possessed abilities that were esteemed by older people.

In addition to identifying unexpected strengths in young students, Spectrum can also locate surprising difficulties. Gregory was an excellent student in first grade, apparently destined for a bright scholastic future; he displayed skill in the acquisition of notational and conceptual knowledge. He performed poorly, however, across a number of Spectrum areas. His teacher thought that perhaps Gregory was able to perform well only in situations in which there was a correct answer and a person in authority had somehow indicated that answer to him. The Spectrum materials posed problems for the boy because many of the activities are open-ended and are not associated with any evident correct answers; he was thus frustrated and looked to the teacher or to other students for ideas about what he should do. After seeing what Gregory's participation in Spectrum revealed, his teacher began to look for ways to encourage him to take risks, to try things out in new ways, to acknowledge that there are not always correct answers, and to appreciate that any response entails certain advantages as well as certain costs.

Over time, Spectrum evolved from serving as a means of assessing strengths to constituting a rounded educational environment. In collaboration with classroom teachers, we developed curricular materials in the form of kits that draw on the range of intelligences as they may figure in the development of a broad theme, such as "Night and Day" or "About Me." With younger children, these materials are used primarily in an exploratory mode. With older children, they are tied more closely to the traditional goals of school, promoting preliteracy or literacy attitudes, approaches, and skills. Thus, children encounter the basics of reading, writing, and calculating in the context of themes and materials in which they have demonstrated interest and an emerging expertise. As they gain proficiency in a board game, for example, children can be introduced to numerical tally systems, and as they create adventures at the storyboard, they can begin to write them down as well as recite or dramatize them.

The adaptability of Spectrum has proved to be one of its most exciting features. Teachers and researchers from several regions of the country have used Spectrum as a point of departure for a variety of educational ends. The Spectrum approach has been adapted with children ranging in age from four to eight for purposes of diagnosis, classification, or teaching. It has been used with average students, gifted students, handicapped students, and students at risk of school failure, in programs designed for research, for compensatory purposes, and for enrichment. It was made the center of a mentoring program in which young children have the opportunity to work with adults from their neighborhood who exemplify different combinations of intelligences in their jobs. As researchers-turned-implementers, we have had the privilege of sitting in on discussions among people who have never met each other but who have adapted Spectrum to their varied needs. It seems clear from such conversations that the Spectrum school-museum blend is appropriate for young children of diverse interests, backgrounds, and ages.

In our own work we have made explicit the ties to the children's museum. Working with the Boston Children's Museum, we have transformed our theme-based kits so that they can be used at home and in the museum as well as at school. The home and school furnish regular stimulation, while the museum provides the opportunity to encounter a related display in an awe-inspiring setting, such as the moon and the stars viewed in a planetarium. It is our hope that encountering a similar cluster of themes, materials, and skills in disparate settings will help children make this cluster their own; we speak of a "resonance" among these milieus that ultimately leads to the child's internalization of important understandings.

Naturally this kind of cross-fertilization works best when children have the opportunity to visit the museum regularly. Thus, we were excited by the installation of a Spectrum-inspired model early learning preschool classroom in the Capital Children's Museum in Washington, D.C.—an ambitious melding of school and museum (Lewin-Benham, 2006). But even when visits are less frequent, a well-prepared class of students can profit from the opportunity to interact with skilled professionals at a children's museum, particularly if they then have the opportunity to revisit related experiences and lessons on a more leisurely basis at home or at school.

Working primarily with disadvantaged children, our former colleague Jie-Qi Chen has extended the Spectrum approach (Chen & Gardner, 2005). She has reviewed a number of additional studies with young children, each of which underscores the appearance of jagged cognitive profiles, particularly among children at risk; she has also documented the power of personalized instruction with this challenging population. In her project "Bridging: Assessment for Teaching," Chen and her colleagues have constructed curricula for early childhood that build on the children's particular strengths. Having identified a profile of performance levels, the Bridging team then determines the curriculum and pedagogy that is best suited for a particular child or set of children. For example, with respect to arithmetical competence, a child receives scores on number sense, spatial relations, part-whole relations, and mathematical understanding, and a description is written of the child's dominant working styles. From an ensemble of recommendations, the teacher then can determine the optimal point of entry and structure for organizing lessons and exercises.

In a number of respects, Project Spectrum epitomizes the way the theory of multiple intelligences catalyzed the creation of effective educational interventions—in this case, with young children. Beginning with a scholarly interest in the existence and identification of talents in very young children, we have seen Spectrum evolve naturally over time into a full-scale approach to early education. This approach was inspired by aspects of MI theory, but in no way did MI theory dictate the exact contents or the precise steps in the implementation of Spectrum. We altered the program considerably in response to our own observations, to feedback from parents, teachers, researchers, and students, and to the changing conditions within which we attempted to implement the approach. Add to that the very different uses made of Spectrum ideas by researchers and practitioners in different parts of the country, and a picture emerges of a family—indeed a spectrum—of variations of Project Spectrum. It is fitting that a program rooted in the celebration of individual differences among young children should itself generate a family of highly individualized approaches.

Chapter 7

PROJECTS DURING
THE ELEMENTARY YEARS

About two years after *Frames of Mind* was published, I was scheduled to give a talk in Kutztown, Pennsylvania. Shortly before I left Boston to make the trip there, I received a phone call from a teacher in Indianapolis. She said that she and some of her fellow teachers had read *Frames of Mind* and wanted to speak with me about some of the ideas in the book. Was I available for a meeting in Kutztown?

Unbeknownst to me, a group of eight teachers from the Indianapolis public school system drove for fourteen hours in order to have a relatively brief meeting with me in Kutztown. At that eventful meeting they showed me a videotape that they had recently completed and told me that they were interested in starting their own K–6 elementary school inspired in part by the ideas of MI theory. I was as surprised as I was delighted.

While I was becoming increasingly interested in educational applications of the theory, it had never dawned on me that someone might take these ideas so seriously as actually to plan a school based on them. I told the "Indianapolis 8" quite frankly that I would be happy to help them but that I knew little about schools. "You are the school people," I insisted, "and it will have to be your school."

AN MI SCHOOL

Few groups of teachers anywhere can have worked harder than the "Indianapolis 8" did over the next two years. Under the guidance of the energetic and visionary Patricia Bolanos, who eventually became the school principal, they raised funds, lobbied, and planned curricula, and after many moments of suspense and some disappointments, they were eventually allowed to have their own inner-city public "options" school in downtown Indianapolis, the Key School (Olson, 1988; Winn, 1990). While I deserve no credit for the launch of this project, I have met regularly with the teachers to talk with them about what they are doing, and, in the way of these things, I have been given excessive credit in the popular media for having inspired the Key School.

The Key School, now called the Key Learning Community, has proved to be a remarkable success in many ways. One of its founding principles is the conviction that each child should have his or her multiple intelligences stimulated each day. Thus, every student at the school participates regularly in the activities of computing, music, and bodily-kinesthetics, in addition to mastering theme-centered curricula that embody standard literacies and subject matter.

While an MI curriculum is the Key Learning Community's most overtly innovative aspect, many other facets of the school suggest an education that strives toward diverse forms of understanding. Three practices are pivotal. First, each student participates every day in an apprenticeship-like "pod," where students work with peers of different ages and a competent teacher to master a craft or discipline of interest. Because the pod includes a range of ages, students can enter into an activity at their own level of expertise and develop at a comfortable pace. Working alongside a more knowledgeable person, students have what may be a rare opportunity to see an expert engage in productive work. At any one time, there are perhaps a dozen pods in a variety of areas ranging from architecture to gardening, from cooking to "making money." Because the focus of the pod falls on the acquisition of a real-world skill in an apprenticeship environment, the chances of securing genuine understandings are enhanced.

Complementing the pods are strong ties to the wider community. Once a week, an outside specialist visits the school and demonstrates an occupation or craft to all the students. Often the specialist is a parent, and typically the topic fits into the school theme at that time. For example, if the current theme is "Protection of the Environment," visitors might talk about sewage disposal, forestry, or the political process of lobbying. The hope is that students will not only learn about the range of activities that exist in the wider community but will also have the opportunity to follow up in a given area, possibly under the guidance of the visiting mentor. One way of achieving this end is through participation in the Center for Exploration at the Indianapolis Children's Museum; students can enter into an apprenticeship of several months, in which they can engage in such sustained activities as animation, shipbuilding, journalism, and monitoring the weather.

The final—and to my mind the most important—avenue for growth at the Key Learning Community involves student projects. During any given year, the school features a number of different themes, introduced at approximately ten-week intervals. The themes can be quite broad, such as "Patterns" and "Connections," or more focused, such as "The Renaissance Then and Now" and "Mexican Heritage." Curricula focus on these themes, and, whenever possible, desired literacies and concepts are introduced as natural adjuncts to an exploration of the theme.

As part of school requirements, each student is asked to carry out a project related to the theme. Thus, students execute three or four new projects each year. These, projects are placed on display at the conclusion of the theme period, so that students can examine what everyone else in the school has done (students prove to be very interested in monitoring the work of friends and peers). Students present their projects to their classmates, describing the project's genesis, purpose, problems, and future implications; they then answer questions raised by classmates and by the teacher.

Of special importance is the fact that all project presentations are videotaped. Each student thus accumulates a video portfolio in which his or her succession of projects has been recorded. The portfolio may be considered an evolving cognitive model of the student's development over the course of his life in the Key Learning Community. On graduating, students receive a copy of their entire video portfolio—an amazing record of personal and intellectual development. Our research collaboration with the Key Learning Community has centered on the uses that might be made of these video portfolios.

PROJECT ASSESSMENT

Most students in the United States, in the course of their scholastic careers, take hundreds, and perhaps thousands, of tests. In the process, they develop skill—often to a highly calibrated degree—in an exercise that will essentially become useless immediately after their last day in school. In contrast, when one examines life outside of school, projects are ubiquitous. Some projects are assigned to the person, and some are carried out strictly at the person's initiative, but most projects represent an amalgam of personal and communal needs and ends. Although schools have sponsored projects for many years—indeed, the progressive era of the 1920s and 1930s featured an educational approach called the "project method"—such involvement in projects over the years has been virtually invisible in records of a child's progress.

Here our research team has sought to make a contribution. We believe that projects are more likely to be taken seriously by students, teachers, parents, and the wider community if they can be assessed in a reasonable and convenient way. We have therefore sought to construct straightforward ways of evaluating the developmental sophistication and the individualized characteristics of student projects. We view projects and student portfolios in terms of the following five separate dimensions, each of which can be assessed (see Krechevsky & Seidel, 1998; Seidel & Walters, 1991; Seidel et al., 1997):

Individual profile. At issue here is what the project reveals about the specific cognitive strengths, weaknesses, and proclivities of the student. The profile includes the student's disposition toward work (taking risks, persevering) as well as the student's particular intellectual propensities (linguistic, logical, spatial, interpersonal, and the like).

Mastery of facts, skills, and concepts. Projects can be quite marvelous to behold and yet be remote from—or directly at odds with—what is being taught in school. When invoking this dimension, we are able to look at the students' capacity to showcase their command of factual knowledge, mastery of concepts, and skills in deploying the standard curriculum. Customarily a bargain is struck between student and teacher: the teacher can ask the student to draw on school knowledge and understanding in creating a project, and the student can select the facts, skills, and concepts to draw on in the project.

Quality of work. Each project is an instance of a certain genre—a comic play, a mural, a science experiment, a historical narrative. These genres harbor within them certain specific criteria of quality that can be invoked in their evaluation—skits are not assessed in the same way as lectures. Among the aspects of quality that are customarily examined are innovation and imagination, aesthetic judgment and technique, the development of a project in order to foreground a particular concept, and the execution of a performance. As a student continues to create in a genre, he or she gains greater familiarity with the criteria of that genre and learns increasingly to think *in* the symbol system of that domain.

Communication. Projects offer an opportunity for students to communicate with a wider audience: with peers in collaborative efforts, with teachers and other adults, and with their own prior goals and concerns. Sometimes the communication is quite overt, as in a theatrical or musical performance. But even in a more "desktop" science or history project, students have to communicate their findings skillfully, and that process is distinct from the work of conducting the experiment or the library research.

Reflection. One of the most important but most neglected features of intellectual growth is the capacity to step back from one's work, to monitor one's goals, to assess what progress has been made, to evaluate how one's course can be corrected, how to make use of knowledge that has been obtained in the classroom or from others, and the like. Projects provide an excellent occasion for such "metacognitive" or reflective activity. Teachers and students can review work together, and ponder how it relates to past work, longer-term goals, working styles, and so on. Equally important, students can come to internalize these reflective practices, so that they are able to evaluate their work even in the absence of outside agents.

It should be stressed that there is nothing magical or final about these dimensions. They reflect a distillation of much discussion in our group and can be expected to evolve further. Despite our belief that these dimensions constitute a powerful set of lenses for the examination of student work, we do not believe that it would be efficacious simply to impose them on a school or a school system. Rather, we believe that a consideration of such dimensions will arise naturally, as teachers (and students) learn to look at work together and think about projects' distinctive qualities and their evolution over time (Seidel et al., 1997).

Still, there is a distinct place for a research team in such an effort. As researchers, we can present teachers with rich examples for discussion and help guide the discussion—for example, avoiding terminological dead ends or confounding of dimensions. We believe that groups of teachers who are engaged in serious evaluation of student efforts will eventually come up with an ensemble of dimensions much like the one I described above. In that sense, the five dimensions can serve as a kind of supermatrix—what we have humorously dubbed "the mother of all scoring systems." Should such a system be adopted, it will be possible for schools to compare the works of students with one another—a desirable outcome if such scoring systems are to achieve a more enduring stature in American assessment.

Naturally, part of the evaluation of student projects focuses on the quality of the projects. But we are also interested in two other facets. One is the extent to which the project reveals something about the individual student—his or her own particular strengths, limitations, idiosyncrasies, and overall cognitive profile. The other is the extent to which the project involves cooperation with other students, teachers, and outside experts as well as the judicious use of other kinds of resources, such as libraries and computer databases.

Students are not graded up or down if projects are more individualistic or more cooperative. Rather, we describe projects in this way because we feel that these features represent important aspects of any kind of project in which a person will ever participate, aspects that should be noted rather than ignored. In particular, in working with others, students become sensitive to the varying ways in which a project can be conceived and pursued; moreover, in reflecting on their own particular styles and contributions, students receive a preview of the kinds of project activities in which they are most likely to become involved after they finish school.

PROJECT SCAFFOLDING

As researchers we have also become involved in the preparation of projects. Somewhat naively, researchers and teachers originally thought that students could readily create and present projects on their own. In the absence of help at school, however, most projects either are executed by parents or, if done by children, are pale imitations of projects already carried out before or observed elsewhere. Particularly common are book reports or television-style presentations in front of displays resembling weather maps. If students are to conceptualize, develop, and present their own projects effectively, they need to be guided—"scaffolded" is the term of choice—in the various phases and aspects of this activity.

Far from undermining the challenge of making one's own projects, such support actually makes participation in projects possible and growth in project-execution abilities likely. Just as students benefit from apprenticeships in literacy or in a craft, discipline, or pod, they also benefit from an apprenticeship in the formulation and execution of projects. Some students are fortunate enough to have had this apprenticeship at home or in some community activity, such as organized sports or music lessons. But for the vast majority who have not had such opportunities, elementary school is the most likely place where they can be apprenticed in a "project" way of life—unless they happen to go to graduate school fifteen years later!

The course of project construction facilitates new understandings. A project provides an opportunity for students to marshal previously mastered concepts and skills in the service of a new goal or enterprise. The knowledge of how to draw on such earlier forms of representation or understanding to meet a new challenge is a vital acquisition. Planning the project, taking stock along the way, rehearsing it, assembling it in at least a tentatively final form, answering questions about it, and viewing the videotape critically afterward should all help enhance the student's understanding of the topic of the project as well as his or her own contributions to the project's realization.

These features of the Key Learning Community point up some aspects of effective education during the period of middle childhood. To an immersion in the richly furnished environment provided by Project Spectrum, one now adds a more or less formal apprenticeship. Skills are acquired in a domain-appropriate form, and the purposes and uses of these skills remain vivid in the consciousness of the apprentice. At the same time, disciplines are encountered not in an isolated form that provides little motivation, but rather as part of encompassing themes that reverberate throughout the curriculum of the school. The student's emerging knowledge and skills are mobilized in the course of executing a project of his or her own devising, one that has meaning for the student, for his or her family, and within the wider community. Such skills and projects are assessed as much as possible within the context of daily school activities; the assessment involves not only the teacher but also peers and, increasingly, the student him- or herself. The student comes to view the project from a variety of perspectives as it speaks to a variety of audiences and as he or she observes it evolving, often in unpredictable ways.

It would be a mistake to consider projects a panacea for all education ills or as the royal road to a nirvana of knowledge. Some materials need to be taught in more disciplined, rote, or algorithmic ways. Some projects can become a license for fooling around, whereas others may function as a way of hiding fundamental deficiencies in the understanding of vital disciplinary content. But at their best, projects can serve a number of purposes well. They engage students over a significant period of time, spurring them to produce drafts, revise their work, and reflect on it. They foster positive cooperativeness in which each student can make a distinctive contribution. They model the kind of useful work that is carried out after the completion of school in the wider community. They allow students to discover their areas of strength and to put their best foot forward; they engender a feeling of deep involvement or "flow," substituting intrinsic for extrinsic motivation (Csikszentmihalyi, 1990b). Perhaps most important, they offer a proper venue in which to demonstrate the kinds of understandings that the student has (or has not) achieved in the course of the regular school curriculum.

Although the project method has a long history within American educational circles, I am not alone among my contemporaries in being in debt to the Key Learning Community for clarifying these possibilities during the past two decades. Alas, projects are under siege in American education circles today, and they are vulnerable elsewhere in the world as well. The reason is simply stated: Various national and international tests now occupy center stage in nearly all educational systems. Indeed, I would go so far as to say that improvement (or, in the happy instance, maintenance) of a country's standing in international comparisons drives curriculum and pedagogy everywhere. To the extent that scores on such instruments hold sway over educational regimes, it is difficult to carry out well-rounded projects.

The demise of projects, especially in the secondary school years, would be tragic. Through well-designed project work, students learn invaluable lessons of in-depth research, clear expression, use of media, and cooperation with peers. Projects are highly motivating and can be memorable; many students remember best those projects in which they invested much time and much effort. The challenge to those of us who value projects is clear. We must make the best case we can for continuing to feature them in the curriculum. A reasonable consensual method for evaluating such student work would bolster the case significantly.

Chapter 8

Multiple Entry Points Toward Disciplinary Understanding

Amid the enormous amount of attention directed toward educational re-form in the United States and elsewhere over recent decades, surprisingly little discussion has occurred on the *reasons* that we should educate our children—or ourselves. This silence with respect to goals also largely characterizes the first part of this volume, where I have focused on human intellectual potentials.

In this chapter, I hope to remedy this imbalance. I begin with a discussion of the major purpose of education, as I conceive of it, and then survey the ways in which this goal should guide educational priorities across the age span. I focus on the acquisition of disciplinary understanding, which I see as a particular challenge of the later years of school—secondary school and beyond. I show how understanding of crucial ideas and concepts is most likely to be achieved if important subject matter is approached from a variety of perspectives, which can activate the range of our multiple intelligences.

Understanding: A Straightforward Goal for Education

Few would challenge the claim that education should seek to inculcate understanding. However, once one asks, "What is understanding, and how do we know that it has been achieved?" the difficulties inherent in the concept of understanding readily emerge. Indeed, I would claim that most individuals involved in education do not have a clear sense of the nature of understanding, nor do they know how to document that it has (or has not) been achieved.

In *The Unschooled Mind* (1991c), I offer a definition of understanding. I argue that an individual understands whenever he or she is able to apply knowledge, concepts, or skills (abbreviated, hereafter, as knowledge) acquired in some kind of educational setting to a new instance or situation in which that knowledge is relevant. By inference, an individual fails to understand if he or she cannot apply that knowledge, or if he or she brings inappropriate knowledge to bear on the novel situation.

As a convenient example of kinds of understanding, let me refer to the short-lived Gulf War of 1991, in which the United States led a consortium of nations in an effort to wrest Kuwait from Iraqi hands, and, in the process, imposed a new balance of power on that region of the world. Someone with a political or historical understanding of the region could have approached this novel situation and predicted which kinds of outcomes were likely or unlikely to occur after the war, including the unlikelihood of a permanent alteration of the antebellum state of affairs. Someone with an understanding of the principles of physics could have specified how to aim a Patriot missile to intercept a Scud missile in flight and predicted how the resulting debris was likely to distribute itself on the ground. Finally, someone who understood the principles of economics could have anticipated the effect on the U.S. economy (and other economies) of an unanticipated large expenditure of money. (As I write in early 2006, the final story on the Iraq war that began in March 2003 remains to be told.)

By virtue of a considerable amount of cognitive research in the past few decades, we know a very unsettling fact: Most students in the United States and, so far as we can tell, in other industrialized countries do not understand the materials they have been presented in school. That is, when confronted with an unfamiliar situation, they are generally unable to mobilize the appropriate concepts from school, even if they have been good students. The "smoking gun" is particularly visible in physics: Students who received high grades in physics at redoubtable institutions like MIT and Johns Hopkins frequently are unable to apply their classroom knowledge to games or demonstrations encountered outside of school. (In fact, they often answer physics-related questions in the same way as do "unschooled" five-year-olds.)

But, as documented in *The Unschooled Mind*, this problem is by no means restricted to the hard sciences. Indeed, whether one looks at student learning in statistics, mathematics, psychology, literature, history, or the arts, one encounters essentially the same situation. In class, students often appear as if they understand—they are able to give their instructors the factual and rule-governed information they have committed to memory. But once they are expected to figure out on their own *which* of the school-learned concepts, facts, or skills are applicable to a new situation, they show themselves incapable of understanding—again mired at the level of the proverbial five-year-old. It may be superfluous to add that few adults in our society constitute an exception to this rule: As the above instances from the Gulf War suggest, understanding of events and processes is not widely distributed in our society.

Needless to say, this state of affairs is distressing. While our better schools certainly succeed in teaching students the basics of reading, writing, and reckoning, they fail a more stringent and perhaps more fundamental test. Even our better students, by and large, can be said not to understand the worlds of the sciences, mathematics, humanities, and arts. It is perhaps not too much to say that ten or even twenty years of education fail to achieve the goal that it is most reasonable to expect of "the system."

HOW TO ACHIEVE AND DEMONSTRATE UNDERSTANDING

I propose that the achievement of understanding in the major scholarly areas should be a primary goal—perhaps *the* primary goal—of the American educational system. Alas, unless it becomes a central goal of our entire educational enterprise, understanding is most unlikely to be achieved. For starters, educators must agree about which sorts of understanding they wish their students to have. I think it would be advisable to have such a conversation at the national level—and having it at the international level might be fruitful as well. While each school needs to wrestle with the problem of understanding, it makes little sense to have every individual school or school system start from scratch in laying out its own preferred understandings. Let me list some plausible candidates for understandings in several disciplines:

- Students of physics should be able to explain the actions of objects and phenomena that they encounter in their everyday world, as well as demonstrations staged for various purposes within the physics laboratory.
- Students of mathematics should be able to measure relevant quantities in their lives, make plausible investments for the short term and the long run, understand the principles of mortgages and insurance, and fill out their tax returns.
- Students of history should be able to read a daily newspaper or weekly newsmagazine and draw on relevant historical principles both to explain what is happening and to make plausible predictions about what is likely to happen next.
- Students of literature and the arts should be able to create at least simple works in relevant genres, understand and appreciate the qualities of works from their cultures and others, and relate these works to their own lives and concerns, even as they bring those personal agendas to any work that they themselves create or appreciate.

I do not think these aspirations are particularly controversial, nor do I think they would be that difficult to achieve. But it is worth noting that very few schools actually articulate such "understanding goals," and even fewer formulate the "performances of understanding" that their students should ultimately be asked to exhibit.

It has sometimes been convenient to contrast *performances* with *understanding*, a dichotomy that I myself used in *To Open Minds* (1989b). Some educational systems highlight performances—ritualized, memorized sets of sequences and patterns that are initially exhibited by teachers and that students are expected to model with increasing fidelity. Various traditional educational systems, such as China's, are often cited as examples of systems that stress performance. In contrast, the West is thought to highlight understanding—the capacity to probe beneath the surface, to figure out underlying causes, to dissect a text or a work of art and illustrate the principles on which it is built. One can think of Confucius as exemplifying a focus on performance, whereas Socrates emerges as the exemplar incarnate of understanding.

On closer examination, it is clear that understandings can be apprehended and appreciated only if they are *performed* by a student. We cannot know whether a student understands a principle of physics unless he or she can produce a relevant performance. Such a performance might include correctly employing a formula that explains the relation between two variables, or predicting what will happen when two objects collide under certain circumstances. Each of these are *performances of understanding*. By the same token, we cannot know whether a student understands a period of American history unless he or she can produce relevant performances: explicate that period to someone ignorant of American history, relate that period to ones that came before and after, explain an event in today's newspaper in the light of important historical antecedents, or illuminate works of art of the period by invoking contemporary events or personages that animated those works. These, too, are performances of understanding.

Work I carried out in collaboration with Tina Blythe, Veronica Boix-Mansilla, Lois Hetland, David Perkins, Vito Perrone, Stone Wiske, and several other researchers at Harvard indicates that although it is by no means an easy matter for teachers to define such performances, it is possible for them to do so. Following such a delineation, the next step is to share these performances with students; they need to become familiar with the kinds of performances their teachers want them eventually to be able to carry out alone or in cooperation with fellow students. Moreover, rather than requiring such performances solely at the end of a course or unit, teachers should have the students begin to practice these performances from the first days of class. By the same token, students ought to become partners in the processes of assessment as soon as possible. Rather than having assessment occur at the end of the term and at the hands of a teacher or an outsider examiner, assessment ought to be an activity of mutual engagement, in which students take regular and increasing responsibility for reflecting on the nature of their performances and on the means for improving them.

IMPLICATIONS FOR CURRICULUM

The most serious consequence of the decision to educate for understanding is a radical foreshortening of the curriculum. If one wishes to have any chance of securing understanding, it becomes essential to abandon the misguided effort to "cover everything." Broad coverage ensures superficiality: at best, heads become stuffed with facts that are forgotten almost as soon as the short-answer test has been administered. Rather, one must move toward "un-coverage," or, to cite another current slogan, one must embrace the principle that "less is more."

In my version of education for understanding, it is important to define at the outset the kinds of concepts that one wishes students to understand and the kinds of performances that one wishes students to exhibit by the time they finish school. Once defined, these end-states or "final exhibitions" become the basis on which curricula and assessments to be used en route are then devised. To the extent possible, students ought to be introduced explicitly to these concepts and performances early in their scholastic careers and have the chance to revisit them periodically. Thus, for example, if an understanding of democratic institutions is a major goal for history or social studies, curricula and assessments ought to be directed toward such understandings from the first years of school. By the same token, if an understanding of the processes and principles of evolution is a major goal for biological studies, then primary school children should be involved in activities that begin to acquaint them with the phenomena of evolution and give them practice in issuing the sought-after kinds of performances. In short, education for understanding entails a "spiral curriculum" in which rich, generative ideas are revisited time and again across a student's career in school.

One can immediately see that such a process requires regular, substantive interchanges among teachers and considerable continuity in student learning. I have been astonished at how frequently a teacher of one age group has no idea what the students did the previous year or what they are likely to be doing the following year. It is as if each year were sacrosanct and each fall begins from scratch. Students and parents are equally culpable. Quite typically, they do not look for continuities across years, semesters, or even classes. What was done in math or English last year is not considered to be related to the tasks for this coming year: tips about writing picked up in, say, history class, are rarely thought to be relevant to the tasks of writing posed in English or science classes. Here, again, some kind of curriculum coordination, certainly across the school and possibly across the nation, seems to be indicated.

From the preceding discussion, it should be clear that I favor some forms of "core knowledge," materials that all students should know. Note that this preference does not take the form of a canonical list of books or principles: I do not feel that such a mandate is appropriate or well founded. Rather I search for a consensus on certain very rich or generative concepts, such as evolution and democracy, and for attention to the kinds of performances that can reveal understanding, such as the application of those concepts to newly encountered biological phenomena or recently reported political occurrences. It is reasonable to expect every graduate in our land to be able to understand the significance of a new biological discovery or to anticipate the political implications of an economic downslide or a long-awaited judicial opinion.

BALANCING SPECIALIZED AND COMPREHENSIVE KNOWLEDGE: AN EDUCATIONAL CHALLENGE

But how can one mediate between the understandable desire for common forms of knowledge within a society and the need to recognize individual interests and gifts, which is so central to the notion of multiple intelligences? I believe that part of the answer lies in an alertness to what makes pedagogical sense at different stages or levels of development.

It is surely no coincidence that children throughout the world begin schooling in earnest at around the age of seven. In my own view, most children have by this age proceeded as far as they can in coming to know the physical and social worlds and the world of symbols through the use of their natural learning processes. For some purposes, this untutored absorption of patterns may be enough. Indeed, in certain nontechnological cultures, it already makes sense to consider these children young adults.

In literate and technologically oriented cultures, however, children are still remote from the concerns and capacities of competent adults. They must become able to read and to master the various notational systems of the culture: mathematical ones, scientific ones, graphing techniques (like maps and charts), and perhaps other specialized notations, such as those used in music, dance, and engineering. It is the job—and the genius—of schooling to transmit this notational knowledge in the succeeding decade or so.

School-age children differ in other ways from their younger counterparts. Preschoolers enjoy free exploration, fantasy, and experimentation with boundaries; their speech favors metaphors, and they readily embrace synesthetic connections. By the age of eight or nine, however, most children have become quite different creatures. They want to master the rules of their culture and of specific vocations and avocations. They want to use language precisely, not allusively; they want to draw pictures that are photographically realistic, not fanciful or abstract; and they expect a strict adherence to rules in dress, behavior, games, moral situations, and other cultural activities, brooking little deviation.

These shifts in mood and focus offer pedagogical opportunities. Certainly the first years of school are a time when it is important for children to master the notational systems of the culture. By and large, children cannot master these notations on their own; that is why formal school begins around the age of six or seven the world over. Mastering notational systems proves to be a more difficult task than previously thought, because such systems are not mastered in a knowledge vacuum. Rather, they must build on and relate to the commonsensical understanding of domains that have been achieved in the preschool years. Thus, written language must be related to oral language skills; musical notational skills to the child's intuitive or "figural" perception of music; scientific concepts to commonsense understandings of the physical world. Effecting this connection is a crucial challenge. Otherwise, the child may be burdened with two disembodied systems of knowledge, neither adequate on its own, rather than one integrated understanding.

Also at this age, children are both ready and eager to master skills in specific areas. They want to be able to draw in perspective, to compose in rhyme, to perform chemical experiments, or to write a computer program. It would be desirable, in the best of all possible worlds, for all children to be exposed to each of these activities. Human finitude, however, guarantees that such a goal is utopian. An attempt to train children in all art forms, all athletic forms, and all scholastic activities would be certain to achieve superficial knowledge at best and a breakdown due to overload in less happy circumstances.

It is for these reasons that I recommend some degree of specialization during middle childhood—roughly from the ages of eight to fourteen. While children are mastering the crucial literacies, they should have the opportunity to attain significant levels of skill in a small number of domains: perhaps, on average, in one art form, one area of physical training, and one or two scholastic subjects. Thus, a ten-year-old might take music or art lessons, engage in one after-school sport, gymnastic, or dance activity, and have regular cumulative lessons in a subject such as history, biology, or mathematics.

I favor this early specialization for two reasons. First, I think it is important that youngsters receive early on some demonstrations of what it means, on a day-to-day basis, to master a subject matter or a cluster of skills—to drill, practice, monitor their own progress, reflect on it, and compare it to that of peers at work in the same domain. Without this opportunity, children may be at a severe disadvantage later on, when it becomes essential to achieve mastery in a vocational area. The need to experience mastery firsthand is nowhere more acute than in contemporary America, where so many of the cultural signals favor the quick fix rather than the lengthy apprenticeship.

The second reason relates more directly to subsequent careers. In my own view, an individual is most likely to achieve a satisfactory life, make a contribution to society, and gain self-esteem if he or she finds vocational and avocational niches that complement his or her own aptitudes. If a child has had plenty of exposure to the range of domains and intelligences in early life, it seems reasonable that he or she should begin to narrow the focus to some extent in the years of middle childhood. At best, the child will then have already begun to gain needed expertise for later life. At the very least, he or she will have had the experience of gaining some competence and monitoring that process.

How to go about choosing these areas? In a pluralistic and democratic society, the choice should be that of the child and the family, making use of whatever evidence and advice they can obtain from other sources. I believe that reasonable assessments of a child's strengths can already be made in middle childhood; therefore, the matching of child and discipline can be informed. It is possible, however, that even when these couplings are made at random, the results need not be unhappy. My observation in China, where such early matching seems to be made in a relatively unsystematic manner, is that children become quite attached to the areas to which their attention has been directed and in which their skills have been assiduously cultivated.

To say that students need to find some areas of specialization and attain clear skills through apprenticeships in these areas might imply a serious and even painful experience. However, specialization need not resemble a diet of castor oil. An inspired teacher, a lively curriculum, a sympathetic mentor, a congenial group of peers can make the early stages of mastery a wonderful, enjoyable experience. In fact, I would urge that at the beginning of any specialization, there be a period of relatively unstructured "search-light" exploration, during which the possibilities of the medium or symbol system are widely sampled. More constrained "laser" training thereafter can build on this initial survey and can be integrated with it as the incipient master begins to handle the medium in a more personal and more assured way.

There is never a need to suggest a single right answer or a prescribed way to do things. Indeed, just because children at this age are likely to make these erroneous assumptions, it is important for their elders to stress a plurality of approaches and responses.

In contrast to the realm of the "middle-aged" child, the world of the adolescent bursts open in at least three directions. It becomes wider: the youth's arena is now the larger society, even the world, and not merely the family or the local community. It becomes higher: the youth is capable of more abstract forms of reasoning, of speculation, and of dealing with the hypothetical and the theoretical. It also becomes deeper: the youth probes more insistently into his or her own life, dealing with personal feelings, fears, and aspirations in a much fuller way than a few years before.

While Piaget's characterization of formal operational thought is no longer accepted in its original form, it is still useful to think of the adolescent as one who can deal comfortably with whole systems of thought. The preadolescent is interested in facts, rules, and "sheer" skills, whereas the adolescent in our culture becomes more involved with values, with wide-reaching principles, with pregnant exceptions, and with the legitimacy of uses to which skills are put. The adolescent becomes newly concerned with the relations among different bodies of knowledge, different points of view, and different fields in which individuals can become productive. He or she tries to relate these issues to personal concerns—the emerging sense of identity and decisions about career, schooling, and personal relationships, including those with individuals of the other sex and of quite different backgrounds.

In our culture, adolescence is a time of "higher school"—high school and college. In many parts of the world, developed as well as underdeveloped, this period is thought of as a time for increased specialization. In my view, from a developmental perspective, this trend is ill timed and unfortunate. Since adolescents are defining themselves with reference to a wider arena, it is particularly important that they remain (or become) exposed to a broad range of topics, themes, subject matter, value systems, and the like and that they be encouraged to engage in thinking that spans these topics.

Thus, in contrast to the years of middle childhood and in opposition to educational practices in many places, there should be a shift of emphasis toward more comprehensive knowledge during the ages fourteen to twenty-one. In old-fashioned terms, this would be viewed as a call for the liberal arts, but defined in such a way as to include scientific and technological subjects as well as the humanistic classics. It is also a call for the inclusion within the curriculum of a consideration of ethical issues, current events, and communal and global problems. It recommends student involvement in rich and multifaceted projects, encouraging them to sample widely and to make well-motivated and diverse connections.

Of course, any constraints that applied to middle childhood do not mysteriously disappear in adolescence. If it is not possible in the years from seven to fourteen to survey the universe, it is obviously equally impossible to do so in the succeeding seven-year period. Nonetheless, I still call for a more catholic emphasis, for three reasons: (1) such a broadening of curricula and concerns is consistent with the youth's own expansive information-processing propensities at this life stage; (2) it is desirable that every growing individual in the world has at least a modicum of exposure to the principal disciplines and concerns of our planet; and (3) youths in this phase are far more willing to transcend boundaries and to welcome inter-disciplinary thinking.

Nearly all educators wrestle with how to ensure that students have such exposure. They search for shortcuts—for example, core curricula, major and minor subjects, and courses that convey concepts or ways of thinking rather than attempting to provide all information from the ground up. Some go so far as to recommend a specific list of facts and terms that everyone who would be educated needs to know.

Even if I had arrived at a universal curriculum for adolescence, there would be no room here to introduce it. Nor do I feel that every student needs to study every subject or the same set of subjects as a matter of course. Rather, what I want to urge is that the third seven-year period of life, like the first years of life, be a time when relatively wide-ranging explo-ration is encouraged and narrow specialization is put aside or suspended, at least for most students, and that activities that synthesize, draw connec-tions, or link school knowledge to extrascholastic concerns be encouraged and even mandated.

To this point, I have introduced understanding as the proper goal for education, outlined the kinds of performances of understanding for which students might strive, and indicated certain curricular options that schools might adopt. It should be clear that most classrooms in the United States and elsewhere are not currently set up so as to encourage, let alone achieve, such an education. If anything, the insistence on having twenty to fifty students in a classroom seated at desks while the teacher lectures, and moving arbitrarily from one subject to another at preordained timed in-tervals, makes the achievement of an education for understanding virtu-ally impossible.

MUSEUMS AS PLATFORMS FOR PERFORMANCES OF UNDERSTANDING

There is, alas, no formula for achieving understanding—although there may well be numerous formulas for thwarting it. Nevertheless, important clues for a more effective education do exist in two institutions about which something is known: the very ancient apprenticeship and the very modern children's museum.

Imagine an educational environment in which youngsters at the age of seven or eight, in addition to—or perhaps instead of—attending a formal school, can enroll in a children's museum, a science museum, or some kind of discovery center or exploratorium.[1] As part of this educational scene, adults are present who actually practice the disciplines or crafts represented by the various exhibitions. Computer programmers are working in the technology center, zookeepers and zoologists are tending the animals, workers from a bicycle factory assemble bicycles in front of the children's eyes, and a Japanese mother prepares a meal and carries out a tea ceremony in the Japanese house. Even the designers and mounters of the exhibitions ply their trade directly in front of the observing students.

During the course of their schooling, youngsters enter into separate apprenticeships with a number of these adults. Each apprentice group consists of students of different ages and varying degrees of expertise in the domain or discipline. As part of the apprenticeship, the child is drawn into the use of various literacies—numerical and computer languages when enrolled with the computer programmer, reading manuals with the bicycle workers, Japanese language while interacting with the Japanese family, preparation of wall labels with the exhibition designers. The student's apprenticeships deliberately encompass a range of pursuits, including artistic activities, activities requiring exercise and dexterity, and activities of a more scholarly bent. In the aggregate, these activities incorporate the basic literacies required in the culture—reading and writing in the dominant language or languages, mathematical and computational operations, and skill in the notations used in the various vocational or avocational pursuits.

Most of the learning and assessment is done cooperatively; that is, students work together on projects that typically require a team of people having different degrees of and complementary kinds of skills. Thus, the team assembling the bicycle might consist of half a dozen youngsters whose tasks range from locating and fitting parts together to inspecting the

---

1. Many of these ideas presented in this section were developed over the years in conversation with my longtime colleague Tina Blythe.

newly assembled systems to revising a manual or preparing advertising copy. The assessment of learning also assumes a variety of forms, including the student's monitoring his or her own learning by keeping a journal on the "test of the street": for example, does the bicycle actually operate satisfactorily, and does it find any buyers? Because the older people on the team, or "coaches," are skilled professionals who see themselves as training future members of their trades, the reasons for activities are clear, standards are high, and satisfaction flows from a job well done. Because the students are enrolled from the first in a meaningful and challenging activity, they come to feel a genuine stake in the outcome of their (and their peers') efforts.

Some readers might be skeptical about the possibility of youngsters' attending such an intensive museum program rather than or in addition to the public school. The connotations of the two types of institutions could scarcely be more different. *Museum* suggests an occasional, casual, entertaining, enjoyable outing; as Frank Oppenheimer, founder of San Francisco's Exploratorium, was fond of commenting, "No one flunks museum." *School*, in contrast, connotes a serious, regular, formal, deliberately decontextualized institution. Would we not be consigning students to ruination if we enrolled them in museums instead of schools?

I believe we would be doing precisely the opposite. Attendance in many schools today does risk ruining the children. Whatever significance schooling might once have held for the majority of youngsters in our society, it no longer holds sway over many of them. Too many students (and, for that matter, too many parents and teachers) cannot provide compelling reasons for attending school. The reasons cannot be discerned within the school experience, nor is there faith that what is acquired in school will actually be utilized in the future. Try to justify the quadratic equation or the Napoleonic wars to an inner-city high school student or his parents! The real world appears elsewhere: in the media, in the marketplace, and, all too frequently, in the demimonde of drugs, violence, and crime. Much if not most of what happens in schools happens because that is the way that practice was done in earlier generations, not because we have a convincing rationale for maintaining it today. The often-heard statement that school is basically custodial rather than educational harbors more than a grain of truth.

Certainly there are exemplary schools, and just as certainly there are poorly designed and poorly run museums. Yet, as institutions for learning, schools have become somewhat anachronistic, whereas museums have retained the potential to engage students, to teach them, to stimulate their understanding, and, most important, to help them assume responsibility for their own future learning.

Such a dramatic reversal of institutional significance has come about for two complementary sets of reasons. On the one hand, youngsters live in a time of unparalleled excitement, where even the less privileged are exposed daily to attractive media and technologies, ranging from video games to space exploration, from high-speed transportation to direct and immediate means of global communication. In many cases, these media can be used to create compelling products. Activities that might once have engaged youngsters—reading in classrooms or hearing teachers lecture about remote subjects—seem hopelessly tepid and unmotivating to many of them. On the other hand, science museums and children's museums have become the loci for exhibitions, activities, and role models drawn precisely from those domains that do engage youngsters; their customary wares represent the kinds of vocations, skills, and aspirations that legitimately animate and motivate students.

I have documented some of the difficulties students have in coming to understand the topics presented in school. It is of course possible that even if one cannot flunk museum, one might fail to appreciate the meanings and implications of exhibitions encountered there. Indeed, I suspect that such miscomprehension often happens on one-shot visits to museums.

An active and sustained participation in an apprenticeship, however, offers a far greater opportunity for understanding. In such long-term relationships, novices have the opportunity to witness on a daily basis the reasons for various skills, procedures, concepts, and symbolic and notational systems. They observe competent adults moving readily and naturally from one external or internal way of representing knowledge to another. They experience firsthand the consequences of a misguided or misconceived analysis and derive pleasure from seeing a well-thought-out procedure work properly. They undergo a transition from a situation in which much of what they do is based on adult models to one in which they are trying out their own approaches, perhaps with some support or criticism from the master. They can discuss alternatives with more accomplished peers, just as they can provide assistance to peers who have recently joined the team. All these options, it seems to me, guide the student toward a state of enablement. The student displays the capacity to use skills and concepts in an appropriate way—the hallmark of an emerging understanding.

If we are to configure an education for understanding, suited for the students of today and for the world of tomorrow, we need to take seriously the lessons of the museum and the institution of the apprenticeship. The goal need not be to convert each school into a museum, nor each teacher into a master craftsman, but rather to think of the ways in which the strengths of a museum atmosphere, of apprenticeship learning, and of engaging projects can pervade all educational environments, from home to school to workplace. Knowledge of a student's intellectual profile should aid in choosing a mentor or directing the student to exhibitions that he or she might find of interest. Yet, intellectual profiles are not sclerotic, and a challenging mentor or exhibition can stimulate the development of an intelligence as well. Finally, the evocativeness and open-endedness of the children's museum need to be wedded to the structure, rigor, and discipline of an apprenticeship. The basic features I have just listed may assume a central place in educational environments that span the gamut of disciplines and the full range of ages from preschool through retirement.

MULTIPLE ENTRY POINTS TO UNDERSTANDING

It may seem odd that so little heed has been paid in this chapter to the different human faculties and intellectual strengths exhibited by students. This omission has in fact been deliberate. I believe that in laying out educational goals and processes, we need to acknowledge the common links among students and the kinds of expectations that we may properly hold with respect to their collective accomplishments.

But it is now time to remedy this omission. The preceding chapters have provided ample evidence that individuals learn in different ways and display different intellectual configurations and proclivities. Certainly, we would dismantle the entire edifice of MI theory if we were to bypass these differences and insist on teaching all students the same contents in the same way.

At first consideration, it may seem that MI theory renders the already formidable task of education even more difficult. After all, it would be highly desirable if all individuals exhibited pretty much the same faculties and learned in pretty much the same way. And, indeed, for a teacher faced with thirty students a class and four or five classes a day, the prospect of in-dividualizing education may appear daunting. But since such individual differences do exist, and since a person's own particular intellectual config-uration will necessarily color his or her trajectory and accomplishments throughout life, it is a disservice to ignore these conditions.

So long as one tries to cover a huge amount of material in school, it is vir-tually impossible to deliver an education nuanced in the light of multiple intelligences. But once it is determined that one will teach for understand-ing and probe topics in depth over a significant period of time, then the ex-istence of individual differences in cognitive profiles can actually be an ally.

My research has suggested that any rich, nourishing topic—any concept worth teaching—can be approached in at least seven different ways that, roughly speaking, map onto the multiple intelligences. We might think of the topic as a room with at least seven doorways into it. Students vary as to which entry point is most appropriate for them and which routes are most comfortable to follow once they have gained initial access to the room. Awareness of these entry points can help teachers introduce new materials in ways that can be easily grasped by a range of students, and as students explore other entry points, they can develop multiple perspectives, which are the best antidote to stereotypical thinking.

Let us look at these seven entry points and provide an example of how each entry might be used in approaching a topic in the natural sciences (evolution) and a topic in the social sciences (democracy).

In using a *narrational entry point,* one presents a story or narrative about the concept in question. In the case of evolution, one might trace the course of a single branch of the evolutionary tree, or perhaps even the gen-erations of a specific organism. In the case of democracy, one would tell the story of its beginnings in ancient Greece or, perhaps, of the origins of constitutional government in the United States.

In using a *logical entry point*, one approaches the concept through a structured argument. Darwin arrived at the theory of evolution through an analogy with what happens to human beings when they struggle for existence in a space that is too crowded and impoverished to sustain them all. Democracies are forms of government that involve the population, or its duly chosen representatives, in decision making.

A *quantitative entry point* deals with numerical quantities and relations. Darwin began to ponder evolutionary questions when he observed different numbers of different species of finches on varioius of the Galápagos Islands. An examination of congressional voting patterns illuminates the ways in which democratic institutions operate—or run into problems.

A *foundational (or existential) entry point* examines the philosophical and terminological facets of the concept. This tack proves appropriate for people who like to pose fundamental questions of the "why" sort associated with young children and philosophers rather than with more practical (or more "middle-aged") spirits. A foundational approach to evolution might consider the difference between evolution and revolution, the reasons that we look for origins and changes, the epistemological status of teleology and finality. A foundational approach to democracy would ponder the root meaning of the word, the relationship of democracy to other forms of decision making and government, and the reasons that a nation might adopt a democratic rather than an oligarchic approach. The philosopher Matthew Lipman has developed engaging materials for introducing such a foundational approach to students in middle childhood (Lipman, Sharp, & Oscanyan, 1990).

We shift gears quite sharply in considering an *aesthetic approach*. Here the emphasis falls on sensory or surface features that will appeal to, or at least capture the attention of students who favor an artistic stance toward the experiences of living. In the case of evolution, the examination of the structure of different evolutionary trees, or the study of the shifting morphology of organisms over time, might activate the aesthetic sensibility. With reference to democracy, one intriguing approach would be to listen to musical ensembles characterized either by group playing or by playing under the control of a single individual—the string quartet versus the orchestra. Another, less exotic tack might be to consider various forms of balance or imbalance as they are epitomized in different voting blocs.

A sixth entry point is an *experiential approach.* Some students—old as well as young—learn best with a hands-on approach, dealing directly with the materials that embody or convey the concept. Those bent on mastering concepts of evolution might breed numerous generations of drosophila and observe the mutations that take place. Nowadays, of course, such replication also can be simulated with computer software. Those in the social studies class might actually form groups that have to make decisions in accordance with various governmental processes and observe the pros and cons of representative democracy as compared with other forms of government.

A final entry point features a *collaborative approach* among students. In recent years, the advantages of well-designed group work have been demonstrated. Students who work comfortably with others are especially likely to learn from group projects, discussions, debates, role-play, and "jigsaw" activities—in which each child in a group makes a special, distinctive contribution. Students who like debate could recreate the famous debates about evolution between T. H. Huxley and Samuel Wilberforce. As noted, students can simulate various forms of democracy—direct, representative, town meetings—and see the strengths and limitations of each option.

In one formulation, a skilled teacher is a person who can open a number of different windows on the same concept. In our example, rather than presenting evolution and democracy only by definition, or only by example, or only in terms of quantitative considerations, such a teacher would make available several entry points over time. An effective teacher functions as a "student-curriculum broker," ever vigilant for educational prostheses—texts, films, software that can help convey the relevant contents in as engaging and effective a way as possible to students who exhibit various learning modes.

It should be evident that using multiple entry points can be a powerful means of dealing with student misconceptions, biases, and stereotypes. So long as students take only a single perspective on a concept or problem, it is virtually certain that they will understand the concept in the most limited and rigid fashion. Conversely, the adoption of a family of stances toward a phenomenon encourages students to come to know that phenomenon in more than one way, to develop multiple representations, and to seek to relate these representations to one another.

Multiple entry points have two important additional advantages. First, by approaching a topic in more than one way, one reaches more students. Some students learn better through narration, some through works of art. Some might learn science better through quantitative entry points, and poetry better through foundational entry points. Second, the use of multiple entry points is the best way to convey what it is like to have expert knowledge. An expert is an individual who can think about his or her area of expertise in multiple ways—verbal description, graphic sketches, behavioral embodiment, humorous renditions, and so on. In encountering different representations of the key ideas, and in having the opportunity to think about these ideas in multiple ways, the student partakes of the heady atmosphere of the expert.

A WORD ABOUT SPECIAL POPULATIONS

This review suggests that even in cases where one wishes to have a core curriculum mastered by all students, it is possible to craft an educational regimen that exploits the existence of multiple intelligences. Education needs to transcend common knowledge, however. Important as it is for all students to know about the history and literature of their land, and about the major biological and physical principles that govern the world, it is at least as important for students to identify their strengths and to pursue areas in which they are comfortable and can expect to achieve a great deal.

My own observations suggest that rarely in life are the fates of individuals determined by what they are unable to do. Their life trajectories are much more likely to be molded by the kinds of abilities and skills they have developed, and these in turn are determined in significant measure by the profile of intelligences with which they were endowed or that was nurtured in their early life. Many of the most creative people in history have had significant learning problems: Thomas Edison, Winston Churchill, Pablo Picasso, and even Albert Einstein come to mind. Far from being crippled by these difficulties, these individuals were able to build on their strengths to make remarkable, and remarkably distinctive, contributions to their particular domain of achievement. Accordingly, those entrusted with education need to pay special attention to the strengths and the proclivities of youngsters under their charge.

It is probably no accident that my work came early to the attention of professionals who are involved with what one might call "special populations"—children who are gifted and talented, children who have learning difficulties, children who are exceptional or handicapped (or both) in one intellectual form or another. What characterizes these children is precisely the fact that they do *not* acquire the lessons of school in the ordinary way. Those who teach them are thus faced with the choice of either writing them off or finding educational regimens and prostheses that are effective. (Incidentally, this problem can prove as acute with students who are highly gifted as with students who are considered disabled by current educational standards.)

MI theory can be of considerable help here. Not only does it supply a categorical scheme and a set of definitions that are useful for diagnostic and training purposes, but it may also actually suggest steps that could be useful for students who exhibit one or another unusual learning pattern.

Take, for example, the case of children with dyslexia. In a significant number of cases, such children show enhanced facility with visual or spatial activities. These strengths can be mobilized to help students excel in vocations and avocations that exploit visual-spatial capacities, and, at least sometimes, these strengths can be drawn on in presenting linguistic materials. While I would scarcely recommend the imposition of a disability on any person, the experience of dealing with and overcoming a disability can itself become a great ally in dealing with subsequent challenges. Perhaps this is another reason why many individuals of singular accomplishment turn out to have been dyslexic, ranging from the inventor Thomas Edison to the politician Nelson Rockefeller to John Chambers, CEO of Cisco Systems.

Or take the case of an individual whose native language is not English. While it is often thought that learning a new language simply involves substituting one language for another, that view turns out to be an oversimplification. Different cultures and subcultures use languages in different ways (for example, one group stresses storytelling and fantasy; another highlights exposition in a truthful fashion; a third is terse and allusive). In addition, language may interact in different ways with other modes of communication, such as gesturing, singing, or demonstrating what one means. Sensitivity to multiple intelligences may help a teacher determine which modalities are most effective for the presentation of a new language as well as how to make sure the linguistic intelligence is interacting in optimal fashion with other intelligences that may participate in the communicative process.

Speaking more generally about students with learning problems, it is possible to use MI information in a number of ways. The most straightforward is simply to identify an area of strength—for example, through a Spectrum-style assessment instrument—and to give the child the opportunity to develop that strength. The child thus can become skilled at endeavors that may have vocational or avocational linkages. Also, the feeling of self-esteem that accrues from a job well done may encourage the child to take up challenges that might previously have been intimidating.

Identification of strengths can have a more integral effect on educational achievement. Sometimes it is possible to use an area of strength as a bridge to an area that has posed difficulties. For example, as suggested above, a child who is especially gifted with narratives may be introduced to difficult mathematical, musical, or scientific concepts through the comfortable vehicle of a story.

Structural affinities sometimes obtain between domains in which the child has talent and domains in which the child appears to be impaired. For example, there are common numerical structures in mathematics and music, and common spatial structures in geometry and the arts. Provided that the transfer is attempted in a sensitive way, it may be possible for a child gifted in art or music to accomplish more in traditional subject matters by exploiting the structural analogues that exist across domains customarily thought to be disparate.

Even when executed indifferently, education is a very complicated process; when it is done well, it turns out to be amazingly complex, intricate, and subtle. Brief lists alone of the interest groups and concerns associated with education threaten to overwhelm our information-processing capacities: the teachers, students, parents, union leaders, school board members, administrators, opinion leaders, and the general public; the texts, tests, curricula, guidelines, schedules, teaching procedures, syllabi, building, grounds, and supplies. And both lists could be extended!

I have sought to provide some degree of focus by insisting on four elements: (1) the goal of an education that is geared to understanding; (2) an emphasis on the cultivation of performances of understanding, which can be assessed primarily in context; (3) a recognition of the existence of different individual strengths; and (4) a commitment to mobilizing these elements productively in the education of each child. To orchestrate these different elements into a seamless educational regimen is no mean task. But there are promising signs that progress can be made and that we can secure an education that celebrates our common heritage as human beings, the particular cultural backgrounds from which we come, and the ways in which each of us is a unique individual.

Chapter 9

DISCIPLINED INQUIRY IN HIGH SCHOOL:
AN INTRODUCTION TO ARTS PROPEL

In the early 1990s, I noted the renaissance of interest in education in the arts. And indeed, for a variety of reasons, the arts had gained—or regained—a place in the American curriculum in the 1980s. Alas, those days seem distant. With the hegemony of high-stakes testing in the first decade of the twenty-first century, quality arts education seems under siege in all but the most well-resourced public schools. Nonetheless, those of us who believe that an education bereft of the arts is, so to speak, "half-brained" will continue to advocate for the arts and will try to do so on the basis of sound arguments and quality curricula.

At the rhetorical level it is easy to find areas of consensus among the various participants in the national arts education movement. Nearly everyone would call for more class time spent on the arts, better-trained teachers, and some kind of graduation requirement. Yet, lurking beneath the surface agreement are vexed issues that engender sharp controversy (Burton, Lederman, & London, 1988; Davis, 2005; Dobbs, 1988; Eisner, 1987; Ewens, 1988; Getty, 1986; Jackson, 1987; Winner & Hetland, 2000; Zessoules, Wolf, & Gardner, 1988).

Some of the questions seem practical in nature. Should we call for specialist teachers or train regular classroom teachers in the arts? Should we focus on one or two art forms or provide the whole menu of genres and forms? Should we have a uniform curriculum across cities or states? Should we employ standardized tests? But one soon encounters issues that exceed the merely practical. To what extent should arts classes be used to foster creativity? Should art be taught separately or infused across the standard curriculum? Is there a privileged canon of Western art, or does the art of our civilization merely take its place among many other equally meritorious traditions? Should art training focus on productive skills, or should there be an emphasis on connoisseurship? Is artistic knowledge primarily factual, or does it involve unique forms of cognition and metacognition?

None of these questions is new to arts educators, but they take on special significance at a time when the allocation of resources is under review. Decisions made (or avoided) are likely to have reverberations.

In this chapter I introduce an approach to curriculum and assessment in the arts, principally at the high school level, called Arts PROPEL. While a number of the features of Arts PROPEL are shared with other contemporary initiatives, the approach differs both in terms of its intellectual origins and its particular mix of components. This chapter thus also serves as an introduction to the general approach to arts education devised over the past four decades at Project Zero at the Harvard Graduate School of Education and to a particular form it has currently assumed in the practical arena.

Project Zero has involved hundreds of researchers over the decades, and they have made contributions in a variety of corners of the humanities and social sciences. Our collective work has been reviewed in a number of summary publications (Gardner, 1982, 2000; Goodman, Perkins, & Gardner, 1972; Perkins & Leondar, 1977; Winner, 1982; see also www.pzweb. harvard.edu) and was the subject of an issue of the *Journal of Aesthetic Education* (Gardner & Perkins, 1988). Hence, it is not necessary to recapitulate our principal research findings here.

It is appropriate, however, to introduce the lines of analysis that led most directly to the Arts PROPEL undertaking. In our early work, we applied the pathbreaking methods of investigation devised by Jean Piaget (1950) in his study of children to the kinds of symbol-using competences described by Nelson Goodman (1968). This focus eventually gave rise to three principal lines of investigation. First, we carried out cross-sectional experimental studies of specific capacities (such as style sensitivity and metaphoric competence) in order to determine the "natural" developmental trajectory of these important skills (Gardner, 1982). Second, we carried out naturalistic longitudinal studies of the development in early childhood of various kinds of symbol-using capacities (Wolf & Gardner, 1981, 1988; Wolf et al., 1988). Third, in a scientifically related body of work, we investigated the breakdown, under conditions of brain damage, of the very symbolic skills whose ontogenesis we had been probing (Kaplan & Gardner, 1989). A number of important and sometimes unexpected findings emerged from these early studies:

1. In most areas of development, children simply improve with age. In several artistic spheres, however, evidence suggests a surprisingly high level of competence in young children followed by a possible decline during the years of middle childhood. This jagged or U-shaped curve in development is particularly evident in certain areas of artistic production, although it can perhaps be manifest as well in certain other areas of perception (Gardner & Winner, 1982).

2. Notwithstanding certain deficiencies in their performance, preschool children acquire a tremendous amount of knowledge about and competence in the arts. As is the case with natural language, this acquisition can occur without explicit tutelage on the part of parents or teachers. The evolution of children's drawings constitutes a particularly vivid example of this self-generated learning and development (Gardner, 1980). In this respect artistic learning stands in sharp contrast to most traditional school subjects.

3. In nearly every area, an individual's perceptual or comprehension capacities develop well in advance of productive capacities. Once again, however, the picture in the arts proves far more complex, and at least in some domains, comprehension actually appears to lag behind performance or production capacities (Winner et al., 1983). This finding underscores the importance of giving young children ample opportunity to learn by performing, making, or doing.

4. According to classical developmental theory, children's competence in one cognitive sphere should predict the child's level of competence in other spheres. Along with other investigators, we discovered much less synchrony across areas. This result can be explained readily by MI theory. Indeed, it was entirely normal for children to be

strong in one or two areas—for example, sculpture—while being average or below average in other areas—such as painting (Gardner, 1983b; Winner et al., 1986).

5. It had been thought for some decades that the brain was "equipotential" with each area capable of subserving the range of human capacities. Neuropsychological research called this finding into doubt. A better description indicates that specific areas of the cortex have particular cognitive functions, and that, particularly after early childhood, there is relatively little plasticity in the representation of cognitive capacities in the nervous system (Gardner, 1975, 1986a).

It would be misleading to suggest that we now understand artistic development, even to the same extent that researchers have illuminated scientific development or the development of linguistic competence. As the taunting "zero" in our name, Project Zero, reminds us, research on this topic is still in its infancy. Our work has established that artistic development is complex and follows multiple pathways; generalizations are hard to come by and often fall by the wayside. Still, it has been important for us to try to tie together our major findings about artistic development, and this we have attempted in a number of places (Davis, 2005; Gardner, 1973, 1990a, 1990b; Winner, 1982; Wolf & Gardner, 1980).

THE THEORY OF MULTIPLE INTELLIGENCES

In my own work, these various insights came together particularly in MI theory (see chapters 1 and 2). In light of a pluralistic view of the intellect, the question immediately arises whether there is a separate artistic intelligence. According to my analysis, there is not (Gardner, 1983a; see also chapter 5). Rather, each of these forms of intelligence can be directed toward artistic ends: that is, the symbols entailed in a domain of knowledge may, but need not, be marshaled in an aesthetic fashion. Thus, linguistic intelligence can be used in ordinary conversation or for the purpose of authoring legal briefs; in neither case is language employed aesthetically. The same intelligence can be used for writing poems or novels, in which case it is deployed aesthetically. By the same token, spatial intelligence can be used by sailors or sculptors, and bodily-kinesthetic intelligence can be exploited by dancers, mimes, athletes, or surgeons. Even musical intelligence can be used nonaesthetically (as in a communication system based on bugle calls), just as logical-mathematical intelligence can be directed in an aesthetic vein (for instance, when one proof is deemed more elegant than another). Whether an intelligence is mobilized for aesthetic or nonaesthetic ends turns out to be an individual or a cultural decision.

ALTERNATIVE ACCENTS IN ARTS EDUCATION

Over the course of history, human intelligences have been trained primarily in one of two contrasting ways. On the one hand, individuals have become participants from an early age in activities that mobilize and channel their intelligences. This process occurs in traditional apprenticeships as well as in informal scholastic activities that feature observation, demonstration, and coaching-in-context (Collins & Brown, 1988; Gardner, 1991a; Resnick, 1987; Schon, 1984). On the other hand, human intelligences have been trained in more formal scholastic settings and formats. Students attend lectures or read textbooks on various subjects and are expected to memorize, understand, and draw from this material for homework, examinations, and "later life." According to my analysis, the scholastic approach has come to dominate our thinking about learning and to exercise a near stranglehold on school activities. Yet people can also train intelligences—including a much wider band of their intelligences—through informal or nonscholastic regimens.

In few areas of knowledge has the distinction between these two forms been more salient than in the field of arts education. For hundreds if not thousands of years, students have learned much of artistry through apprenticeships. They observe artistic masters at work. They are gradually drawn into these activities. They at first participate in simple, carefully supported ways, then gradually tackle more difficult assignments with less support from their coach or master. Certainly this was the procedure of choice in the ateliers of the Renaissance, and versions of it persist in private art and music lessons today. Artists-in-the-Schools programs are efforts to exploit the power of these traditional learning schemes. Here, appropriate intelligences are mobilized directly, without the need for extensive linguistic, logical, or notational interventions.

Over the past few hundred years, a second front has opened in arts education. With the emergence of fields such as art history, art criticism, aesthetics, communications, semiotics, and the like, an ensemble of scholastic understandings about the arts has gained importance in the academy. Rather than being acquired through observation, demonstration, or apprenticeship, these "peri-artistic" bodies of knowledge are mastered primarily through traditional scholastic methods: through lectures, texts, and writing assignments, in the same manner as history, economics, and sociology.

Now there is no necessary link between these aspects of the arts and the modes of teaching. Art history could be taught through observation or demonstration, just as painting or playing the violin could be taught (if not learned!) through lecturing or reading a textbook. And yet, for evident reasons, each of these artistic disciplines has tended to favor one form of pedagogy over its rival.

THE SCENE IN ARTS EDUCATION

Various surveys of American education paint a generally consistent picture. In the younger grades, arts education is relatively abundant. More often than not, artistic instruction is provided by the regular classroom teacher, and, in general, it focuses very much on artistic production. Children paint, draw, and model clay, and they sing, participate in rhythm bands, or, less often, play an instrument, dance, or tell stories. When teachers are gifted or inspired, these productions may achieve a high level, but for the most part youthful artistic productions are not noteworthy. In middle childhood, arts education declines in frequency; by high school, specialists handle instruction, but only a minority of students participate. With few exceptions, the accent continues to fall on production. The actual classroom procedures often involve apprenticeship methods, particularly at the older age levels, but typically the initiative for production is placed almost entirely in the students' hands.

In a few school systems, efforts have been made to train children in "peri-artistic" activities like history or connoisseurship. Traditionally there has been little constituency in the community for this activity; only with the advent of discipline-based arts education, an approach developed in the early 1980s by the Getty Trust, has there been a call for training in artistry outside the production sphere.

Within the professions of arts education, however, a consensus has emerged over recent decades that production alone will not suffice. While arts educators differ in their assessment of the importance of artistic production—and its putative connection to creativity, more broadly framed—they concur that for the majority of the population, such an exclusive emphasis no longer makes sense. Thus, nearly all reform efforts call for an arts education that encompasses some discussion and analysis of artworks themselves and some appreciation of the cultural contexts in which artworks are fashioned.

THE PROJECT ZERO APPROACH TO ART EDUCATION

Given our cognitive approach to artistic education, these general trends have been applauded within Project Zero. (Indeed, in our more chauvinistic moments, we claim a bit of credit for some of the recent reorientation in arts education.) We believe that students need to be introduced to the ways of thinking exhibited by individuals involved in the arts: practicing artists and those who analyze, criticize, and investigate the cultural contexts of art objects.

Yet, in contrast to some advocates of discipline-based arts education, we nuance this position. While not pretending to speak for all of Project Zero—past or present—I call attention to the following points:

1. Particularly at younger ages (below, say, age ten), production activities ought to be central in any art form. Children learn best when they are actively involved in their subject matter; they want to work directly with materials and media; in the arts these strengths and inclinations almost always translate into the making of something. Moreover, young children have considerable gifts

for figuring the crucial components or patterns in an artistic object, and they should have the opportunity to do such "ferreting out" on their own (Bamberger, 1982b). This accent is a legacy of the Progressive Era that deserves to endure, even in a more "disciplinary epoch" (see Dewey, 1959; Lowenfeld, 1947).

2. Perceptual, historical, critical, and other "peri-artistic" activities should be closely related to and, whenever possible, emerge from the child's own productions. That is, rather than being introduced in an alien context to art objects made by others, children should encounter such objects in relation to the particular artistic products and problems with which they are themselves engaged—and, whenever possible, in intimate connection to the child's own art objects. (Older students and adults can also benefit from such contextualized introductions to "peri-artistic" activities.)

3. Arts curricula need to be presented by teachers or others with a deep knowledge of how to think in an artistic medium. If the area is music, the teacher must be able to think musically—and not merely introduce music via language or logic. Likewise, education in the visual arts must occur at the hand—and through the eyes— of someone who can think visually or spatially (see Arnheim, 1969). To the extent that teachers do not already possess these skills, they ought to enroll in training regimens that can develop these cognitive capacities.

4. Whenever possible, artistic learning should be organized around meaningful projects that are carried out over a significant period of time and that allow ample opportunity for feedback, discussion, and reflection (see chapter 7). Such projects are likely to interest students, motivate them, and encourage them to develop skills; and they may well exert a long-term impact on the students' competence and understanding. As much as possible, one-shot learning experiences should be spurned.

5. In most artistic areas, it will not be profitable to plan a strict K–12 sequential curriculum. (I have in mind here simple-minded but all too frequent curricular goals: can provide four color names; can sing three intervals; can recite two sonnets.) Such a formula may sound attractive, but it flies in the face of the holistic, contextually

sensitive manner in which people customarily gain mastery in crafts or disciplines. Artistry involves a continuing exposure, at various developmental levels, to certain core concepts, such as style, composition, and genre, and to certain recurrent challenges, such as performing a passage with feeling or creating a powerful artistic image. Curricula need to be rooted in this "spiral" aspect of artistic learning. A curriculum may be sequential in the sense that it revisits concepts and problems in an increasingly sophisticated way, but not in the sense that one set of problems, concepts, or terms is addressed in second grade and another set in third grade, and so on.

6. Assessment of learning is crucial in the arts. The success of an arts program cannot be asserted or taken on faith. Assessments must respect the particular intelligences involved—musical skill must be assessed through musical means and not via the intervening screens of language or logic. Assessments also must probe those abilities and concepts that are most central to the arts. Rather than crafting the curriculum to suit the assessment, we must devise assessments that do justice to what is most pivotal in an art form.

7. Artistic learning does not merely entail the mastery of a set of skills or concepts. The arts are also deeply personal areas, through which students confront their own deepest feelings as well as the feelings of others. Students need educational vehicles that allow them such exploration; they must see that personal reflection is a respected and important activity; and be assured that their privacy will not be violated.

8. In general, it is risky—and, in any case, unnecessary—to teach artistic taste or value judgments directly. However, it is important for students to understand that the arts are permeated by issues of taste and value that matter to anyone who is seriously engaged in the arts. These issues are best conveyed through contact with individuals who care about these issues and are willing to introduce and defend their values, but who also are open to discussion and countenance alternative views.

9. Arts education is too important to be left to any one group, even that group designated as "art educators." Rather, arts education

needs to be a cooperative enterprise involving artists, teachers, administrators, researchers, and the students themselves.

10. While ideally all students would study all art forms, this is not a practical option. There are simply too many subjects—and, in my terms, too many intelligences—competing for space on the calendar, and the school day is already excessively fragmented. In my view, no art form has any intrinsic priority over others. Thus, at the risk of offending aficionados of a particular art form, I assert that students should all have extended exposure to some art form—but it need not be one of the visual arts. Indeed, I would rather students be well versed in music, dance, or drama than have a smattering of knowledge across the several lively arts. Then they would at least know what it is like to think in an art form, and they would retain the option of assimilating other art forms in later life, rather than be forever consigned to dilettante status, or even to drop out of the world of arts altogether.

Arts PROPEL[1]

The above points could give rise to any number of programs in arts education. For us at Project Zero, they contributed to an approach called Arts PROPEL. In 1985, with encouragement and support from the Arts and Humanities Division of the Rockefeller Foundation, Project Zero joined forces with the Educational Testing Service and the Pittsburgh Public Schools in a five-year project to devise a set of assessment instruments that could document artistic learning during the later elementary and high school years.

As anyone involved in educational experiments can readily appreciate, it proved easier to state our goal than to implement it. We began by attempting to delineate the kinds of competences that we sought to measure in our students. We decided to work in three art forms—music, visual art, and imaginative writing—and to look at three kinds of competences: production

---

1. Many researchers were involved in Arts PROPEL, including Lyle Davidson, Larry Scripp, Steve Seidel, Ellen Winner, and Dennie Wolf. I thank Reineke Zessoules for her help in developing the ideas in this essay.

(composing or performing music; painting or drawing; engaging in imaginative or "creative" writing); perception (effecting distinctions or discriminations within an art form—"thinking" artistically); and reflection (stepping back from one's own perceptions or productions, or those of other artists, and seeking to understand the goals, methods, difficulties, and effects achieved). PROPEL captures acronymically this trio of competences in our three art forms, with the final L emphasizing our concern with learning.

Ideally, we would have liked simply to devise adequate assessment instruments and administer them to students in the target age groups. However, we soon arrived at a simple but crucial truth: there is no point in assessing competences or even potentials unless the student has had some significant experience in working directly with relevant artistic media. Just as baseball scouts look at students who are already playing baseball, it is necessary for educational assessors to examine students who are already engaged in artistic activities. Similarly, just as baseball rookies need well-trained and skilled coaches, so, too, do art students require teachers who are fully acquainted with the goals of an educational program and able to exemplify the requisite artistic skills and understandings.

To bring about these goals, therefore, we devised curriculum modules and linked them to assessment instruments. We implemented a careful procedure of curriculum and assessment development. For each art form, we assembled an interdisciplinary team charged with defining the central competences in that form. In writing, we looked at students' capacities to create instances of different genres—for example, writing a poem and creating dialogue for a play. In music, we examined the ways in which students learn from rehearsals of a work-in-progress. And in the area of visual arts (from which I will draw most of my examples here), these competences focused on sensitivity to style, appreciation of various compositional patterns, and ability to plan and create a work such as a portrait or a still life.

Two Educational Vehicles

For each of these nominated competences, we generated a set of exercises called a *domain project* that had to feature perceptual, productive, and reflective elements. Domain projects do not in themselves constitute an entire curriculum, but they must be curriculum compatible: that is, they should fit comfortably into a standard art curriculum.

The domain projects are first explored and critiqued by teachers. After revision, they are administered in pilot form to students. A preliminary assessment system is then tried out by the teachers. An iterative process is invoked until the domain project is considered adequate from the perspective of each of its audiences. Once the project has been completed, it can be used as-is by teachers or adapted in various ways to fit a particular curriculum or the teaching style or goals of a specific teacher. Part of the assessment procedure is rough-and-ready—simply giving students and teachers a feeling for what the student is learning. However, it is also possible to make more fine-grained analyses (for research purposes) as well as to produce a summary score for use by the central school administration.

As one example, let me briefly describe the "composition" domain project, which has already been used quite widely in Arts PROPEL. This project is designed to help students notice how arrangements and interrelationships of shapes affect the composition and the impact of artistic works. Students are given an opportunity to make compositional decisions and to reflect on the effects of such decisions in their works and in works created by acknowledged artistic masters.

In an initial session, students are given a set of ten odd, black, geometric shapes. They are asked simply to drop those shapes on a piece of white paper. The exercise is then repeated, although this time students are asked to put together a set of shapes that they find pleasing. They are then asked to reflect on the differences between the "random" and the "deliberate" work. In a notebook they record the differences they see and state the reasons that motivated their own "deliberate" choices. Most students find this exercise fun, although at first they may not quite know what to make of it.

In a second session, students encounter informally certain principles of composition. The teacher introduces the students to a number of artistic works of different styles and periods that differ significantly from one another in the kinds of symmetry or balance they epitomize or violate. Students are asked to describe the differences among these works and to develop a vocabulary that can capture these differences and convey them effectively to others. Achievements (or violations) of harmony, cohesion, repetition, dominant forces, radial patterns, surprise, or tension in the works are noted. At the conclusion of the session, students are asked to jot down in their notebooks similarities and differences in a contrasting set of slides. They are also given an assignment: during the next week, they should search their daily environment for instances of different compositions—both compositions already achieved by an artist and those that the students can create by "framing" a scene in nature.

In a third session, students report on the compositions they observed in their own environment and discuss them with reference to those observed in the art class. The students then return to the deliberate composition of session one. Now they are asked to make a "final work." Before proceeding, however, they are asked to indicate their plans for this work. Then they go about realizing and, if they wish, revising their final composition. On a worksheet they indicate what they found most surprising about their composition and which further changes they might want to make in a future work.

In addition to the student's own compositions, perceptual discriminations, and reflections, the teacher also has his or her own assessment sheet. The teacher can evaluate students in terms of the kinds of compositions attempted or achieved. Other kinds of learning—for instance, the students' success in discovering interesting compositions in their environments or their ability to connect their own compositions with those of well-known artists—can also be assessed. This domain project can be repeated, in its initial or an altered form, to determine the extent to which the students' grasp of compositional issues has developed over time.

The "composition" domain project works with a traditional element of the visual arts—the arrangement of form—and seeks to tie this element to students' own productive and perceptual experiences. A quite different approach is taken in a second domain project called the "biography of a work." In this instance our goals are much broader. We want to help students synthesize their learning from previous domain projects in composition, style, and expression, and to do so through tracing the development of a complete work.

In the "biography of a work" students first observe a large set of sketches that Andrew Wyeth prepared before he completed *Brown Swiss*. They survey a companion set of sketches and drafts of Picasso's *Guernica*. After these perceptual explorations of the roots of masterworks, students are asked to draw their room at home in a way that expresses something about themselves. They are given a range of media (paper, pencil, charcoal, pen and ink, and so on) as well as some pictorial material, such as magazines and slides. In an initial session, students are asked to choose any element(s) of their room, to add whatever props or objects might be revealing about themselves, and to use these in preparing a preliminary sketch. Their focus should be on composition, but they are encouraged to think about how the range of artistic elements can reveal themselves and not just what is represented literally in the picture. A few examples are given of how aspects of form can convey metaphorically a property of an individual.

In a second session, students begin by examining slides that show how artists have used objects metaphorically in their work and how particular objects or elements can carry a multiplicity of meanings. They are also shown slides of artists' studios or rooms and asked how these rooms might bring out something about the artists' view of their particular world. Students then return to their own preliminary sketches and are asked to make provisional decisions about the media that they wish to use and the style, color, line, texture, and so on that they plan to employ. As in the earlier session, students fill out worksheets in which they are asked to reflect on the choices they made, the reasons for these choices, and their aesthetic consequences.

In a third session, students review all of their preliminary sketches and "trial sheets," think about whether they are satisfied with them, and then begin their final work. Students discuss their works-in-progress with other students. Then, in a final session during the following week, the students complete their works, critique one another's efforts, and review their sketches, trial sheets, and reflections. The activities in this final week serve as a model for the kinds of reflections that are used as well in the student portfolio compilations (described below).

In Arts PROPEL we sought to create an ensemble of domain-projects for each art form. These prototypes should encompass most of the important concepts in an art form. One should be able to develop a general theory of domain projects: what set of exercises qualifies as a domain project, what kinds of learning one can expect to take place, and how best the student can be assessed within and across domain projects.

In addition to the ensemble of domain projects, we introduced a second educational vehicle. While this vehicle is often called a *portfolio*, I prefer the term *processfolio*. Most artists' portfolios contain only their very best works, the set by which the artist would wish to be judged in a competition. In contrast, processfolios are much more like works-in-progress. In their processfolios, students include not just finished works but also original sketches, interim drafts, critiques by themselves and others, artworks by others that they admire or dislike and that bear in some way on their current project. Sometimes students are asked to present the whole folder of materials; at other times they are asked to select those pieces that appear particularly informative or pivotal in their artistic development (see Brown, 1987; Wolf, 1988a, 1988b, 1989).

The maintenance of high standards, so crucial to the success of any arts education program, is heavily dependent at the outset on the stance the teacher takes vis-à-vis artistic performance and productivity; with time, students' effects on one another may well become the chief means of conveying and maintaining standards (Berger, 1991). The teacher's role in a processfolio environment differs from the role of the master in a classical apprenticeship in that no single model of progress—no set of discrete levels—underlies the instruction; still, in the sense that the teacher serves as an exemplar of productive artistry and as an embodiment of the standards of the community, an Arts PROPEL classroom does resemble a classical atelier.

Given our initial charge, much of the energy in Arts PROPEL went into the construction of assessment systems. Each domain project features a set of self-assessment procedures that can be used during the life of that project. In the case of the "composition" project, students have the opportunity to step back and reflect on the strengths and weaknesses of each composition, the expressive effects achieved in each composition, and just how these effects are (or are not) fully realized. In the case of the "biography of a work" project, students reflect on the changes they have made, the reasons motivating the changes, and the relation between the early and late drafts. The students' drafts and final product, along with their reflections, are then assessed on a variety of qualitative dimensions, such as engagement, technical skills, imaginativeness, and critical evaluative skills. While the primary assessment for the domain project occurs within the class, it is also possible to assess these projects off-site; such assessment sessions have been carried out with reasonable success by external arts educators brought together under the auspices of the Educational Testing Service.

Whereas domain projects lend themselves to a number of familiar forms of assessment, the assessment of processfolios is a more challenging and delicate operation. Processfolios can be assessed on a large number of dimensions. Some are straightforward, such as the regularity of the entries, their completeness, and the like. Others are more complex and subjective, but still familiar: the overall quality of the final products, on technical and imaginative grounds. Of special interest to us are those dimensions that help illuminate the unique potential of processfolios: students' awareness of their own strengths and weaknesses, capacity to reflect accurately, ability to build on self-critique and to make use of critiques of others, sensitivity to their own developmental milestones, ability to use lessons from domain projects productively, capacity to find and solve new problems, ability to relate current projects to those undertaken at earlier times and those that one hopes to undertake in the future, and capacity to move comfortably and appropriately from one aesthetic stance or role to another and back again. The goal is not only to assess along a variety of potentially independent dimensions, but also to encourage students to develop along these dimensions. Such an assessment system has the potential to alter what is discussed—and what is valued—in the classroom.

The Arts PROPEL team, under the direction of Ellen Winner (1991–1993), set down dimensions of production, perception, reflection, and "approach to work" that can be applied to student processfolios and the projects contained therein. The four dimensions are summarized in table 9.1. Even to list these dimensions is to convey something of the difficulty of the assessment task and the extent to which it breaks new ground. It would be misleading to suggest that we have solved the problems involved in any of these facets of assessment: indeed, as we sometimes jest, we simply have several years more experience than others in recognizing what does *not* work! It is sobering to note that took a century for standardized tests to reach their present, hardly glorious status; it is unreasonable to expect as-

TABLE 9.1
PROCESSFOLIO ASSESSMENT SYSTEM

(Based on art, music, and writing. Can be expanded to other artistic domains.)

I. PRODUCTION: Thinking in the Domain

Evidence: The evidence for assessing work on the dimension of production lies in the work itself. Thus, these dimensions can be scored by an outsider looking at drafts and final works as well as by the classroom teacher.

A. *Craft:* The student is in control of the basic techniques and principles of the domain.

B. *Pursuit:* The student develops works over time, as evidenced by revisions that are productive and thoughtful. She pursues the problem in depth. She returns to a problem or theme from a variety of angles.

C. *Invention:* The student solves problems in a creative manner. She experiments and takes risks with the medium. She sets her own problems to solve.

D. *Expression:* The student expresses an idea or feeling in the work (or in the performance of the work, as in music).

II. REFLECTION: Thinking About the Domain

Evidence: The evidence for assessing reflection comes from the student's journals and sketchbooks and from observations of the kinds of comments the student makes in class. Thus, these dimensions need to be scored by a classroom teacher who knows the student.

A. *Ability and proclivity to assess own work:* The student can evaluate her own work. She can articulate and defend the perceived strengths and weaknesses of her own work. She can engage in "shop talk" about her own work.

B. *Ability and proclivity to take on role of critic:* The student has developed the ability to evaluate the work of others (peers, published artists). She has a sense of the standards for quality work in the domain. She can engage in "shop talk" about others' work.

C. *Ability and proclivity to use criticisms and suggestions:* The student can consider critical comments about her own work and can incorporate suggestions where appropriate.

D. *Ability to learn from other works of art within domain:* The student can use work by artists for ideas and inspiration.

E. *Ability to articulate artistic goals:* The student has a sense of herself as an artist, as evidenced by the ability to articulate goals for a particular work, or more general artistic goals.

III. PERCEPTION: Perceiving in the Domain

Evidence: The evidence for assessing a student's perceptual skills comes from the student's journal entries and from observations of the student's comments made in critique sessions. Thus, only a classroom teacher can assess a student on this dimension.

A. *Capacity to make fine discriminations about works in the domain:* The student can make discriminations in works from a wide variety of genres, cultures, and historical periods.

B. *Awareness of sensuous aspects of experience:* The student shows heightened sensitivity to physical properties of the environment related to the domain in question (for example, she responds to visual patterns made by shadows, to sounds of cars honking in different pitches, to patterning of words on a grocery list, and so on).

C. *Awareness of physical properties and qualities of materials:* The student is sensitive to the properties of the materials that she is working with as she is developing a work (for example, textures of different papers, timbres of instruments, sounds of words).

IV. APPROACH TO WORK

Evidence: The evidence for assessing a student's approach to work lies in observations of the student in classroom interactions and from the student's journal entries. Thus, a student's approach to work can be assessed only by the classroom teacher.

A. *Engagement:* The student works hard and is interested in what she is doing. She meets deadlines. She shows care and attention to detail in the presentation of the final project.

B. *Ability to work independently:* The student can work independently when appropriate.

C. *Ability to work collaboratively:* The student can work collaboratively when appropriate.

D. *Ability to use cultural resources:* The student knows where to go for help: books, museums, tools, other people.

sessment of domain projects and processfolios to mature in just a few years with the modest resources we have at our disposal. Still, our progress to date, and our belief that we are assessing in a way that is worthy of the subject matter, emboldens us to continue our work.

Even if we should fall short of our goal of adequate psychometric measures of processfolios, our effort has utility. As noted earlier, an important aspect of artistic learning is the opportunity for students to become involved in meaningful projects in which their own understanding and growth can come to the fore. It is already clear to us that both students and teachers find these processfolio activities engaging, exciting, and useful in their own right. Teachers find that their classrooms come alive. By encouraging the development of processfolios, and by looking at them sympathetically and systematically, we may be able to increase the use of these materials and activities in schools. While it may be too much to expect that colleges will ever base admissions decisions chiefly on such processfolio information, we hope that such educational vehicles may allow students to recognize and develop their own cognitive strengths.

Educators and educational critics frequently lament the gap between theory and practice—and between theorists and practitioners. It is no doubt true that the professional goals of the two groups are different—the theorist's triumph often leaves the practitioner untouched; the practitioner's pleasures seem uninteresting to the theorist. For some time, it was fashionable to criticize Project Zero for its remoteness from educational practice. That remoteness had two senses: (1) our work focused more on "natural" development than on what could be explicitly taught in the classroom; and (2) our ideas, whether or not they were considered generally appealing, had little or no direct implication for what happens in the classroom on Monday morning.

While these charges sometimes left us a bit offended and made us a tad defensive, we are on the whole comfortable with them as characterizations of our project's youth and early adolescence (1960s and 1970s). We feel that it is important to look at "natural" development before examining interventions, and we believe that it is important to establish the psychological facts and to develop one's educational philosophy before attempting to influence practice—especially since it is always possible that one might influence practice for the worse!

Having had the luxury of a relatively ivory-tower exploration of arts education, it has certainly been opportune for us to become more directly involved in educational experimentation. The fact that arts educational practice is being widely discussed only heightens the need for us to get our feet wet. Arts PROPEL represents one concerted effort to do just that. It is too early to know how successful this effort will prove to be and, if it is successful in its "hothouse" atmosphere, whether it can be successfully transported to more remote soils. Still, it is not premature to indicate that researchers can learn a great deal from attempting to implement their ideas in a school setting. So long as we are on the alert for any disruption that we may cause, this intermingling of theory and practice should redound to the good of all those involved in arts education.

Arts PROPEL received a tremendous accolade in the early 1990s, when it was selected by *Newsweek* magazine as one of only two "model educational programs" in the United States—the other being graduate education at the California Institute of Technology (Chideya, 1991). Now that several years have passed since the Arts PROPEL project came to an official end, it is germane to ask about the extent to which it has gained a foothold. Arts PROPEL has suffered from the retrenchment surrounding arts education in the United States and elsewhere; implementation of the program requires trained staff and sufficient resources. Still, I am happy to report that I often encounter teachers of the visual arts and music, both in the United States and abroad, who know about Arts PROPEL and have used some of its approach.

Even more surprising, and especially gratifying, is the fact that the ideas undergirding PROPEL have proved attractive to educators in other subject matters. Although the notion of projects and processfolios has a long history in the arts, teachers and curriculum supervisors in domains ranging from history to mathematics have come to appreciate the usefulness of rich and engaging projects and the desirability of that systematic cast of thought involved in reflecting on one's work and keeping a regular journal. As a longtime arts educator who is used to seeing his field treated as a backwater, I gain special satisfaction from the present circumstance: our ideas and practices may actually provide inspirations to areas of the curriculum that have traditionally been more prestigious.

Chapter 10

Assessment in Context: The Alternative to Standardized Testing

A familiar scene almost anywhere in the United States today: Several hundred students file into a large examination hall. They sit nervously, waiting for sealed packets to be handed out. At the appointed hour, booklets are distributed, brief instructions are issued, and formal testing begins. The hall is still as students at each desk bear down on number two pencils and fill in the bubbles that punctuate the answer sheets. A few hours later, the testing ends and the booklets are collected; some time later, a sheet bearing a set of scores arrives at each student's home and at the colleges to which the students have directed their scores. The results of a morning's testing become a powerful factor in decisions about the life chances of each student.

An equally familiar scene in most preindustrial societies over the centuries: A youth of ten or eleven moves into the home of a man who has mastered a trade. Initially, the apprentice is asked to carry out menial tasks as he helps the master prepare for his work or clean up the shop at the end of the day. During this initial phase, the lad has the opportunity to watch the master at work, while the master monitors the youth to discover his special talents or serious flaws. Over the months, the apprentice slowly enters into the practice of the trade. After initially aiding in the more peripheral aspects of the trade, he eventually gains familiarity with the full gamut of skilled work. Directed not only by tradition but also by the youth's particular skills and motivation, the master guides his charge through the various steps from novice to journeyman. Finally, after several years of supervised training, the youth is ready to practice the craft on his own.

While both of these scenes are idealized, they should be readily recognizable to anyone concerned with the assessment and training of young people. Indeed, they may be said to represent two extremes. The "formal testing" model is conceived of as an objective, decontextualized form of assessment that can be adopted and implemented widely with some assurance that similar results will be obtained. The "apprenticeship" model is implemented almost entirely within a naturally occurring context in which the particularities of a craft are embedded. The assessment is based on a prior analysis of the skills involved in a particular craft, but it may also be influenced by subjective factors, including the master's personal views about his apprentice, his relationship with other masters, and his need for other kinds of services.

It should be evident that these two forms of assessment were designed to meet different needs. Apprenticeships made sense when the practice of various crafts was the principal career path for nonrural youths. Formal testing is a contemporary means of comparing the performance of hundreds of thousands of students who are being educated in schools. Yet these forms of assessment are not limited to the two prototypical contexts described earlier. Despite the overwhelmingly agrarian nature of Chinese society, formal tests have been used there in selecting government officials for over two thousand years (Gardner, Kornhaber & Wake, 1996). And in many art forms, athletic practices, and areas of scientific research (Polanyi, 1958), apprenticeships and the concomitant ongoing, context-determined forms of assessment continue to be used in our highly industrialized society.

Thus, the choice of formal testing as opposed to apprenticeship is not dictated solely by the historical era or the primary means of production in the society. It would be possible in our society to utilize the apprenticeship method to a much greater extent than we do. Very few people today lament the passage of the obligatory apprenticeship system with its frequent excesses and its blatant sexism. From several points of view, contemporary formal testing represents a fairer and more easily justifiable form of assessment. And yet aspects of the apprentice model are consistent with current knowledge about how individuals learn and how their performances might best be assessed.

Our society has embraced the formal testing mode to an excessive degree. I contend that aspects of the apprentice model of learning and assessment—which I term *contextualized learning*—could be profitably reintroduced into our educational system (see Collins, Brown, & Newman, 1989). In this chapter, after presenting an account of the origins of standardized testing and the one-dimensional view of mentation typically implied by such testing methods, I suggest the need for a far more capacious view of the human mind and of human learning than that which informed earlier conceptions. My task here is to envision forms of education and modes of assessment that have a firm rooting in current scientific understanding and that contribute to enlightened educational goals. In the latter half of the chapter, I will sketch the nature of an "assessing society."

BINET, THE TESTING SOCIETY, AND THE "UNIFORM" VIEW OF SCHOOLING

The widespread use of formal testing can be traced to the work on intelligence testing carried out in Paris at the dawn of the twentieth century by Alfred Binet and his colleagues (see chapter 1). So great was the appeal of the Binet method that it soon became a dominant feature of the American educational and assessment landscape. To be sure, some standardized tests—ranging from the California Achievement Tests to the SAT—are not direct outgrowths of the various intelligence tests. And yet it is difficult to envision the proliferation of these instruments over just a few decades without the widely esteemed examples of the Stanford-Binet, the Army Alpha, and the various Wechsler intelligence instruments (Brown & Herrnstein, 1975).

Especially in the United States, with its focus on quantitative markers and its cult of educational efficiency, there has been a virtual mania for producing tests for every possible social purpose (Gould, 1981; Hoffmann, 1962). In addition to tests for students, we have standardized tests for teachers, supervisors, soldiers, and police officers; we use adaptations of these instruments to assess capacities not only in standard areas of the curriculum but also in civics and the arts; and we can draw on short-answer measures for assessing personality, degrees of authoritarianism, and compatibility for dating. The United States is well on the way to becoming a "complete testing society." We could encapsulate this attitude as follows: If something is important, it is worth testing in this way; if it cannot be tested in this way, then it probably should not be valued. Few observers have stopped to consider the domains in which such an approach might *not* be relevant or optimal; most have forgotten the insights that might be gained from modes of assessment favored in an earlier era.

It is risky to attempt to generalize across the thousands of formal instruments that are described in books such as the *Mental Measurements Yearbooks*. Yet, at the cost of doing some violence to certain instruments, it is worth specifying the features that are typically associated with such instruments.

There is within the testing profession considerable belief in "raw," probably genetically based, potential (Eysenck, 1967; Jensen, 1980). The most highly valued tests, such as IQ tests and the SAT, are thought to measure ability or potential performance. There is no reason why a test cannot assess skills that have been learned, and many "achievement" tests claim to do this. Yet for tests that purport to measure raw ability or potential, it is important that performance cannot be readily improved by instruction; otherwise, the test would not be a valid indicator of ability. Most authorities on testing believe that performance on ability and achievement tests reflects inherent capacities.

Adherents of testing also tend to embrace a view of human development that assumes that a young organism contains less knowledge and exhibits less skill than a more mature organism but that no qualitative changes occur over time in human mind or behavior (Bijou & Baer, 1965). Making such assumptions enables test makers to use the same kinds of instruments for individuals of all ages; and they can legitimately claim that descriptions of data at a certain point in development can be extended to later ages because one is dealing with the same kind of scale and the same property of mind or behavior.

Reflecting general American technological pressures as well as the desire for elegance and economy, most test makers and buyers place a premium on instruments that are efficient, brief, and easy to administer. In the early days of testing, assessment sometimes took hours and was individually administered; now, group-administered instruments are desired. Virtually every widely used test has spawned a "brief" version. Indeed, some of the staunchest supporters of formal intelligence tests hope to strip them down even further: Arthur Jensen (1987) has embraced "reaction time" measures, Michael Anderson (1987) looks to sensory discrimination, Hans Eysenck (1979) calls for the examination of patterns of brain waves, and many influenced by the genetics revolution hope to identify the crucial gene(s) or chromosome(s) governing inherent capacities.

Accompanying a fealty to formal testing is a view of education that I have termed the "uniform view of schooling." In this view, progress in school should be assessed by frequent formal tests administered under uniform conditions, and students, teachers, and parents should receive quantitative scores that detail the student's progress or lack thereof. These tests should be nationally normed for maximum comparability. The most important subject matters are those that lend themselves readily to such assessment, like mathematics and science. In other content areas, value is assigned to the aspects that can be efficiently assessed (grammar rather than voice in writing; facts rather than interpretation in history). Those disciplines that prove most refractory to formal testing, such as the arts, are least valued in the uniform school.

In presenting this picture of Binet, the testing society, and the uniform view of schooling, I am aware that I am overemphasizing certain tendencies and lumping together views and attitudes in a way that is not entirely fair to those who are closely associated with formal testing. Some of those intimately involved with testing have voiced the same concerns (Cronbach, 1984; Messick, 1988). Indeed, had I put this picture forth a quarter century ago, it might have seemed an outrageous caricature. However, the trends in American education since 1980 bear a strong resemblance to the views I have just sketched. At the very least, these views serve as a necessary contrast case to the picture of contextualized and individualized assessment and schooling that I present later in the chapter; they should be taken in that contrastive spirit.

Sources for an Alternative Approach to Assessment

While the testing society has responded more to pragmatic needs than to scientific dictates, it does reflect a certain view of human nature. The scientific ideas on which the testing society has been based derive from an earlier era in which behaviorist, learning-theoretical, and associationist views of cognition and development were regnant (see Gardner, 1985 for a summary). According to these views, it made sense to believe in "inborn" human abilities, a smooth and probably linear curve of learning from infancy to old age, a hierarchy of disciplines, and the desirability of assessing potential and achievement under carefully controlled and maximally decontextualized conditions.

Over the past few decades, the various assumptions on which this testing edifice was based have been gradually undermined by work in developmental, cognitive, and educational studies; a quite different view has emerged. It is not possible in this chapter to review all the evidence underlying this shifting psychological conception. Still, because my alternative picture of assessment builds on the newly emerging picture of human development, it is important to highlight the principal features of this perspective and to indicate where it may clash with standard views of testing.

The Need for a Developmental Perspective

Owing to the pioneering work of Jean Piaget (1983), it is widely recognized that children are not simply miniature versions of adults. The infant or the toddler conceives of the world in a way that is internally consistent but that deviates in important particulars from a more mature conception. Children pass through a number of qualitatively different stages, called sensorimotor, preoperational, concrete operational, and formal operational. A child at one stage in one area of knowledge will necessarily be at the same stage in other domains of experience. Few investigators still hold to a literal version of this structured-stage perspective; there have been too many findings that do not support it (Brainerd, 1978; Gelman, 1978). But most developmental psychologists continue to subscribe to the view that the world of the infant or toddler has its own peculiar structures; many developmentalists believe that there are stage sequences within particular domains of experience (for example, language, moral judgment, understanding of physical causality); and nearly all emphasize the need to take into account the child's perspective and level of understanding (Case, 1985; Feldman, 1980; Fischer, 1980).

Another feature of this approach is its assumption that development is neither smooth, nor unilinear, nor free of perturbations. While details differ among theorists, most researchers believe that there may be critical or sensitive periods during which it is especially easy—or especially diffi-cult—to master certain kinds of materials. Similarly, since youngsters tend to improve in most areas with age, there will be periods of more rapid growth and periods of stasis. And a minority of researchers believe that in some domains there may actually be regressions or performances that ex-hibit a U-shaped curve: younger children and adolescents perform in a more sophisticated or integrated fashion than students in middle child-hood (Strauss, 1982).

It is possible to construct measurement instruments that reflect the de-velopmental knowledge recently accrued. In fact, some batteries of tests have been devised that build specifically on Piagetian or allied notions (Uz-giris & Hunt, 1966). For the most part, however, American tests have been insensitive to developmental considerations.

The Emergence of a Symbol-System Perspective

At the height of the behaviorist era there was no need to posit any kind of mental entity, such as an idea, a thought, a belief, or a symbol. Psycholo-gists identified and observed behaviors or actions of significance as scrupulously as possible; so-called thoughts were considered simply to be "silent" movements of vocal musculature.

Over the past several decades, psychologists have recognized the impor-tance of the capacity to use various kinds of symbols and symbol systems (Gardner, Howard, & Perkins, 1974; Goodman, 1968). Human beings are deemed the creatures par excellence of communication; we garner mean-ings through words, pictures, gestures, numbers, musical patterns, and a whole host of other symbolic forms. The manifestations of these symbols are public: all can observe written language, number systems, drawings, charts, gestural languages, and so on. However, the mental processes needed to manipulate such symbols must be inferred from the perform-ances of individuals on various kinds of tasks. Unexpectedly potent sup-port for the belief in internal symbol-manipulation has come from the development and widespread use of computers; if these human-made ma-chines engage in operations of symbol use and transformation, it would seem ludicrous to withhold attribution of the same kinds of capacities from the humans who invented them (Newell & Simon, 1972).

Considerable effort has been expended in various branches of science to investigate the development of the human capacity for symbol use. It is widely (though not universally) agreed that infants do not use symbols or exhibit internal symbolic manipulation and that the emergence of symbol use during the second year of life is a major hallmark of human cognition. Thereafter, human beings rapidly acquire skill in the use of the symbols and symbol systems that are featured in their culture. By the age of five or six, most children have acquired a "first-draft" knowledge of how to create and understand stories, works of music, drawings, and simple scientific explanations (Gardner, 1982).

In literate cultures, there is a second level of symbol use. Children must learn to utilize the *invented symbol* (or *notational*) systems of their culture, such as writing and numbers. With few exceptions, this assignment is restricted to school settings, which are relatively decontextualized. Mastering notational systems can be difficult for many students in our society, including those whose mastery of practical knowledge and first-order symbol systems has been unproblematic. Even students who prove facile at acquiring notational systems face a nontrivial challenge: they must mesh their newly acquired second-order symbolic knowledge with the earlier forms of practical and first-order symbolic knowledge they brought with them to school (Bamberger, 1982b; Gardner, 1986b; Olson, 1996; Resnick, 1987).

Nearly all formal tests presuppose that those taking them will be literate in the second-level symbol systems of the culture. These tests thus pose special challenges for individuals who, for whatever reason, have had difficulty in attaining second-level symbol knowledge or cannot map that knowledge onto earlier forms of mental representation. Moreover, it is my belief that those with well-developed second-level symbolic skills can often "psych out" such tests, scoring well even when their knowledge of the subject matter that is ostensibly being assessed is modest (Gardner, 1983b). At any rate, the exact relations among practical, first-order, and second-order symbolic knowledge and the best way to assess these remain difficult issues to resolve.

Emergence of a Multiple Intelligences Perspective

When intelligence tests were first constructed, there was little attention paid to the underlying theory of intelligence. But soon the idea gained currency that the different abilities being tapped all fed into or reflected a single general intelligence. This perspective has remained the view of choice among most students of intelligence, although a minority have been open to the idea of different "vectors of mind" or "products, content, and operations" of intellect (Guilford, 1967; Thurstone, 1938). This group has based its conclusions on the results of factor analyses of test results; however, it has been shown that one can arrive at either unitary or pluralistic views of intellect, depending on which assumptions guide specific factor analytic procedures (Gould, 1981).

In recent years, there has been a resurgence of interest in the idea of a multiplicity of intelligences. Mental phenomena have been discovered that some researchers construe as evidence for mental *modules*—fast-operating, reflexlike, information-processing devices that seem impervious to the influence of other modules. The discovery of these modules has given rise to the view that separate analytic devices may be involved in tasks such as syntactic parsing, tonal recognition, and facial perception (Fodor, 1983; Tooby & Cosmides, 1990).

A second source of evidence for a multiplicity of intelligences has been the fine-grained analyses of the mental operations involved in the solution of items used in intelligence tests (Sternberg, 1977, 1985). These analyses suggest the existence of different components that contribute to success on any standard intellectual assessment. Individuals may differ from one another in the facility with which the different components operate, and different tasks may call on a differential use of the various components, metacomponents, and subcomponents (see Sternberg, 1977, and chapters 1 and 2 of this book). The various "multiple intelligences" perspectives, including my own, all concur on the following proposition: Instead of a single dimension called intellect, on which individuals can be rank-ordered, vast differences obtain across individuals in their intellectual strengths and weaknesses and also in their styles of attack in cognitive pursuits (Kagan & Kogan, 1970). Our own evidence suggests that these differences may be evident even before the years of formal schooling (see chapter 6).

The literature on different individual strengths, as well as the findings on diverse cognitive styles, have crucial educational implications. To begin with, it is important to identify strengths and weaknesses at an early point so that they can be incorporated into educational planning. Striking differences among individuals also call into question whether all students should be taking the same curriculum and whether, to the extent that there is a uniform curriculum, it needs to be presented in the same fashion to all students.

Formal tests can be an ally to the recognition of different cognitive features, but only if the tests are designed to elicit—rather than mask—these differences (Cronbach & Snow, 1977). It is particularly important that instruments used in for "gatekeeping" purposes (such as college admissions) be designed to allow students to show their strengths and to perform optimally. Thus far, little effort has been made in this regard, and tests are used more frequently to point up weaknesses than to designate strengths.

A Search for Human Creative Capacities

During most of the first century of formal testing, interest fell heavily on assessment of individual intelligence, and there was relatively little concern with other cognitive capacities. In the post-Sputnik era, when scientific ingenuity was suddenly at a premium, American educators became convinced of the importance of imaginativeness, inventiveness, and creativity. They called for the devising of instruments that would assess creativity or creative potential (Guilford, 1950, 1967). Regrettably (from my perspective), in their search for measures of creativity, they repeated most of the mistakes that had been made throughout the history of intelligence testing. That is, they tried to devise short-answer, timed measures of the abilities they thought central to creativity—the capacity to come up with a variety of answers to a question (divergent thinking) or to issue as many unusual associations as possible to a stimulus (ideational fluency).

While the field of intelligence testing is filled with controversy, there is consensus that creativity tests have not fulfilled their potential (Wallach, 1971, 1985). These instruments are reliable, and they do measure something other than psychometric intelligence, but they cannot predict which individuals will be judged as creative on the basis of their productions within a domain. Rather than attempting to devise more and better creativity tests, researchers have instead begun to examine more closely what actually happens when individuals are engaged in problem-solving or problem-finding activities (Getzels & Csikszentmihalyi, 1976; Gardner, 1993; Gruber, 1981; Sternberg, 1988b).

Recent studies have yielded two major findings. On the one hand, creative individuals do not seem to have at their disposal mental operations that are theirs alone; they make use of the same cognitive processes others do, but they use them in a more efficient and flexible way and in the service of goals that are ambitious and often quite risky (Perkins, 1981). On the other hand, highly creative individuals seem to lead their lives differently than most others. They are fully engaged in and passionate about their work; they exhibit a need to do something new and a strong sense of their purpose and ultimate goals; they are extremely reflective about their activities, their use of time, and the quality of their products (Csikszentmihalyi, 1996; Gardner, 1993; Gruber, 1985).

Except rhetorically, the quest for creativity has not been a major goal of the American educational system. However, to the extent that fostering creative individuals is a desirable goal for an educational institution, it is important that this goal be pursued in a manner consistent with current analyses of creativity (Gardner, 1988a).

The Desirability of Assessing Learning in Context

When standardized tests and paradigmatic experimental designs were first introduced into non-Western cultural contexts, they led to a single result: people from preliterate cultures and others from non-Western societies appeared to be much less skilled and much less intelligent than Western control groups. An interesting phenomenon was then discovered: Simple alterations of materials, test setting, or instructions frequently elicited dramatic improvements in performance. The performance gap between the subjects from other cultures and those from our own culture narrowed or even disappeared when familiar materials were used, when knowledgeable and linguistically fluent examiners were employed, when revised instructions were given, or when the "same" cognitive capacities were tapped in a form that made more sense within the non-Western context (Laboratory of Comparative Human Cognition, 1982).

Now a huge body of experimental evidence indicates that assessment materials designed for one target population cannot be transported directly to another cultural setting; there are no purely culture-fair or culture-blind materials. Every instrument reflects its origins. Formal tests that make some sense in a Western context do so because students are accustomed to learning about quite abstract materials at a site removed from the habitual application of such materials. However, in unschooled or lightly schooled environments, most instruction takes place in situ, and so it only makes sense to administer assessments that are similar in context.

Building on this cross-cultural research, investigators have also generated findings about the cognitive abilities of experts in traditional societies. It has been shown that experts often fail on decontextualized measures of their calculating or reasoning capacities, but they can exhibit precisely those same skills in the course of their ordinary work—such as tailoring clothes, shopping in a supermarket, loading dairy cases onto a truck, or defending their rights in a dispute (Lave, 1980; Rogoff, 1982; Scribner, 1986). In such cases, it is not the person who has failed but rather the instrument that purported to measure the person's level of competence.

Locating Competence and Skill
Outside the Head of the Individual

This avenue of research yields another novel conceptualization. In many cases it is erroneous to conclude that the knowledge required to execute a task resides completely in the mind of a single individual. This knowledge can be "distributed." That is, successful performance of a task may depend on a team of individuals: no single person possesses all of the necessary expertise, but, working together, members of a team can accomplish the task in a reliable way (Scribner, 1986). Similarly, it is too simple to say that an individual either has or does not have the requisite knowledge; he or she may demonstrate that knowledge reliably in the presence of the appropriate human or mechanical triggers, but the knowledge might be otherwise invisible to probing (Squire, 1986).

It makes sense to think of human cognitive competence as an emerging capacity, one likely to be manifest at the intersection of three different constituents: the *individual,* with his or her skills, knowledge, and aims; the structure of a *domain of knowledge* within which these skills can be aroused; and a set of institutions and roles—a surrounding *field*—that judges when a particular performance is acceptable or even constitutes a creative breakthrough as well as when it fails to meet specifications (Csikszentmihalyi,

1988a; Csikszentmihalyi & Robinson, 1986; Gardner & Wolf, 1988). The acquisition and transmission of knowledge depends on a dynamic that sustains itself among these three components. Particularly beyond the years of early childhood, human accomplishment presupposes an awareness of the different domains of knowledge in one's culture and the various "field forces" that affect opportunity, progress, and recognition. By focusing on the knowledge that resides within a single mind at a single moment, formal testing may distort, magnify, or grossly underestimate the contributions that an individual can make within a larger and supportive social setting.

The foregoing research findings point to a differentiated and nuanced view of assessment that, at least in certain ways, might more closely resemble traditional apprenticeship measures than formal testing. Any assessment initiative being planned today should, in light of these findings, be sensitive to developmental stages and trajectories. Such an initiative should investigate human symbolic capacities in an appropriate fashion in the years following infancy and investigate the relationship between practical knowledge and first- and second-level symbolic skills. It should recognize the existence of different intelligences and of diverse cognitive and stylistic profiles. It should incorporate an awareness of these variations into assessments. It should be built on an understanding of those features that characterize creative individuals in different domains. Finally, any new assessment initiative should acknowledge the effects of context on performance and provide the most appropriate contexts in which to assess competences, including contexts that extend beyond the individual being assessed.

It is a tall order to meet all of these needs and desiderata. Indeed, an attraction of formal testing is that one can bracket or minimize most of the features that I have just outlined. However, if we seek an assessment that is both true to the individual and reflective of our best understanding of the nature of human cognition, we cannot afford to ignore these lines of thinking.

GENERAL FEATURES OF A
NEW APPROACH TO ASSESSMENT

If one were to return to the drawing board today and lay out a fresh approach to assessment, one might attempt to incorporate eight principal features.

1. Emphasis on Assessment Rather Than Testing

The penchant for testing in America has gone too far. While some tests are useful for some purposes, the testing industry has taken off in a way that makes little sense from the point of view of a reflective society. Many who seek to understand the underlying theoretical or conceptual basis of findings are disappointed. It seems that many tests have been designed to create, rather than to fulfill, a need.

While I have ambivalent feelings about testing, I have little ambivalence about assessment. To my mind, it is the proper mission of educated persons, as well as those who are under their charge, to engage in regular and appropriate reflection on their goals, the various means of achieving them, their success (or lack thereof) in achieving them, and the implications of the assessment for rethinking goals or procedures.

I define assessment as the obtaining of information about a person's skills and potentials with the dual goals of providing useful feedback to the person and useful data to the surrounding community. What distinguishes assessment from testing is the former's favoring of techniques that elicit information in the course of ordinary performance and its general uneasiness with the use of formal instruments administered in a neutral, decontextualized setting.

In my view, those in the psychological and educational communities charged with the task of evaluation ought to facilitate such assessment (see Cross & Angelo, 1988). We should be devising methods and measures that aid in regular, systematic, and useful assessment. In some cases we would end up producing formal tests, but in most cases we would not.

2. Assessment as Simple, Natural, and Occurring on a Reliable Schedule

Rather than being imposed by external authorities at odd times during the year, assessment ought to become part of the natural learning environment. As much as possible, it should occur "on the fly," as part of an individual's natural engagement in a learning situation. Initially, the assessment would probably need to be introduced explicitly; but after a while, much assessment would occur naturally on the part of student and teacher with little need for explicit recognition or labeling on anyone's part.

The model of the assessment of the cognitive abilities of the expert is relevant here. On one hand, it is rarely necessary for the expert to be assessed by others unless competitive conditions obtain. It is assumed that experts will go about their business with little external monitoring. However, it is also true that the expert is constantly in the process of assessing; such assessment occurs naturally, almost without conscious reflection, in the course of working. When I first began to write scholarly articles, I was highly dependent upon waves of detailed criticism by teachers and editors; now most of the needed assessment occurs at a preconscious level as I sit at my desk scribbling, or typing a first draft, or editing an earlier version of the material.

As assessment gradually becomes part of the landscape, it no longer needs to be set off from the rest of classroom activity. As in a good apprenticeship, the teachers and the students are always assessing. There is also no need to "teach for the assessment" because the assessment is ubiquitous; indeed, the need for formal tests might atrophy altogether.

3. Ecological Validity

A problem with most formal tests is their validity—that is, their significant correlation with some consensually valued criterion (Messick, 1988). As noted, creativity tests are no longer used much because their validity has never been adequately established. The predictive validity of intelligence tests and scholastic aptitude tests is often questioned in view of their limited usefulness in predicting performance beyond the next year of schooling.

Returning to our example of the apprenticeship, it would make little sense to question the validity of the judgments by masters. They are so intimately associated with their respective novices that they can probably predict each novice's behaviors with a high degree of accuracy. When such prediction does not occur reliably, trouble lies ahead. I believe that the assessments used today have moved too far away from the territory that they are supposed to cover. When individuals are assessed in situations that more closely resemble actual working conditions, it is possible to make much better predictions about their ultimate performance. It is odd that most American schoolchildren spend hundreds of hours over their scholastic careers engaged in a single exercise—the formal test—when few if any of them will ever encounter a similar instrument once they have left school.

4. Instruments That Are "Intelligence-Fair"

As already noted, most testing instruments are biased heavily in favor of two varieties of intelligence—linguistic and logical-mathematical. People blessed with strengths in this particular combination are likely to do well on most kinds of formal tests, even if they are not particularly adept in the domain actually under investigation. By the same token, those with problems in either or both linguistic and logical-mathematical intelligences may fail at measures that purport to sample other domains, just because they cannot master the particular format of most standard instruments.

The solution—easier to describe than to realize—is to devise instruments that are intelligence fair, that peer directly at the intelligence in operation rather than proceeding via the detour of linguistic and logical faculties. Spatial intelligence can be assessed by having a person navigate around an unfamiliar territory; bodily intelligence by seeing how the person learns and remembers a new dance or physical exercise; interpersonal intelligence by watching him or her handle a dispute with a sales clerk or navigate an agenda through a difficult committee meeting. These homely instances indicate that "intelligence-fairer" measures could be devised, although they cannot necessarily be implemented in the psychological laboratory or the testing hall.

5. Uses of Multiple Measures

Few practices are more nefarious in education than the drawing of widespread educational implications from the composite score of a single test—like the Wechsler Intelligence Scale for Children. Even intelligence tests contain subtests, and, at the very least, recommendations ought to take into account the differences among these subtests and the strategies for approaching particular items (Kaplan, 1983).

Attention to a range of measures designed specifically to tap different facets of the capacity in question is even more desirable. Consider, for example, the admission standards of a program for gifted children. Conservatively speaking, 75 percent of the programs in the United States simply admit solely on the basis of IQ—as noted in chapter 1, if the cutoff is 130 and you have only 129, then you do not qualify. How unfortunate! I have no objection to the use of IQ as one consideration, but why not attend as well to the products that a child has already fashioned, the child's goals and desire for a program, performance during a trial period alongside other "gifted" children, and other unobtrusive measures? I often feel that enormous educational progress would be made if the Secretary of Education simply appeared in front of the television cameras, not accompanied by a single one-dimensional chart, but against the backdrop of a half-dozen disparate graphic displays, each monitoring a distinct aspect of learning and productivity.

6. Sensitivity to Individual Differences, Developmental Levels, and Forms of Expertise

Assessment programs that fail to take into account the vast differences among individuals, developmental levels, and varieties of expertise are increasingly anachronistic. Formal testing could, in principle, be adjusted to take these documented variations into account. But it would require a suspension of some of the key assumptions of standardized testing, such as uniformity of individuals in key respects (for example, in developmental level) and the penchant for cost-efficient instruments.

Individual differences should also be highlighted when educating teachers and assessors. Those charged with the responsibility of assessing youngsters need to be introduced formally to such distinctions; one cannot expect teachers to arrive on their own at empirically valid taxonomies of individual differences. Such an introduction should occur in education courses or during teaching apprenticeships. Once teachers are introduced to these distinctions and given the opportunity to observe and work with children who exhibit different profiles, these distinctions come to life for them.

It then becomes possible to take these differences into account in a tacit way. Good teachers—whether they teach second grade, piano to toddlers, or research design to graduate students—have always realized that different approaches prove effective with different kinds of students. Such sensitivities to individual differences can become part of the teacher's competence and can be drawn on in the course of regular instruction as well as during assessment. It is also possible—and perhaps optimal—for teachers to season their own intuitive sense of individual differences with judicious occasions of assessment crafted with the particular domain of practice in mind.

7. Use of Intrinsically Interesting and Motivating Materials

One of the most objectionable, though seldom remarked upon, features of formal testing is the intrinsic dullness of the materials. How often does *anyone* get excited about a test or a particular item on a test? It was probably only when, as a result of "sunshine" legislation, it became possible for test takers to challenge the answer keys used by testing organizations that discussion of individual test items ever occupied space in a publication that anyone would voluntarily read.

It does not have to be that way. A good assessment instrument can be a learning experience. But more to the point, it is extremely desirable to have assessment occur in the context of students working on problems, projects, or products that genuinely engage them, that hold their interest and motivate them to do well. Such exercises may not be as easy to design as the standard multiple-choice entry, but they are far more likely to elicit a student's full repertoire of skills and to yield information that is useful for subsequent advice and placement.

8. Application of Assessment for the Student's Benefit

An equally lamentable aspect of formal testing is the use made of scores. Individuals receive the scores, see their percentile ranks, and draw conclusions about their scholastic, if not their overall, merit. In my own oft-stated view, psychologists spend far too much time ranking individuals and not nearly enough time helping them. Assessment should be undertaken primarily to aid students. The assessor should provide feedback to the student that will be helpful immediately: identifying areas of strength as well as weakness, giving suggestions on what to study or work on, pointing out which habits are productive and which are not, indicating what can be expected in the way of future assessments, and the like. It is especially important that some of the feedback take the form of concrete suggestions and indicate relative strengths to build on, independent of the student's ranking in a comparable group of students.

Armed with findings about human cognition and development, and in light of these desiderata for a new approach to assessment, it should be possible to begin to design programs that are more adequate than those that exist today. Without having any grand design to create a "new alternative to formal testing," my colleagues and I at Project Zero have become engaged in a number of projects over the last several years that feature new approaches to assessment. In the preceding four chapters, I described several of our current efforts to assess student intellectual strengths in context. Here I attempt to place these efforts within the broader picture of assessment in the schools.

Toward the Assessing Society

I have presented a brief in favor of regular assessment occurring in a natural fashion throughout the educational system and across the trajectory of lifelong learning. I have reviewed a sizable body of evidence, which, by and large, points up problems with standard formal testing as an exclusive mode of assessment. Many of these findings suggest that it would be more fruitful to create environments in which assessments occur naturally and to devise curricular entities, like domain projects and processfolios, that lend themselves to assessment within the context of their production. It would be an exaggeration to say that I have called for a reintroduction of the apprentice method. Yet I do claim that we have moved too far from that mode of assessment; contemporary assessment might well be informed by some of the concepts and assumptions associated with traditional apprenticeships.

Indeed, if one considers formal testing and apprentice-style assessment as two poles of assessment, it could be said that America today has veered too far in the direction of formal testing without adequate consideration of its costs and limitations. Even outside the realm of physics, an excessive action calls for a reaction—one reason that this chapter stresses the advantages of more naturalistic, context-sensitive, and ecologically valid modes of assessment. Standard formal tests have their place—for example, in initial screening of certain at-risk populations—but users should know the limitations of such tests as well.

Some objections to the perspective introduced here can be anticipated. One is the claim that formal testing is, as advertised, objective and that I am calling for a regression to subjective forms of evaluation. I reject this characterization for two reasons. First, there is no reason in principle to regard the assessment of domain projects, processfolios, or Spectrum-style measures as intrinsically less objective than other forms. Statistical reliability can be achieved in these practices as well. The establishment of reliability has not been a focus of these projects; however, the conceptual and psychometric tools exist to investigate and achieve reliability in these cases. Moreover, these assessment measures are more likely to possess ecological validity.

A second rebuttal of this characterization has to do with the alleged objectivity or nonbias of standard formal tests. In a technical sense, it is true that the best of these instruments avoid the dangers of subjectivity and statistical bias. However, any kind of instrument is necessarily skewed toward one or a few kinds of individual and one or a few intellectual and cognitive styles. Formal tests are especially friendly to those who possess a certain blend of linguistic and logical intelligences and who are comfortable in being assessed in a decontextualized setting under timed and impersonal conditions. Correlatively, such tests are biased against individuals who do not exhibit this blend of intelligences or whose strengths show up better in sustained projects or when they are examined in situ or without time limits.

I believe that, especially when resources are scarce, everyone should have the opportunity to exhibit strengths. There is no objection to a high scorer being able to show off a string of College Board 800s to a college admissions staff. By the same token, individuals with other cognitive or stylistic strengths ought to have their day as well.

There are those who might be in sympathy with the line of analysis pursued here and yet would reject its implications because of considerations of cost or efficiency. According to this argument, it is simply too inefficient or expensive to mobilize the country around more sustained forms of assessment; hence, even if formal testing is imperfect, we will have to settle for it and simply try to improve it as much as possible.

This argument has a superficial plausibility, but I reject it as well. To be sure, formal testing is now cost-effective, but it has taken millions, perhaps billions, of dollars expended over many decades to bring it to its current, far-from-perfect state. Spending more money on it, I believe, could improve it only marginally if at all.

Our Project Zero pilot projects, which depend on research funds, are modest by any standard. In each instance we believe that the main points of the approach can be taught readily to teachers and made available to interested schools or school districts. We subscribe to the estimate made by educator Theodore Sizer that a move toward more qualitatively oriented forms of education (and perhaps also to higher-quality education) might increase costs by 10 to 15 percent but probably not more.

The major obstacle I see to assessment in context is not shortage of resources but lack of will. There is in the United States an enormous desire to make education uniform, to treat all students in the same way, and to apply the same kinds of one-dimensional metrics to all. This trend is inappropriate on scientific grounds and distasteful on ethical grounds. The current sentiment is based in part on an understandable disaffection with some of the excesses and limitations of earlier educational experiments. But, to a disturbing degree, it is also based on a general hostility to students, teachers, and the learning process. In other countries, in which the educational process is held in higher regard—for example, Finland—it has proved possible to have higher-quality education without subscribing to some of the worst features of one-dimensional educational thinking and assessment.

It is not difficult to sketch the reasons for the tentative national consensus on the need for more testing and more uniform schools. Understandable uneasiness with poor student performance in the latter half of the twentieth century resulted in a general indictment of contemporary education, which was blamed for a multitude of societal ills. Government officials entered the fray; the price paid for increased financial support was more testing and more accountability based on the results of these tests. The fact that few experts in education were entirely comfortable with the diagnosis or the purported cure was not relevant. After all, political officials rarely pore over the relevant literature; they almost reflexively search for scapegoats and call for the quick fix.

It is unfortunate that few public officials or societal leaders have offered alternative views on these issues. If significant forces or interest groups in this country were to dedicate themselves to a different model of education—for example, the assessment and schooling philosophy outlined here—I have every confidence that they could implement it without breaking the bank. It would be necessary for a wider array of people to pitch in; for college faculty to examine the processfolios that are submitted; for community members to offer mentorships, apprenticeships, or "special pods"; for parents to find out what their children are doing in school and to work with them (or at least encourage them) on their projects. These suggestions may sound revolutionary, but they are daily occurrences in excellent educational settings in the United States and elsewhere. Indeed, it is hard to imagine quality education in the absence of such a cooperative ambience.

To my way of thinking, the ultimate policy debate is—or at least should be—centered on competing concepts of the purposes and aims of education. As I have intimated above, the formal standard testing view harbors a concept of education as a collection of individual elements of information that are to be mastered and then spewed back in a decontextualized setting. On this "bucket" view, it is expected that those who acquire a sufficient amount of such knowledge will be effective members of the society.

The assessment view advanced here values the development of productive and reflective skills cultivated through long-term projects. The animating impulse seeks to bridge the gap between school activities and productive activities outside school, with the thought that the same habits of mind and discipline can be useful in both kinds of undertakings. Special attention is paid to individual strengths. Assessment should occur as unobtrusively as possible during the course of daily activities, and the information obtained should be furnished to gatekeepers in useful and economical form.

The assessment view fits comfortably with a vision of individual-centered schooling. Some observers sympathetic to a focus on assessment might still object to the individual-centered view, seeing it as an impractical or romantic conception of education. They would prefer more naturalistic modes of assessment in the service of a rigorous curriculum. To these individuals I would respond, perhaps surprising them, by unequivocally endorsing the importance of rigor. There is nothing in an individual-centered approach that questions rigor; indeed, in any decent apprenticeship, rigor is assumed. If anything, it is the sophomoric multiple-choice-cum-isolated-fact mentality that sacrifices genuine rigor for superficial conformity. I fully embrace rigorous curricula in an individual-based school: I simply call for a broader menu of curricular options (Gardner, 1999b).

Karl Marx hoped that one day the state would simply wither away, no longer needed and hardly missed. In my personal millennial vision, I imagine the apparatus of intelligence testing as eventually becoming unnecessary, its waning unmourned. An hour-long standardized test may at certain points in history have served as a reasonable way of indicating who should be performing better at school or who is capable of military service or of performing at officer rank. But as we come to understand the variety of roles and the variety of ways in which scholastic or military accomplishment can come about, we need far more differentiated and far more sensitive ways of assessing what individuals are capable of accomplishing. In place of standardized tests, I hope that we can develop environments (or even societies) in which individuals' natural and acquired strengths would become manifest—environments in which their daily solutions of problems or fashioning of products would indicate clearly which vocational and avocational roles most suit them.

As we move toward constructing such environments, there will be less need for formal and context-free kinds of evaluations because the distance between what students are doing and what they will need (or want) to do in the society will be correspondingly narrowed. We do not have tests to determine who will become a good leader because leadership abilities emerge under naturally occurring circumstances, and this kind of evidence speaks for itself. Nor do we have tests for sex appeal, football playing, musical performance, or for much the same reasons, legislative skills. We designed tests for intelligence because this alleged global property is not easy to observe in the real world; but it may well be elusive precisely because the notion of intelligence as a single, measurable capacity was never well conceived to begin with.

If the kinds of naturally occurring cognition that I have described are valid, then their several manifestations ought to be readily discernible through judicious observations in the individual's ordinary environment. Far from rendering psychologists or psychometricians unemployable, however, a shift to this kind of subtle measurement would require outstanding efforts from a much larger, more broadly trained, and more imaginative cadre of workers. When one thinks about the enormous human potential currently wasted in a society that values only a small subset of human talents, such an investment seems worthwhile.

In contrast to a testing society, I believe, the assessment approach and the individual-centered school constitute a more noble educational vision. Both are more in keeping with American democratic and pluralistic values (Dewey, 1938). I also believe that this vision is more consistent with what has been established in recent decades by scientific study of human growth and learning. Schools in the future ought to be so crafted that they are consistent with this vision. In the end, whatever the forms and the incidence of official assessments, the actual daily learning in schools, as well as the learning pursued long after formal school has been completed, should be its own reward.

PART THREE

NEW VISTAS

Chapter 11

SOCIETAL CONTEXTS

Coauthored with
Mindy Kornhaber and Mara Krechevsky[1]

A ll definitions of intelligence are shaped by the time, place, and culture in which they evolve. Although these definitions may differ across societies, we believe that the dynamics behind them are influenced by the same forces: (1) the domains of knowledge necessary for survival of the culture, such as farming, literacy, or the arts; (2) the values embedded in the culture, such as respect for elders, maintenance of scholarly traditions, or preference for pragmatic solutions; and (3) the educational system that instructs and nurtures individuals' various competences. In this chapter, we consider not only the familiar territory of the human mind but also the societies in which all minds must operate.

Unlike many other theorists of intelligence, we do not seek to reduce the concept of intelligence to a less complex form in order to devise a test that measures "it." Rather, we wish to explain the diverse manifestations of intelligence within and across cultures. We believe that this more expansive view of intellect designates when and where we might expect to find manifestations of intelligence and how these manifestations might be increased. We favor assessments that are aimed at building on the range of individuals' cognitive potentials or competences. These competences, in

---

1. Article adapted from Kornhaber, M., Krechevsky, M., & Gardner, H. (1990). Engaging intelligence. *Educational Psychologist, 25* (3–4), 177–199.

turn, enable individuals to participate in the variety of end-states human beings and societies have developed over the millennia. We hope, too, that such assessments will help create environments that foster individual as well as group potential.

To establish a theory of intelligence that spans the range of cultures, we first look across this range at two types of societies—traditional and industrial. We consider the domains of knowledge each requires to survive and thrive and how individuals in each type of society are motivated to engage their competences in these domains of knowledge. After defining more precisely the elements of our theory, we examine from that perspective the recent trajectories of two contemporary postindustrial societies, Japan and the United States. Finally, we close with a discussion of the new types of assessment that should be developed in accord with our expanded notion of intelligence.

HUMAN INTELLIGENCE IN SOCIETAL PERSPECTIVE

By definition, a traditional society is one in which the majority of the population is engaged in ensuring an adequate supply of food (LeVine & White, 1986). Obtaining food in these societies is typically very labor intensive. Thus, most people must pursue domains such as fishing, farming, hunting, or herding. But even in these societies, food is not the only source of sustenance. Although there are no formal schools, a kind of curriculum exists nonetheless. Domains of knowledge have evolved around religion, myth, music, dance, and visual art forms. Children must also be socialized into the value system of the society, its religion and ethics, and its social order; the latter is usually determined by age and gender (LeVine & White, 1986).

How are the elements of this crucial curriculum acquired? For the most part, children learn the values and skills of their culture by watching adults and then imitating them. The children's environment is rich with real-life opportunities for applying the skills they learn, and so these skills get regular drill. In fact, practice in these skills usually takes the form of labor on which the community relies. Whatever actual instruction children receive from adults is largely informal. Both instruction and assessment occur in the context of carrying out work within the society's domains and take the form of encouragement, advice, criticism, or the provision of helpful techniques (see chapter 10).

In some traditional societies, the evolution of skilled occupations and prized crafts comes to require a more structured form of learning. These crafts are transmitted to young people primarily through an apprenticeship system. Frequently these apprenticeships are linked to a family's customary occupation and take place at the feet of one's parent. Alternatively, a youngster is assigned to a master who acts *in loco parentis* (Bailyn, 1960). In either case, much of the instruction and evaluation is informal (though not necessarily benign). The child carries out minor tasks related to the master's work and watches what the master does. Gradually, through practice, the apprentice becomes skilled in various, well-defined steps that comprise the making of the final product (Lave, 1977). Eventually, the individual becomes a journeyman, capable of fashioning the final product under supervision of a master. After more years of experience, the individual may create the requisite masterpiece and become a master in turn (Gardner, 1989).

In more complex traditional societies, political and religious organizations evolve and trade routes develop (LeVine & White, 1986). Human memory no longer suffices to maintain and organize the knowledge and skills on which these societies rely. The marks or pictures used in less complex societies must become organized into systems. The first literacy systems, beginning with the invention of writing, were used for financial record keeping, and the first extended texts detailed stark historical records. Later, texts set down the prevalent social virtues of traditional societies; notable among them were "fertility and respect for parents" (LeVine & White, 1986, p. 32).

Because texts ensure the survival of complex traditional societies, and because they serve powerful institutions, people who are literate typically hold highly desirable places within the social hierarchy. However, only an extremely small group of people in these societies possess more than rudimentary literacy skills. Any given society has many roles to fill that do not require literacy. In fact, a society might not withstand the shortage of agricultural labor incurred by a population that spent undue time acquiring and using advanced literacy skills. Therefore, with few exceptions (see, for example, Kobayashi, 1976), formal education in literate skills is reserved for the sons of the hierarchy and for boys who show great promise. Academies or schools develop primarily to prepare young men for leadership roles in political and religious life (and in many societies these roles frequently overlap).

Defining intelligence in remote cultures is neither a simple nor a straightforward matter. Although people in traditional societies may admire literacy, intelligence is not especially defined by skills associated with it. Rather, as LeVine and White (1986) noted:

> If you are intelligent, you behave according to the moral norms of the community because to do otherwise would antagonize those with whom you are permanently connected—which no intelligent adult would want to do. . . . Those who behave in accordance with social convention are assumed to be intelligent in the way that counts the most, i.e., in their maintenance of the social linkages that mean long-term security, though this implies normal rather than exceptional intelligence. Those in the community who are most respected for their moral virtue are credited with being wisest and most intelligent (pp. 39–40).

Thus, we see that in traditional societies, intelligence involves the ability to maintain the community's social ties. In a society that likely depends on the cooperation of many individuals for such basic needs as food and shelter, it makes eminent sense that those who can secure such cooperation would be deemed intelligent.

In contrast to traditional societies, the advances of industrial societies in science and technology have freed—and indeed compelled—large portions of the population to engage in labor unrelated to the production of food. These societies develop a wide range of occupations that both stem from and further the use of technological knowledge. Thus, coal miners and steelworkers help support the infrastructure of new industry; factory employees are needed to churn out a great variety of mass-produced goods; and scientists and engineers are trained to develop new equipment and processes as well as new forms of information and knowledge. The demand for new inventions, as well as the increased economic complexity of trade, banking, and distribution, requires literacy from a greater proportion of the population. Literacy is necessary in order for people to draw on science, mathematics, and the other vast stores of knowledge generated in these societies.

Although children continue to learn much from their elders, parents in industrial societies rarely provide instruction for their children's future occupations. In traditional societies, occupations were largely passed on from one generation to another; in industrial societies, parents may work outside the home, or they may not want their children to follow in their footsteps, or be in a position to compel them to do so. Furthermore, those footsteps may be erased by technological advances. For these and other reasons, the young in industrial societies acquire literacy and learn domains of knowledge primarily through schooling. Governments reinforce this change in parental responsibility by legislating schooling because widespread literacy is regarded as a social good (see Kobayashi, 1976).

As in traditional societies, the activities of schooling in industrial societies do not resemble the daily routines of the surrounding adult community. In schools, skills and knowledge are assessed with little recourse to other persons, and evaluation is more formal and less frequent. In addition, schoolwork often does not engage the experiences young people have outside the school setting (Brembeck, 1978; Brown, Collins, & Duguid, 1989; Gardner, 1991a; Resnick, 1987; Sarason, 1983).

Schooling in industrialized societies differs in important ways from schooling in traditional societies. In the latter, the texts that are emphasized form the core values and often the political guidelines of the surrounding community. Therefore, what youths study in schools carries status in the larger community, even if their activity is removed from the community's daily routine of trade and agriculture (Gardner, 1991a). Unlike the situation of schools in traditional societies, the decontextualized tasks of schooling in industrialized societies may or may not bear a meaningful connection to the values held by the surrounding community. The extent of connection depends in part on the relationship of a school's population to the larger society and also on the values of the society.

A change in the conception of intelligence attends the increased demand for literacy and the legislation of schooling. Whereas initially, honorifics like "intelligent" or "wise" were applied to the virtuous or moral individual, regardless of that person's level of education in industrialized societies, those who are illiterate are unlikely to attain positions of social power or influence. And because community ties are lessened, so is the importance of intelligence that is associated with maintaining social cohesion, at least in some societies. For example, among the Gusii tribe in Kenya, after the introduction of Western schooling, the label of intelligent changed from being identified with morality and virtue to describing successful performance in school (LeVine, personal communication, 1989).

A NEW CONCEPTION OF INTELLIGENCE

The social contexts described previously suggest two different ways in which intelligence has been defined. In traditional societies, intelligence is linked to skill in interpersonal relations, whereas in many industrial societies, intelligence centers more on advanced abilities in the three Rs. Yet despite these differences, the two definitions are derived in a similar way. Both are intertwined with issues of cultural survival—maintaining the necessary social cohesion in traditional societies, and providing the means to shape technology and advance industry in industrial societies.

We believe that these disparate definitions make sense in their societies of origin. As Keating (1984) argued, our notions of intelligence have been profoundly distorted by our continued failure to consider the social, historical, and political contexts from which such ideas arise. If intelligence is conceptualized as representing a dynamic between individual proclivities and a society's needs and values (as opposed to a characteristic of an individual), then it appears that the realization of individual potentials and the needs of the aforementioned cultures were organized in a way that proved effective for the society's particular social and economic structures. It is our claim that the capacity of individuals to acquire and advance knowledge in a cultural domain and apply it in some purposeful fashion toward a goal has equally to do with the competences inside a person's head and with the values and opportunities afforded by society to engage these competences.

Hence, we might construe intelligence primarily as the manifestation of engagements between two components: (1) individuals who are capable of using their array of competences in various domains of knowledge; and (2) the societies that foster individual development through the opportunities they provide, the institutions they support, and the value systems they promote. Individual competences represent only one aspect of intelligence; intelligence also requires social structures and institutions that enable the development of these competences. In this framework, intelligence becomes a flexible, culturally dependent construct. Either the individual or the societal agent may play a dominant role, but both must take part if intelligence is to be achieved. To borrow a distinction from the physical sciences, in *field* societies such as Japan, the action takes place much more on the society's part; in our own *particle* society, the human agent plays a more significant role.

For roughly a century, Western industrialized societies and their schools could afford to mobilize the competences of only a minority of their populations. However, with the rise of postindustrial economies, it is no longer feasible to enable only those who are adept at decontextualized learning to develop their competences. We need to broaden our notion of what can be considered intelligence in terms of both individual and cultural components. Along with new attitudes about intelligence, new forms of schooling and assessment are needed to foster the competences of the majority.

Individuals: The Case for Multiple Intelligences

In postindustrial societies, the notion that intelligence is a trait of individuals may be tied to the innovations in psychological testing that took place at the beginning of the twentieth century. Binet's intelligence scales were developed to identify children who were performing poorly in school and who might benefit from special education (Binet & Simon, 1905). Although Binet never intended to reify intelligence, and although he did not maintain that intelligence was a unitary trait (Gould, 1981), the fact that his test results could be summarized by a single score fostered conceptions of intelligence as a unitary attribute situated in the heads of individuals.

However, several views developed in recent decades (Ceci, 1990; Feldman, 1980; Gardner, 1983b; Sternberg, 1985) suggest a more pluralistic notion of intelligence in order to account for individuals' diverse abilities both to pursue various domains of knowledge and to create new ones. As detailed in part I, the theory of multiple intelligences suggests that individuals are capable of cognitive functioning in several relatively autonomous areas. The different profiles, trajectories, and rates of development that emerge across intelligences enable a person to grasp, more or less readily, the symbol systems in which the domains of his or her culture are transmitted (Gardner, 1983b).

Although individuals are capable of developing a range of competences toward various end-states, they do not do so in isolation. Even in the case of a universally developed competence like language, it is only in the interaction of adult and child that such a faculty develops. Not only does learning generally take place in the context of social interaction, but the great majority of what is learned after the age of two is socially constructed (Snow & Ferguson, 1977). Societies teach their children the bodies of facts, theories, skills, and methods that constitute various domains of knowledge, ranging from fishing to physics (Csikszentmihalyi & Robinson, 1986). We maintain that human cognition is best developed and nurtured through tasks within the bounds of such *domains*—that is, in socially valued disciplines, in which an individual can acquire skills and knowledge through effort over time, typically with feedback from people knowledgeable in the discipline.

MI theory provides a useful framework within which to consider the broad range of individual competences, the first component of our proposed theory. However, to flesh out our theory more fully, we need to consider the dynamic between individuals and the societies in which they operate. A discussion is needed of two contemporary societies from the perspective of the theory's cultural component. The first society illustrates a case in which intelligence seems to be abundantly manifested, and the second, one in which such manifestations are far less conspicuous.

CONTEMPORARY POSTINDUSTRIAL SOCIETY: TWO EXAMPLES

Given our definition of intelligence as representing effective engagements between individuals and the societies in which they live, we might expect Japan to serve as a particularly instructive example. In Japan, the development of intelligence is fostered by widely shared values, which in turn are supported by the institutions of the society. Among these values are school achievement and diligent study. Parents demand high-quality schools and have high expectations for their children. They believe children can fulfill these expectations through hard work and commitment rather than through innate capacity. Thus, mothers actively tutor their children, and teachers are held in high regard. It is regarded as a social responsibility to maximize the child's potential, not only on a rhetorical level but also in actual practice (White, 1987).

The concern with developing children's potential is reinforced by the structure of the Japanese educational system and its connection to job security and success. In the United States, there are scores of colleges whose reputations themselves could ultimately enable students to secure high-level professional careers. However, there are very few such institutions in Japan, and most employers look only to these few when they hire for top positions. The competition to attend these universities calls for a seriousness of purpose—and entails a level of stress—that is world renowned.

In Japan, performing at one's highest level is not simply promoted as a way to make it through the narrow pipeline to professional success. The motivation to realize individuals' competences stems from the fact that doing so helps secure one's place in a society that emphasizes and values interpersonal bonds. Failure to study hard and contribute within the larger society threatens these bonds (Shimizu, 1988).

The influence of social connection on achievement is also evident in Japanese employment. In the work world, employees identify strongly with their firms, in part because they expect to have lifelong careers with them. Furthermore, employees do not feel especially competitive with their fellow workers, and no particular premium is placed on a single individual's possessing all the requisite competences him- or herself. Indeed, the Japanese corporation seems to recognize the profile of human competences and accepts the notion that individuals with different profiles can make their own distinctive contributions to the success of the firm (Gardner, 1983b).

Japan, then, seems to exemplify some of the elements of our normative—as opposed to descriptive—theory. The engagements between individuals and society are evident at many levels: between individual and family, family and school, school and work, and employee and employer. Furthermore, societal values support both schooling and an emphasis on effort and motivation rather than innate ability. Individual competences are nurtured by institutions that encourage their development in a supportive context. When all of these forces align, according to our analysis, intelligence is likely to be manifested.

The United States provides a useful contrast to Japan. By now, we are all too familiar with the reports showing that American schoolchildren score lower on standardized tests than children in most other Western, industrialized, or nonindustrial nations. We see national studies indicating that large proportions of American youngsters do not master basic school subjects. There is no reason to believe that our affluent country contains disproportionate numbers of people whose capacities are inherently limited. To determine how our society might better elicit intelligence, it may prove edifying to examine the course that led us to this point.

The social connections afforded by widely shared values between parent and child were threatened in America from the first colonial days. Although the Puritans had every intention of educating their own children, maintaining traditional apprenticeships, and schooling boys to become ministers, the environment undermined these plans. Unlike other societies, the solder of traditional society—respect for one's elders and dependence on them—had disintegrated in America long before industrialization prevailed. The Puritan leaders, fearing that the next generation was at risk of becoming barbarians, decided to build schools to perpetuate their unraveling culture (Bailyn, 1960). However, it was clear to the young people in this society that the tradition-bound knowledge of their elders was not especially useful for surviving in the wilderness. Labor was at a premium, land was abundant, and young people moved until they found a comfortable niche (Bailyn, 1960).

As the United States became an industrial society, the dubious regard for school-based knowledge remained in effect. Literacy, numeracy, and an acquaintance with texts that captured our cultural legacy were accepted to a certain extent, but competent, active engagement in practical affairs was generally more valued. As Andrew Carnegie put it, "In my own experience I can say that I have known few young men intended for business who were not injured by a collegiate education" (cited in Callahan, 1962, p. 9). The popular view was that intelligent people applied themselves in practical domains and that a traditional school curriculum was of little utility (Bailyn, 1960; see also Hofstadter, 1963). Thus, the close alignments existing in

Japan between individual and family, family and school, and school and work never took hold in the United States.

America's break with tradition-bound learning (Bailyn, 1960), coincident with its love of new technology, may have rendered it especially vulnerable to explanations of intelligence that claimed to be scientific. In any case, it was easy for a variety of hereditarian views and the eugenics movement to take hold here, especially in light of the influence of Darwin's (1859) *On the Origin of Species* and the social Darwinism that followed (Gould, 1981). The adaptation of intelligence tests for mass administration to American military recruits in World War I hastened the shift from social to scientific designations. Science, with its paper-and-pencil tests, formulae, and factor analysis—rather than social judgments about performance in different domains of knowledge—supported the view that white, Christian, northern Europeans possessed the most intelligence. In the minds of many, these people came from the best genetic stock. Thus, in America, we came to believe that intelligence was born and not made. As Gould (1981) noted, the rendering of the concept of intelligence into a reified, inherited trait was "an American invention" (p. 147).

At the same time that IQ tests were developed, American schools were subjected to the forces of another science-related trend, the efficiency movement. In business and commerce, people were turning to science and technology to solve the problems of manufacturing. Jobs were broken down into discrete tasks that could be performed on assembly lines. In education, public schools were increasingly pressured to operate efficiently, to minimize retention, and to provide a disciplined workforce (Callahan, 1962). The introduction of principles of scientific management and mass production into the schools dampened educators' efforts to provide remediation for students with scholastic difficulties. Attempts were made to determine children's competences early on and to provide them with education that was fitting for their presumed adult end-state. Although the development of competences among immigrant groups was especially threatened, all children were affected by the schools' adoption of business values and practices (Oakes, 1986a, 1986b; Powell, Farrar, & Cohen, 1985).

Excessive reliance on psychometric instruments tended not only to divorce individuals from teachers or others who evaluated their performance in a social context, but also to estrange people from the domains of knowledge valued by the society. The determination of intelligence by intelligence tests is made outside of what we consider the legitimate boundaries of human cognition. One reason for this state of affairs is that intelligence tests do not operate within the bounds of an authentic domain of human endeavor. In creating an array of such tests—they were assembled in the *Mental Measurements Yearbooks* beginning in 1938 (Buros, 1938)—psychometricians and psychologists established a domain of sorts. Yet, although this domain is subject to the interpretation of experts in the field, it is largely devoid of features that mark authentic domains. Missing from an apparatus built on mental testing are opportunities for practicing domain-relevant tasks and using them in meaningful contexts. Also absent is the possibility of progressing through a series of stages—often with feedback from those more skilled in the domain—toward proficiency in a socially valued end-state. Except perhaps in the domain of television game shows (another American invention), one is rarely expected to repeat series of numbers, to solve analogies, or to identify well-known figures within a few seconds in order to achieve a social reward.

The absence of an authentic domain threatens the grounds on which intelligence experts make their judgments. Their situation is akin to that of other experts who must make judgments in domains in which criteria are not agreed on. As noted earlier, the case of creativity offers a useful model for comparison (see chapters 3 and 10). According to Csikszentmihalyi (1988a), three dynamic systems are at play in determining creativity: (1) the individuals who create works; (2) the domains of knowledge in which they work; and (3) the field of experts in the domain who judge the works of individuals. In this framework, attributions of creativity rely on the recognition of individual efforts by the field of judges. Such attributions are widely accepted in disciplines in which criteria are well established and agreed on (such as mathematics). In disciplines in which criteria are not widely shared (such as contemporary painting), the attribution of creativity is likely to depend less on a person's work within the domain than on the extent to which the person possesses personal traits that are synchronous with those of other members of the field (Getzels & Csikszentmihalyi, 1976).

Attributions of intelligence share similar judgment calls. We believe that, lacking an authentic domain, the attribution of intelligence is even more dependent on the degree to which the experts and those they are evaluating share social characteristics. The history of intelligence testing, before legal and political efforts were made to restrict its use, bears witness to the importance of social synchrony in the attribution of intelligence (Gould, 1981; see Heubert, 1982; Kornhaber, 2004).

Given the above analysis, a focus on testing for an allegedly general ability is no longer tenable. We must look instead at meaningful performances within a culture. Whereas intelligence tests look only at the individual, intelligence must take into account both individuals and societies. Even when intelligence tests have attempted to measure what we are calling individual competences, they have been narrow in scope. Rather than examining the range of human cognition, they have focused on a thin band of human cognitive competences—on certain aspects of linguistic and logical intelligences. Intelligence tests are limited not only in the competences they examine but also in the way they examine them. They require people to deal with atypical, decontextualized tasks rather than probing how people function when they are able to draw on their experience, feedback, prior knowledge, and colleagues, as they typically do. They also may well produce high scores for individuals who excel at taking short-answer tests but who do not function well in organizations that demand other skills.

It is not even clear that the thinking called upon in these tests bears a significant relation to the usual reasoning employed in learning (Keating, 1984). As Resnick and Neches (1984) noted,

> The extensive attention given to the cognitive components of test performance is based on an implicit assumption that the processes required for *performance* on the tests are also directly involved in *learning*. We believe that this is a risky assumption (p. 276).

Test items such as abstract analogies may tell us something about how people attempt to solve highly decontextualized problems—and which people are more capable, or simply more practiced, at solving such test items—but they do not tell us much about intelligence in our expanded view (Johnson-Laird, 1983). Unless assessment is placed in the context of authentic domains and social environments, we doubt it can adequately represent human intellectual performance.

Some contemporary approaches to assessment recommend using standardized tests as only one component of a broad-based evaluation. Although more comprehensive assessments—including observations of the child in his or her setting and interviews with the child's parents—represent an improvement, the world is an imperfect place, and scientific measurements hold disproportionate sway. When funds and staffing are stretched, test score cutoff points serve in the place of more detailed evaluations. Hard-looking data are used to fend off parents hoping to get their children into programs for the gifted and talented; test measurements often furnish the fallback position for deciding who gets remediation. In a society that has advanced far on technology and scientific data, numbers act as the primary basis for triage (Neill & Medina, 1989).

THE NEED FOR A SOCIAL FRAMEWORK

Just as America overly emphasized the technocratic aspects of education with its heavy focus on testing and measurement, it also neglected the social glue that had always been an important part of education, whether in the schools (as in Japan) or in the wider community (as in traditional apprenticeships). Yet, as mentioned earlier, individual competences need to be encouraged within a social framework. Motivation is not simply a function of competence alone; it also depends on interactions with the social world (Fordham & Ogbu, 1986; Ogbu, 1978; see also Scarr, 1981). Such interactions become internalized over time and serve as a guide to individual behavior (Vygotsky, 1978). Our society has tended to ignore the effects of interpersonal experiences, in part because they are not readily abstracted and measured when analyzing differences in competences and achievements. Hence, the educationally disadvantaged have typically been defined in terms of demographic and educational variables (Bereiter, 1985).

Nonetheless, the creation of cooperative, supportive environments in homes, schools, and communities has been shown to have a positive effect on students' social and psychological well-being, a situation that eventually leads to higher academic achievement (Cochran, 1987; Comer, 1980,

1988a; Damon, 1990; Henderson, 1987; Leler, 1983; Zigler & Weiss, 1985). The intervention projects that Comer (1980) and his colleagues designed for low-income children emphasize the importance of relationships: "[W]hen relationships improve in the schools, the children themselves become the carriers of desirable values" (Comer, 1988a, p. 29). Effective schools seem to be determined not so much by the students themselves or their aptitudes as by parental and teacher support and involvement and the transmission of their high expectations (Ascher, 1988; Brookover, 1985; Chubb, 1988; Comer, 1980; Edmonds, undated).

In America, there has always been a lack of continuity among (1) the range of individual competences; (2) what is learned in school; and (3) what our society values. In our postindustrial society, where these discontinuities remain as prominent as ever, the ascertainment of intelligence via decontextualized, scientific instruments is no longer serviceable; the education that flows from them no longer supports the adult end-states that have evolved in our culture. Advances in communication, transportation, and automation and the exportation of manufacturing to other countries mean that many people who were classified and educated under the old system cannot take up meaningful roles. We need to develop alternative assessments that will take into account our expanded notion of intelligence. Ideally, such a development will lead to the creation of assessment environments where the engagement of individuals in meaningful tasks in society can be looked at more directly.

Enabling Intelligences by Contextualized Assessment

Tests of intelligence serve as traps not only for theorists but for educators and students as well. Rather than constructing tests that inevitably sort individuals and potentially limit their growth, we prefer to design vehicles that simultaneously help uncover and foster the individual's competences. Our proposed model considers assessment in terms of meaningful adult end-states that are valued by the community.

The concept of adult end-states is helpful for focusing assessment on abilities that are relevant to achieving significant and rewarding adult roles in our society. Suppose, for example, that we value the roles of novelist and lawyer. A more valid assessment of language skills might examine a young child's ability to tell a story or provide a descriptive account of an experience, rather than examine his or her ability to repeat a series of sentences, define words, or solve antonymic or syllogistic tasks. The latter tasks bear no discernible relationship to an acknowledged domain or adult end-state. The implications of highly contextualized assessments for instruction and remediation are more immediate and direct than those deriving from the decontextualized items of standard tests. For example, mentoring experiences in a domain of knowledge such as the visual arts or mechanical science might be one way to work closely with the central issues and materials of a field.

Apprenticeships also embed learning in a social and purposeful context. They are valuable not only because they build on student interests and strengths, but also because they foster critical thinking through regular, informal assessment in the context of an authentic domain. In this respect, they are much more similar to the robust learning that goes on outside of school (Brown, Collins, & Duguid, 1989; Resnick, 1987). Apprenticeships also serve as a means of providing greater community involvement with schools. As mentioned earlier, the cooperative involvement of parents and others in the surrounding community strengthens the cognitive achievements of the community's schoolchildren (Chubb, 1988; Comer, 1988b; Heath, 1983; Henderson, 1987). Every child should have the opportunity to work closely with an adult who serves as a model of serious study, reflection, and application in the world that has meaning for him. Although the domains of knowledge shift continually over time, it is in human relationships that societies have managed to develop individual competences from their very beginning (see Comer, 1984).

In addition to advocating apprentice-type learning environments where possible, we believe that education should be firmly grounded in the institutions and practices of society—art and science museums, ateliers, scouting, and so on. Science, discovery, and children's museums offer rich and powerful opportunities for children to draw on the different forms of knowledge that are generally left unintegrated, treated in isolation from each other, or perhaps ignored in school. The materials in museums are in a sense already pretested for their appeal to children. Many of these materials are quite educational for children and can be utilized in a variety of ways over long periods of time. A number of interactive technologies allow children to combine intuitive and school-based knowledge in various endeavors, from understanding the principles of physics to appreciating a foreign culture (Bransford, et al., 1989; Wilson, 1988).

In our conception, assessment environments have several desiderata (see also chapter 10). They should integrate curriculum and assessment and invite young people to deploy their various competences in the context of carrying out meaningful projects or activities. Such assessments should also make available a range of intrinsically interesting and motivating materials that would be used over time and that would be sensitive to individual differences. They should also be intelligence-fair, that is, capable of engaging specific competences without the need to rely on linguistic or logical means or abilities as an intermediary. Ideally, these assessments would also meet Fredericksen and Collins's (1989) criteria for "systemically valid tests": tests that induce "in the education system curricular and instructional changes that foster the development of the cognitive traits that the test[s] [are] designed to measure" (p. 1).

In chapters 6 through 9 we examined educational interventions framed in this spirit. Project Spectrum and Arts PROPEL represent attempts to identify a wider range of competences in a context that is both embedded in the culture and meaningful to the child. By building on a child's interest and motivation, schools might have more success in carrying out what may be their most crucial task: empowering children to engage meaningfully in their own learning. As we have seen, one way to develop meaningful engagement is through apprenticeships. These might be arranged for students through school specialists, with some apprenticeships being conducted by teachers and others by people from the surrounding community. Although discovering the rewards of learning in a domain as an end in itself is important (Amabile, 1983; Csikszentmihalyi, 1990a), Comer's (1980, 1984) writings, among others, show that an interpersonal relationship is critical in motivating students to learn.

The Key Learning Community, described in chapter 7, reflects an environment where school, children, and the community come together in a productive way. The school encourages children to develop competence in the various domains through an interdisciplinary curriculum. Equal time is devoted to English, math, music, visual art, computers, movement, and other subjects. In addition, children are allowed to develop in their areas of strength in an apprentice-like situation known as a *pod*. Pods are small classes conducted by teachers along their special lines of interest that children from any grade are free to join. Children can also develop their interests in after-school programs led by the principal and teachers.

As a magnet school, the Key Learning Community draws children from all neighborhoods of the city. An advisory board made up of representatives from local businesses, cultural institutions, and universities helps the school take advantage of local resources. Parents are also involved in the school, through teacher conferences, parent-advisory committees, and occasional presentations in their areas of expertise. Thus, the Key Learning Community attempts to bridge the individual, the school, and the community. Enhancing the development of individual competences is a many-sided effort. We see prospects for it in new forms of assessment, such as Arts PROPEL and Spectrum, in closer working relationships between young people and mentors, and in increased cooperation between schools and communities. We also believe that recently forged ideas about intelligence have a large part to play.

Most theories of intelligence have attempted to answer the question "What's the score?" To the extent that tests have been based on such theories, they have served more to label individuals than to promote their development. Instead, we have focused our search for a new theory around the questions "When?" "Where?" and "How?" We believe the theory generated by these inquiries provides a constructive framework to advance both analysis and practical interventions. We hope that our theory will act as an impetus for the study of intelligence to shift from a focus on individuals to a focus on interactions between individuals and societies. To the greatest extent possible, psychological and cognitive factors must be considered in conjunction with the social contexts in which they operate.

The study of intelligence requires a meeting of the minds. Research based on individual cognition—studies involving information processing approaches, means-ends models, factor analysis, and the like—will continue to be useful. But although these domains may provide insights into the kinds of strategies people use in specific kinds of problem solving, these peculiarly decontextualized problems do not represent the crux of human intelligence (Neisser, 1983). In life, most problems are not presented ready-made to the solver but must be shaped out of events and information from the surrounding environment (Csikszentmihalyi, 1988b). We need a deeper understanding of how social settings motivate people to delve into these kinds of problems, the policies that have discouraged people from engaging their competences as against the policies that encourage engagement, the effect of parents and peer groups and how this effect might be enhanced, and the effects of school organization and curriculum on a variety of students and teachers. In short, because we believe that the great majority of people are capable of using their competences in a skillful way, we need to explore how such use can be encouraged within a social framework. Once we recognize that intelligence evolves through a dynamic of individuals' competences and society's values and institutions, we are more likely to devise policies and support initiatives that effectively engage people's minds.

Chapter 12

AT THE WORKPLACE

Coauthored with Seana Moran

THE WORLD OF EDUCATION
MEETS THE WORLD OF THE WORKPLACE

The educational community embraced the theory of multiple intelligences in part because the intelligences correspond relatively easily to academic subjects: the linguistic intelligence with language arts, logical-mathematical with math and science, bodily-kinesthetic with physical education, musical with band and orchestra, and so on. While this equation represented an oversimplification (there is not a one-to-one mapping between any intelligence and any domain), it opened up new pedagogical and assessment possibilities that excited educators.

At first blush, the workplace is quite different from school. Moreover, there are all kinds of workplaces, ranging from the office in which a social worker meets clients to the factory in which automobiles are assembled to the backrooms in which account books are audited or mail is sent to customers. In this chapter, we consider a range of workplaces but focus particularly on the world of business, with which the vast majority of American workers are connected.

Businesses exist to make products or to provide services; schools provide information, knowledge, and skills presumed to be of use in the future—perhaps especially at the anticipated workplace. Furthermore, businesses must earn a profit in order to stay in business, and ever higher profits are sought. In contrast, most schools are nonprofit ventures, and they are likely to remain so; "market" approaches to education—charter schools, vouchers, and the like—are designed primarily to improve scholastic performance, not to make money. Finally, schools are presumed to serve a civic function—to pass on the models and the motives that help people become law-abiding, actively contributing members of the society. While businesses are certainly free to fulfill a civic function and to educate their workers, there is no imperative that they do so.

These differences should not be allowed to obscure similarities in how business and education have been conceived and carried out and how they might be refashioned in the future. Indeed, the training of one traditional worker—the individual craftsperson—bears a strong resemblance to the ways in which students and pre-professionals have been educated over the centuries. Recently, the modern corporation—the business that we focus on here—has been considered a model for how schools should be managed. For these reasons, we draw, as appropriate, on analyses and proposals that have already been put forth in this volume. In what follows, we consider the recent business interest in a broader range of intelligences; the role played by individual intelligences in the business world; the advantage gained by considering various blends of intelligences, in individual workers as well as in groups of workers; and the ways in which having particular intelligence profiles help people in certain work positions carry out their jobs effectively. Our theme can be readily stated: In a fast-changing world, with a multitude of roles and an ever-greater dependence on teamwork, it is anachronistic to adhere to the notion of a single, all-purpose intelligence that resides in the head of a single individual.

Beyond Traditional Views of Intelligence

Gardner has often quipped that if the intelligence test had been invented by businesspeople rather than academics, it would have been a very different test. A good test of BQ (Business Quotient) should tap marketing skills, risk taking, salesmanship, establishing trust, and ability to predict and perhaps even alter consumer trends—none of which could conceivably be inferred from the items on a typical IQ test. That said, it is notable that until recently, most business analysts, like most educators, believed that there was such a capacity as general intelligence and that IQ could predict one's performance across a wide range of business (and particularly managerial) roles.

Most competence measures for the workplace, as for education, have been based on general aptitude—*g* in shorthand. Several researchers have studied the extent to which a single number predicts performance in various types of work (for example, Carson, 1998; Ellis et al., 2003; Gottfredson, 1986; Hunter, 1986). These general aptitude test scores do correlate with ability to be trained in a skill. That is, adults who score well can grasp job requirements with instruction and practice, just as children with high IQ scores tend to grasp academic material better and more quickly than those with lower scores (Dawis, 1996). But there is little evidence that high scores on such tests directly lead to high performance: according to a widely cited though controversial estimate, *g* predicts only 4 percent of the variation in actual job performance (Dagley & Salter, 2004; Sternberg, 1996). Also, tests of *g* only differentiate occupations across different hierarchy levels within an organization (say, between a manager and a worker) but not within a given level (say, between different types of workers) (Dawis, 1996). Hence, their value in a more complex workplace is suspect.

The enormous interest engendered by Daniel Goleman's writings (1995, 1998) on emotional intelligence (often called EQ) represented the first clear break from the hegemony of IQ and general intelligence in the workplace. Goleman's emotional intelligence is akin to the personal intelligences posited in MI theory, although the latter are purely descriptive (how people understand one another and themselves), not normative (how people *should* treat one another). In the past decade, accordingly, there has been an outpouring of other candidate intelligences—leadership, financial, business, and spiritual intelligences, just to name a few (see chapters 1 and 2). Without commenting here on the merits of these various candidates, we hope that the business community has opened itself to a more variegated view of intellect.

Intelligences and Occupational Roles

Once a taxonomy of various intelligences has been set forth, it is possible to delineate general correspondences of the sort noted in the educational community. For example, journalists, speakers, and trainers tend to draw heavily on linguistic intelligence; scientists, engineers, financiers, and accountants on logical-mathematical intelligence; architects, graphic designers, and taxi drivers on spatial intelligence; salespeople, managers, teachers, and counselors on the personal intelligences; athletes, contractors, and actors on bodily-kinesthetic intelligence; composers, audio effects designers, and advertisers on musical intelligence; taxonomists, ecologists, and veterinarians on naturalistic intelligence; and clergy and philosophers on existential intelligence (see Gardner, 1999a; Martin, 2001; Weller, 1999).

Multiple intelligences can also tie into other popular occupational taxonomies, such as Holland's (1997) RIASEC model, which categorizes occupations into realistic/trades; investigative/sciences; artistic; social; enterprising/business or sales; and conventional/clerical or maintenance. This model aligns clients' interests with the demands of different occupations. Recent research suggests that interests and abilities correlate; therefore, ability assessments may also be used with the RIASEC model (Dagley & Salter, 2004; Prediger, 1999).

We could venture, further, that linguistic and personal intelligences are more important in the social and enterprising, people-oriented occupations; logical-mathematical in the data-oriented, desk-centered occupations; bodily-kinesthetic, naturalistic, and spatial in the realistic, thing-oriented occupations; and linguistic, logical-mathematical, musical, and spatial in artistic and investigative, idea-oriented occupations (see Carson, 1998; Prediger, 1999).

MULTIPLE INTELLIGENCES IN
RAPIDLY CHANGING WORK CONTEXTS

Such straightforward correspondences are useful to a point. But the power of an MI approach can be more fully tapped through an examination of the ways the intelligences interact in individuals or within teams. Looking at intelligences in isolation does not highlight the advantages of having more than one specific intelligence rather than one general intelligence (IQ). A variety of potentials combining into different patterns allows a wider array of competences and performances to arise. People, teams, and organizations can fine-tune their skills to their needs in a more flexible way—often called "business agility." Such adaptability has been the clarion call of the new economy for the past fifteen years (Ellis et al., 2003; Senge,

1992). As a result, MI theory may help individuals, teammates, managers, and leaders gain traction in the increasingly complex workplace.

The well-known set of Lego pieces provides a useful analogy. We can create much more complicated plastic structures using a lot of little pieces than using a few big pieces, because we have more options for arranging them. Similarly, in a more complex workplace, people and companies have more choices about how to think or behave. Bureaucratic organizations with stable, functional units of people in standardized roles—such as the traditional all-purpose airlines—have proved a lot less nimble in adapting to change than more network-like organizations—such as Southwest Airlines and JetBlue Airways. In network organizations, job value stems from effect-on-customer, not from position in a hierarchy; by the same token, jobs involve developing and "packaging" ideas rather than mass producing standardized products (Cascio, 1995; Fisher & Fisher, 1998). Large organizations need to organize work into smaller, more manageable units to be able to respond more effectively to changing business opportunities.

As the context of work changes, so does the profile of desired intelligences. Office and computer work privilege the value of linguistic intelligence. Television and graphical user interfaces increase the importance of spatial intelligence. E-marketplaces initially increased the demand to integrate linguistic, logical-mathematical, and spatial (navigational) intelligences; as these marketplaces become "smarter," they entail interpersonal intelligence on both ends of transactions. Skills that can be taken over by computers and machines, such as some software engineering that now can be done by compilers, leave the so-called "soft skills" of envisioning, alliance-building, opportunity-spotting, communication, and sophisticated pattern recognition for people to do (Coy, 2004; Levy & Murnane, 2004).

Often the amount of information processing required is more than one person can handle. Thus, firms use team-based work in which intelligence is not assessed at the individual level but distributed across teams and cultural tools, such as computer databases and programs (Bennis & Biederman, 1997; Fisher & Fisher, 1998; Jacques, 1989). A helpful image for the contemporary organization may be drawn from the performing arts: a director brings together actors, costume designers, lighting specialists, editors, and other specially trained individuals for a particular movie, play, or dance;

when the production is complete, the organization disappears and these individuals—with their respective intellectual profiles—are free to coagulate into another organization for a different project (see Jackson, 1996).

INTERACTIONS AMONG MULTIPLE INTELLIGENCES

Since intelligences function in combination with each other, attempting to analyze how they do so can become an exceedingly complex task. Thus, a primary analytic challenge is to reduce the possible combinations to a manageable number. We recommend focusing on the ways intelligences might interact with each other to affect performance. In other words, the point is not to "measure" a particular intelligence in some absolute way, but rather to consider the overall configuration of, and relations among, the several intelligences.

Profiles, Not Scores

One approach involves profiling, which provides a snapshot of an individual's intelligences. Almost everyone's profile is jagged; that is, there are peaks and valleys, relative strengths and weaknesses. Rarely does someone have a completely flat profile, signifying equal fitness to process all types of information. Such jaggedness or imbalance may arise from genetic endowment or the development of preferences as a result of different experiences or differential access to types of information. For example, social class or the proximity of one's hometown to cultural centers may affect whether, and how well, musical intelligence develops. Similarly, access to parks, playgrounds, and free time for playing (or, alternatively, sedentary video game and television activities indoors) may affect the development of bodily-kinesthetic intelligence.

As discussed in chapter 2, we have identified two contrasting types of profiles—*laser* and *searchlight*. Laser profiles include one or two intelligences that are particularly strong and dominate a person's perceptions and career choices. For example, extremely strong mathematical potential may so narrow the stimuli to which a person attunes that he does not seek out other stimuli. Such may have been how an Isaac Newton or a John

Nash started out. Extraordinary achievers in the arts and sciences tend to have laser profiles (Moran & Gardner, 2006).

Searchlight profiles balance several intelligences. While the laser mind focuses on one or two forms of information, the searchlight mind is characterized by a capacity—and a proclivity—for regularly sampling diverse forms of information. The prototypical searchlight mind belongs to the politician or the CEO; this person's job is not to be a master of any single topic but rather to post a wide radar screen and to make sure that nothing crucial escapes notice on that screen. Most people, we suspect, have searchlight profiles; and most jobs support them. A study using the Armed Services Vocational Aptitude Battery of tests found that those who hold social and enterprising jobs—sales, counseling, entrepreneurship—tend not to show marked strength in a specific sphere (Kelso, 1977). This finding makes sense, as these types of occupations often are best suited for people with searchlight profiles, which would not show a "spike" indicator as laser profiles would. More generally, searchlight profiles provide multiple possible career options, more so than laser profiles.

In addition to these two primary profile types, there are other ways in which different intelligences can affect each other. We propose three: one intelligence can mediate and constrain the others; one intelligence can compensate for another; and one intelligence can catalyze another.

Bottlenecks

Bottlenecks occur when one intelligence constrains the ability of other intelligences to operate. Most likely, bottlenecks result from weaker intelligences that inhibit the full expression of stronger intelligences. For example, a weak linguistic intelligence may prevent a person from expressing her strength in interpersonal intelligence because she cannot speak well. Or a weak intrapersonal intelligence may keep a person from effectively deploying his logical-mathematical intelligence because he can't regulate his moods or thoughts or he keeps seeking leadership positions for which his personality is ill suited. We suspect that the long-standing stereotype of the cranky or sadistic "eccentric genius" may arise from bottlenecks in the personal intelligences.

Bottlenecks might also result from strong intelligences that overpower others. Such a situation may be more likely with laser profiles. For example, Picasso reportedly had difficulty developing his logical-mathematical intelligence because his exceptionally strong spatial intelligence oriented him to see numbers as images rather than quantities: he saw a 2 as a nose (Gardner, 1993).

In addition, a bottleneck might result from the cultural tools used to develop and assess abilities. A common bottleneck in schools, and probably workplaces, emanates from the linguistic realm. Most tests are language-based paper-and-pencil instruments, regardless of the competence or skill they are actually designed to measure. As a result, workers with weaker linguistic intelligence may be at a disadvantage despite an actual potential in the competence being assessed. In contrast, those whose language and logical abilities allow them to "psych out" such tests may perform well, even when their knowledge of the domain is actually scanty. To be authentic and valid, each intelligence should be assessed in its own medium—bodily-kinesthetic through movement, spatial through images and orientation, and so on. Otherwise, the linguistic (or logical-mathematical if the test is numerically based) intelligence serves as a bottleneck.

Compensation

Compensation occurs when one intelligence makes up for another. For example, strong linguistic or interpersonal intelligence might make up for weak spatial intelligence in a person who may not be able to orient herself in an unfamiliar environment but can talk with people to help keep herself on course. Or a strong bodily-kinesthetic intelligence might compensate for a weak linguistic intelligence by communicating the person's intentions and message through gestures and expressions.

The advantage of compensation is that it supports how a particular job performance might emerge through several different combinations of intelligences. We have seen this at work in the educational sphere, where success on a particular measure—say, geometric skill—can be achieved through various combinations of intelligence. Turning to the workplace, one person might excel at public speaking through linguistic strength in writing speeches, another person through bodily-kinesthetic strength in dramatic motion or "presence" on stage, and still another through the musical qualities of voice or notable rhythm in the words or their expression. One person might excel at accounting through logical-mathematical strength via formulas and another through spatial strength via spreadsheets and visual patterns in data.

Compensation may also mask weaknesses that an employee or his manager may want to identify. Ideally we want to know not only *that* someone can do a certain task, but also *how*, in order to best determine that person's growth potential on a particular career path. Even though both types of accountant might rank equally on a traditional performance review, a formulaic, logical-mathematical accountant may be at a disadvantage with today's more spatially oriented spreadsheet approach to keeping books; in contrast, a more spatially oriented accountant may be at a disadvantage in finding calculation errors. If higher accounting positions require strength in formulaic manipulation, knowing different candidates' profiles could be important for making a judicious decision about a promotion.

Catalysts

As we have seen repeatedly in the educational sphere, a catalytic or "bridge" intelligence can jump-start another intelligence or modify the way it functions. This is also true in the area of scholarship: Einstein's unusually powerful spatial intelligence allowed him to conceptualize problems in ways that eluded other physicists. In the workplace, a strong musical intelligence may lead a person engaged in a linguistic task to be more sensitive to the rhythmic properties of language as well as its meaning. Such a catalyzing interaction would be advantageous for an advertising jingle writer or poet or speaker, but less so for a journalist, especially if such sensitivities keep him or her from turning in stories on time or editing them to fit a word limit. A strong spatial intelligence may lead a person who works with language to be more sensitive to the shape of linguistic symbols. This catalyzing effect would be advantageous for publication editors but less so for speechwriters. A strong interpersonal intelligence may lead a person to be more sensitive to the nuances of another's speech or the effect of his or her own speech on others—which would be advantageous for counselors and therapists. Recognizing such catalyzing interactions can help us determine the potential of various candidates for specific occupational roles.

The Whole Does Not Equal the Sum of the Parts

A critical point about these interactions is that a person's potential does not necessarily equal the sum of his or her intelligences, as various inventory measures assume (see Martin, 2001; Weller, 1999). With bottlenecks, the total potential could equal less. With compensation and catalysts, it could equal more.

Furthermore, conventional wisdom assumes that more of all intelligences is better. But weaknesses can be as important as strengths in matching people to work tasks and roles. It is not the amount of intelligence by itself that matters, but how different levels of the different intelligences affect each other within a particular situation or job. Some studies suggest that in some roles a person can have too much of a certain intelligence: for example, despite the current excitement about emotional intelligence (Goleman, 1998), too much interpersonal or intrapersonal intelligence may actually hamper corporate management and leadership (Feyerhern & Rice, 2002; Kolodinsky, Hochwarter, & Ferris, 2004; Moran & Gardner, 2006). Finally, an employer or human resource manager needs to determine whether the role in question is more likely to be filled successfully by someone with a jagged laser profile or with a relatively flat searchlight profile.

MANAGEMENT

An MI approach need not require an overhaul of an organization's hiring, review, and promotion procedures. Rather, it may call for increased sensitivity to certain tasks that managers, teammates, and human resources professionals already perform. We focus on three such opportunities: interpreting "experience" in a job interview, conducting "experiential" reviews, and "in the moment" sensitivity.

The Role of "Experience"

Most companies prefer to hire or promote people "with experience." But what does that phrase really mean? Often, it just comprises a number: how many years a person has been in a certain role or field. Sometimes it comprises a particular list of tasks a person has done or situations in which he or she has been. An MI approach, however, considers experience as the way a person interacts with the environment.

Experience is critical for determining intellectual strengths and weaknesses as well as for developing the different intelligences. The two are reciprocal. Without music in the environment, musical intelligence is unlikely to develop; without musical intelligence as a potential, it is unlikely people will make music. Without other people around, interpersonal (and probably intrapersonal) intelligence is unlikely to develop; without the personal intelligences as a potential, it is unlikely people will interact civilly and productively. How can managers conducting job interviews or performance evaluations learn about experiences that are meaningful, and how can applicants or employees convey them? One powerful way is through stories (Bruner 1990; Gardner 1995a); both the content of narratives and the ways in which they are conveyed can illustrate experiences. For example, an interview guide might read:

1. Avoid general descriptions of past work, as are often given on résumés. Instead, focus on events. What happened? Then what happened? What worked or didn't work? Why do you think that is so? What did you think about the event at the time? What do you think about the event now? What would you notice or do differently if you could relive it? What's the "bottom line" or key theme of this event?

2. Listen not only to *what* the person is saying, but also *how* he or she is saying it. Does the person tend to convey details that are visual ("I saw . . . ") or auditory ("I heard . . . ") or kinesthetic ("I felt . . ." or "I grasp that . . . ") or logical ("I figure . . ." or "I infer . . . ")? How and how well does she spatially orient herself in relation to objects or others who were there? Is she more concerned

with her personal meaning (intrapersonal) or the event's impact on others (interpersonal)? How elaborate is the language used? How rhythmic is the narrative? Does the story proceed logically, or from different people's perspectives (interpersonal and/or spatial), or according to larger themes (existential)?

3. In the telling, does the person include a lot of body language (kinesthetic) or diagrams (spatial or logical) or word-picture descriptions (spatial)? How do these different aspects of telling enhance, balance, or conflict with each other (how integrated are the person's intelligences)? What are the changes in the perception or evaluation of the event since it occurred? What does the bottom line emphasize?

Such questions may help a manager or a team determine the relative strengths and weaknesses of different potentials. It may be helpful to record the session to have the option of studying it more carefully.

"Experiential" Reviews

Of course, the storytelling approach requires diligence in watching out for a linguistic intelligence bottleneck. In addition, a manager or teammate must be mindful of the possibility of self-report inflation about abilities (Morgeson et al., 2004). A less linguistically oriented way to assess intelligence profiles involves performance and evaluation. This type of assessment has been conducted successfully with young children through Project Spectrum (see chapter 6). Another human resources guide entry might proceed:

1. Put a job applicant or an employee in a room stocked with a variety of materials and tasks that appeal to different intelligences. Materials might include books or books-on-tape for linguistic intelligence; CDs or instruments for musical; a self-development journal for intrapersonal; a coworker (or put two applicants together) for interpersonal; contemplative "big questions" for existential; model-building materials for bodily-kinesthetic; objects and bins for naturalistic; and drawing materials or a maze for spa-

tial. Tasks might include writing a story or giving a speech, solving business math or logic problems, reorganizing a file drawer, interpreting or drawing an image. This list only provides examples; it is not intended to be exhaustive or definitive.

2. The objective is to observe the person in the room for an hour or so. What does the person gravitate toward on his or her own accord? How does the person interact with the different materials? Which tasks seem easier or harder to complete? Toward which problems does the person gravitate, and which materials does he or she deploy?

3. After the allotted time has passed, ask the person what the experience was like from his or her perspective; the person's answer should supply additional clues about intellectual preferences and abilities.

We note that this hypothetical performance evaluation involves actual materials. With computer software and, eventually, virtual reality, it is possible—at least potentially—to sample a much wider range of environments efficiently and inexpensively. However, we cannot assume that people will handle "virtual realities" in the same way that they would manage actual realities.

"In the Moment" Sensitivity

The two opportunities just described provide static, one-point-in-time assessments of potential. As a manager or team member becomes more aware of indicators of the different intelligences, he or she should be able to capture indicators of intelligences dynamically, as they are drawn on during a regular workday. Special sessions, such as interviews or performance reviews, need not be the only times when an MI approach is invoked. How might MI theory help workers and managers make better decisions in the moment, diagnose what is not working, or leverage what does work?

First, each of us should do an intelligence "mirror test." What are our own intellectual preferences and abilities? Otherwise, our intellectual proclivities—even if they are strengths—may become biases or bottlenecks that negatively affect our perceptions, decision making, and performance.

If a manager is not aware of how her linguistic strength may affect her, she may only hire other linguistically strong individuals, whom she finds easier to "understand." Or, even more pointedly, if a manager wants to be communicated with face-to-face, he may underestimate the strength of someone whose communication skills are better conveyed in writing. Allowing personal preferences to drive choices in this way may result in an imbalanced team if the goal is, for example, putting together a "chat" Web site. In addition to language skills, logical-mathematical, spatial, and interpersonal intelligences should also be represented across the team in some way. In this sense, intrapersonal intelligence—knowing one's own strengths, weaknesses, and biases—may underpin the success of other intelligences in the workplace; hence, current emotional intelligence models include self-regulation as a component (Goleman, 1998; Mayer & Salovey, 1997; Prati et al., 2003).

FOUR VIGNETTES

What might a multiple intelligences approach look like in action? We present four hypothetical scenarios of common workplace occurrences: individual career planning, management of roles/jobs, teamwork, and leadership.

Career Planning

Andrea is a twenty-year-old journalism student interning at Hardwick/Davis Public Relations. Traditionally, career planning involves meeting with a counselor during or after high school or college. The objective is to discuss interests or take a few inventories, such as the Myers-Briggs Type Indicator or abilities checklists, to match the student with various possible jobs. Career counselors also may provide information about the growth and salary opportunities in different fields as well as stepping stones—such as college or internships—along the career path (Dagley & Salter, 2004).

An MI approach suggests that Andrea conduct self-assessments, such as those described above (see also Kammeyer-Mueller & Wanberg, 2003). The internship itself can serve as a real-life laboratory for the experiential review. Which tasks can she do more quickly, grasp more easily? Which tasks does she enjoy more? Which coworkers and supervisors does she prefer to work with or understand better? How do they speak and behave, as described above? When she is stuck, toward which resources or recourse does she gravitate? What technology is called for on the job? Which routine tasks might one day be automated, and which seem likely to remain people-dependent? For example, writing and distributing press releases, some aspects of which can be automated through templates and auto-fax or blanket e-mail programs, may become a less valued skill, whereas the ability to think of attention-grabbing campaign concepts will continue to require a creative, thoughtful person.

Second, an MI approach might be helpful with adjustment to the job or field. Recognizing that people process information in different ways might help the "new kid on the block" not take criticisms personally, since they might stem from profile differences. Here are some guidelines for people like Andrea:

Pay attention to the various ways different coworkers complete tasks as a way to increase your repertoire of skills. At the same time, you should continue to value your own profile of intelligences even if it is not the norm for the organization; your addition to the staff expands the organization's repertoire.

Watch for "leverage points," or opportunities to catalyze your own or a coworker's potential by combining forces. Thinking collaboratively from the start of your career can help your career trajectory.

Keep an eye on the big picture to develop intrapersonal and existential intelligences: Where do you derive personal meaning from your work? How do you handle increases or changes in the freedom or self-responsibility to handle tasks? During what tasks or situations do you most feel like your "real self"? (See Cohen, 2003.)

Team Dynamics

Andrea has been assigned to work with George, Brenda, Olivia, and Henry, the campaign team to plan the grand opening of Hot Tamales Restaurant. Most teams in the past have been assembled cross-functionally to include a writer, a designer, a media specialist, and an account executive. A certain amount of conflict would be expected as teammates negotiate campaign concepts and strategy in the traditional "forming, storming, norming, performing" pop model of team functioning.

An MI approach recommends two additional considerations: complementarity of abilities beyond functional training, and heightened awareness of the personal intelligences to aid conflict management. Effective teams entail sharing but not sameness; that is, they involve common goals but not equivalent skills. The advantage of teams emerges through the complementarity of individual members' jagged intelligence profiles; different skills brought to the task catalyze and compensate for one another through sharing information (Conner & Plasman, 2003; Ellis et al., 2003; John-Steiner, 2000). Perhaps the team should be directed by someone who has a searchlight profile.

Because different profiles can lead to the same performance outcome, it does not suffice to say, for example, that this team needs a "word person." It would be helpful to determine whether to hire an intern who is a writer with strong spatial intelligence if that is lacking in the current team's profile, or to hire a charismatic salesperson type with verbal-linguistic, interpersonal, and bodily-kinesthetic strengths.

In addition, when bringing people together, it is helpful to ensure that there is sufficient overlap in intelligences or that the team includes people who can translate among the different information processing potentials. Such redundancy can help smooth communication and operations as well as provide a cushion of skill if a team member is out sick for a while, goes on vacation, or resigns. For example, it is helpful when the writer can look at information from a spatial, designer perspective (or vice versa). Then the ad, poster, or other document the team produces is more likely to be well integrated spatially and linguistically than if the writer and designer cannot understand one other.

Finally, in a team environment, more so than in a hierarchical environment, it is critical that workers are aware of and appreciate differences among intelligences. Without such awareness, trust and respect may falter, spiraling into dissatisfaction and poor performance. Because team members often negotiate norms, conducting "360-degree" performance reviews of each other and the overall team, the personal intelligences become increasingly important. Effective team members are those who know themselves well, can regulate themselves, and understand the impact of their words and actions on others.

Management/Organizing Work

Tim is the division manager with jurisdiction over all teams who work on restaurant accounts. Whereas team effectiveness involved dealing with problem-solving, conflict management, and planning at a local level, management focuses on coping with maintaining order, planning, budgeting, staffing, and problem-solving more globally within the company (Kotter, 1990). Technical skills are still important at the management level but it is ill advised to base the decision to hire or promote a manager solely on who among the candidates is the best writer, designer, or media technician. Individual employees and team members can have laser profiles and be effective if their strengths are balanced against those of others who also have laser profiles. In contrast, managers with searchlight intelligences seem more poised for success, because they are more likely to be able to communicate with a variety of profiles.

As Tim has moved up the corporate ladder, his personal intelligences have become even more important in differentiating himself from other promotion candidates: at the management level, almost everyone has an IQ of 120+ (Spencer & Spencer, 1993). Tim has become more introspective and more focused on alliance building. He must communicate and negotiate across a wider array of intelligences. This wider array presents more opportunities for a "meta-view" of intelligences—sensitivity to bottlenecks, compensations, and catalysts. That is, Tim considers how best to combine individual intelligence profiles into effective team profiles and an even larger divisional unit profile. He must be careful to take his own profile into account so he doesn't hire clones of himself or discriminate against those whose intellectual profiles are alien to him.

Multiple intelligences theory also might aid Tim in job design. Rather than just listing the tasks a team member job might be faced with, he might think of the job in terms of ideal and minimum intelligence profiles. What can his current team do and not do? Where are there holes or lacking overlap? With what types of information will the team member be working, and under what conditions? Such considerations might improve Tim's hiring "hit" rate in expected ways, such as choosing writers with spatial skills. But Tim's approach to hiring might also be beneficial in less expected ways—for example, in declining to hire a writer with strong bodily-kinesthetic or interpersonal needs who wouldn't do well working on a "virtual team" via computer correspondence (compare Fisher & Fisher, 1998).

Leadership

Jane is the president of Hardwick/Davis. Whereas her managers deal more with the day-to-day operational problems, Jane's job is to steer the whole ship (Kotter, 1990). She must maintain a longer-term outlook, take into account the conditions of the marketplace, set a general direction, align her resources, and inspire her employees and customers to stay on board.

As a result, Jane's adaptability in processing information must be even greater than Tim's: she must be able to translate even more widely to understand and communicate with a growing horizon of intelligences, profile types, bottlenecks, compensations, and catalysts. She must contend not only with profiles within her management team but also with her customer base, her shareholders, the whole company as it now exists, and the company as she envisions it in the future. Her personal intelligences are crucial, as she must understand her own skills and biases and work well with a variety of stakeholders within and outside the company. Most crucially, her existential intelligence comes to the fore. She must be able to think in terms of the broad goals of the company, the ever-changing global landscape, the needs and fears of her workers; and she must be able to create a master narrative that captures these realities and conveys meaning to those who look to her to provide a convincing rationale for their collective enterprise (Fisher & Fisher, 1998; Gardner 1995a, 1999a). As Senge (1992) has remarked, the leader's key task is "continually expanding the capacity to create [the company's] future" (p. 14).

A key strategy for leadership success, which corresponds with this event-to-event assessment and characterization, is the creation of dramatic stories (Gardner, 1995a, 2004b). Although obviously language based, stories have a structure that can contain information that can appeal to and be processed by most of the other intelligences: existential themes, bodily action, interpersonal dialogue, intrapersonal reflection, spatial settings, logical progression, and musical pacing. As the world learned during the Hollywood century, stories can be conveyed through many means and many media.

Conclusion

MI theory has implications that extend well beyond the educational realm. It can help individuals, teams, and organizations use human capital more effectively in an ever more complex environment. To begin with, different jobs call for different intellectual strengths, intelligence profiles, and intellectual relations to coworkers. This information is crucial both for the individual worker and for those who are in charge of an enterprise. More explicit recognition and understanding of interaction of the various intelligences—as bottlenecks, compensators, and/or catalysts—can help increase employee productivity and perhaps satisfaction. Intrapersonal intelligence—or knowing our own strengths, weaknesses, and biases—is key in almost any job, and certainly in having a successful career over time.

Intelligence profiles can also be applied at the team and organizational level to see how different workers can constrain, compensate for, or catalyze each other. Whether in the course of interviewing, checking references, or engaging in day-to-day teamwork, awareness that everyone has different profiles might ease tensions and help learning. For example, individuals with strikingly different profiles can work together effectively and synergistically as long as they know how to "translate" ideas into each other's "native medium." Or they can produce disastrous results if they can't step outside their own strengths and weaknesses to see other possible ways of being in the world and processing information. Managers and leaders need to be cognizant of these potentials; they can best catalyze positive potentials if they have a keen understanding of their own intellectual proclivities, the needs of the current era, and the ways in which to inspire those over whom they exercise control.

Finally, on a wider scale, creating and planning the types of work available and desired by a culture—not only immediately but a generation or more in the future—will allow a longer-term perspective on the development and deployment of intelligences for the broader benefit of society.

Right now, our schools and training programs, which still emphasize language and logical-mathematical intelligences to the exclusion of almost all else, overproduce certain skills for the jobs available (Gardner, 1983b). What kind of society do we want? What kinds of intelligences, in what combinations, will create such a society? How can we best develop those intelligences across individuals' lifetimes and even from one generation to succeeding ones? As we seek to answer these questions, we can help channel the biopsychological potentials of intelligences in desirable social-historical directions (Gardner, Csikszentmihalyi, & Damon, 2001).

Chapter 13

THE FUTURE

An anniversary provides an occasion to stand back, survey the terrain, attempt to make sense of what has happened since the original event, and anticipate possible futures. In the case of the theory of multiple intelligences, forecasting the scene in 2030 or 2040 may be as challenging as it would have been to anticipate the scene of 2005 back in 1980. Still, some of the suggestions put forth here may help guide researchers and practitioners who work with the theory in the years ahead.

In these concluding remarks, I begin with a sketch of the phases in the study of intelligence, as I have come to think of them. I then take a look over time at the various audiences that have found MI theory of interest in the United States and abroad. Finally, I describe the lines of work that I expect will be undertaken in the future, under the aegis of MI theory.

EIGHT PHASES IN THE STUDY OF INTELLIGENCE

1. Lay Conceptions

Until 1900, the word "intelligence" was used by ordinary individuals to describe their own mental powers and those of other persons. Like most lay terms, the characterizations "intelligent," "smart," and "clever" were used unreflectively. Thus, in the West, a person was spoken of as smart if he or she was quick, or quick-witted, or capable of mastering and remembering a large amount of material. In non-Western societies, the word "intelligent" (or the closest equivalent) might be used to denote persons who were good listeners, obedient, moral, or wise. No formal efforts were undertaken to determine whether those considered "bright" by one individual or group would be so considered by others.

2. The Scientific Turn

In a sequence of events that I've chronicled in earlier chapters, the crucial event in the history of study of intelligence occurred at the beginning of the twentieth century. French psychologist Alfred Binet responded to a request from the authorities in Paris to create a measure that would predict which students were likely to need special attention in school. In effect, Binet created the first intelligence test, which soon gave rise to the concept of IQ. Binet's work was supported by cognate efforts in Europe, particularly in Britain and Germany, and soon spread to the United States, where standardized tests of intelligence were created. By the 1920s, intelligence tests were ensconced in the educational landscape of the United States and a number of other countries. In general, this work supported a view of intelligence as singular, strongly influenced by hereditary, and susceptible to measurement by a brief intervention.

Work on such mental measurement instruments continues today, among both those who accept the traditional g view of intelligence and those, like me, who are critical of it. Efforts to create paper-and-pencil tests are being supplemented by computer-administered measures as well as efforts to measure intelligence through neuroscientific and genetic means. Progress on a theory of human intelligence has not been notable among those who favor the traditional view.

3. The Pluralization of Intelligence

Although Binet did not take a position on the number and types of intellect, most of his contemporaries and successors chose to believe that intelligence was a single construct that could be adequately measured by a brief test. However, for some time a minority of researchers have been sympathetic to the view that human beings possess a number of intelligences, which are relatively independent of one another and which merit separate assessment. Typically these researchers based their assertion on the statistical technique of factor analysis, a form of correlational analysis that indicates which sets of items in a test "hang together" and which ought to be considered as distinct from one another. Among the researchers who embraced this pluralistic view were L. L. Thurstone (1938) and J. P. Guilford

(1967). Others, dating back to Charles Spearman (1904), take a hierarchical view of intellect that posits an overarching general factor as well as specific factors aligned in subsidiary positions (Carroll, 1993; Thomson, 1939; Vernon, 1971).

As outlined in earlier chapters, my theory of multiple intelligences differs from these psychometric efforts. Rather than creating a series of items and subjecting them to factor analysis, I instead surveyed an ensemble of research literatures spanning evolutionary biology, neuroscience, anthropology, and psychology. I defined an intelligence as an information-processing potential to solve problems or create products that are valued in at least one culture. I laid out a set of criteria for what counts as an intelligence and applied it to various candidate capacities. At present, I believe that human beings possess eight or nine relatively separate intelligences, each of which undoubtedly is itself composed of a number of separate subcapacities.

Much of the criticism of MI theory within psychology derives from the unorthodox way in which I have identified the intelligences; critics would have been mollified if I had developed tests for each intelligence and demonstrated their psychometric independence. Scattered evidence exists for the relative autonomy of intelligences, but the major scientific work on the plurality of intellect remains to be done.

4. The Contextualization of Intelligence

Most psychologists, including me, have a propensity to think of intellect as an attribute of the individual mind, indeed, the individual brain. This position has merit inasmuch as human intellect cannot be conceived of as independent of a mind or brain in which that intellect is exercised.

However, researchers have recently called attention to aspects of intellect that are best construed as external to the individual thinker; these scholars refer to the contextualization of intelligence. Even if the intellectual potential of a human being is contained inside his or her genome, the way in which it will be expressed, and the extent to which it is expressed, will depend on the culture in which the person happens to be born and the experiences that he or she happens to have within that culture.

A vivid example is the case of Bobby Fischer, probably the most gifted chess player of the twentieth century. Clearly, Fischer had the potential to become a great chess player—and others may have that potential as well. For Bobby Fischer's chess career, however, it was fortunate that he happened to be born in the United States at a certain time, that he had the opportunity to learn the rules of chess when he was young, and that the time and resources were available so that he could become a master at an early age. Fischer could not have invented the game of chess—it took hundreds of years for chess to develop. And it is not at all clear that Fischer would have emerged as a great talent in another game—say, bridge or Go—or in another pursuit, say, politics, business, or physics. Indeed, events in Fischer's life after he attained global fame as a chess champion suggest that he is something of a misfit in every activity except the game of chess. As we argue in chapter 11, intelligence or intelligences are always an interaction between biological proclivities and the opportunities for learning that exist in a culture.

This perspective is useful for considering a recent controversy—whether women have less aptitude in science. Empirically, there is no question that there have been fewer scientists, and fewer great scientists, among women than among men. While there is presumably no specific potential to be a scientist (a purely cultural category), there may be differing potentials to master spatial or logical reasoning. Even if women proved less skilled on average at one or another form of reasoning, however, it would be a huge leap to infer that the limits were genetic or that they constrained scientific achievement. Women have fewer role models in science; they are often discouraged from pursuing science; the decision to pursue science may be confounded with many other factors, ranging from motivation to win prizes to willingness to neglect one's children. We could not determine women's suitability for science unless these and other relevant factors were controlled for—just as we could not determine whether there are any racial differences in intelligence unless we lived in a truly color-blind society.

5. The Distribution of Intelligence

Closely related to, but distinct from, the notion that intelligence must be contextualized is the contention that intelligence should be thought of as distributed. The term "distribute" denotes the claim that intelligence is best thought of as extending beyond the skin of the individual. Specifically, one's intellect is not simply the ideas and skills that the individual has obtained and can access him- or herself. Rather, one's intellectual facility depends equally, and perhaps especially, on the various material and human resources to which the person has access.

Starting close to home, consider someone like me who is writing a book about intelligence. From one perspective, inasmuch as I am the acknowledged author, the ideas and skills are mine. And yet, left completely to my own devices, I would find this task onerous indeed, if not impossible. On the one hand, I depend on all kinds of material resources, such as notes, pencils, computer files, the Internet, and so on. On the other hand, I depend equally on all kinds of human resources, ranging from the experts whom I consult on various issues to my outstanding student Seana Moran, who conducts research on various topics, critiques my manuscript, and carries out various other important tasks, sometimes in cooperation with my extremely able assistant Lindsay Pettingill. And once the manuscript leaves our Cambridge office, many persons connected with the publishing and marketing of the books take over the birthing process.

The work undertaken at Project Zero illustrates our commitment to the contextualization and distribution of intelligence. In Project Spectrum (chapter 6), the provision of a rich environment is a necessary step for evoking and developing the several intelligences of the young child—a dramatic demonstration of contextualization. In the project work at the Key Learning Community (chapter 7) and in the portfolios and processfolios featured in Arts PROPEL (chapter 9), we see at work the role played by material resources (such as works of art and video recording equipment) and by human resources (such as supportive teachers and critical peers) in bringing a complex project through to completion.

6. The Individualization of Intelligence

The further we move from a unitary view of intellect in which each person can be represented by a point on a single bell curve, the more apparent it becomes that each individual has a unique intellectual configuration. Indeed, thanks to neuroimaging, we now know that even identical twins use different brain (and mental) resources in attacking the same problem. Just as we look different from one another and have different personalities and temperament, so, too, do we each have different kinds of minds (Levine, 2002).

Confirmation of the uniqueness of each intellect is fascinating from an observer's perspective and challenging to the teacher and the parent. Life is more interesting when each person's mind is unique; and that diversity probably contributes to the robustness of the species (Gould, 1989). However, the uniqueness of minds poses a challenge to those charged with education and nurturance. We must decide how much effort to devote to a determination of the particular configuration of each person, and how to use such information. In a totalitarian society, differences are overlooked or condemned, and efforts are undertaken to make nearly all individuals into carbon copies of one another. The leading apparat controls the context totally, including the resources to which individuals are exposed. However, such an option cannot, or at least should not, be pursued in a democratic society.

7. The Education of Intelligence

Until this point, the phases of intelligence have been largely descriptive; they have not contained within them any imperative. Once one begins to speak of differences across persons, however, the issues surrounding action become patent. Should we cultivate differences among individuals? Should we tolerate them? Or, as in a totalitarian society, should we attempt as much as possible to eradicate these differences and produce a society of clones or, perhaps, a "brave new world" featuring a hierarchy of types of clones?

In this book, I have taken a strong position on the education of intelligences, a position that is avowedly progressive. In my view, psychologists have spent way too much time assessing individuals and not nearly enough time helping them. In the past fifty years, education policy in societies all over the world has undergone an enormous shift. No longer is the purpose of education simply to pick out those students who are intelligent, on one or another definition, and give them special access to higher education. Rather, the purpose of education now is to educate an entire population, for we cannot afford to waste any minds.

And so we face the question of how best to educate a diverse population. We could attempt to minimize the differences among individuals—and this option has typically been followed in East Asian societies with notable success. But I call for a contrasting approach—what I have termed individual-centered education. The assumption here is that individuals have different profiles of abilities; they and the society will be better off if those individual proclivities are honored and nurtured rather than ignored or minimized.

How to educate individuals so that each develops his or her potential to the fullest is still largely a mystery. (Interestingly, the grant from the Bernard Van Leer Foundation that funded my initial research on MI theory was designed explicitly to discover the range of human potentials). I hope that in the preceding chapters I have identified some promising paths.

8. *The Humanization of Intelligence*

According to the analogies introduced above, the several human intelligences can be thought of as separate computers or separate muscles. It is up to us how we use these computers, how we develop these muscles. A computer can be used to compute targets for battle or to plan a campaign to eradicate disease; one's muscles can be used to rescue a drowning person or to slug someone in the course of an argument. As a student of intelligence, my job has been to figure out how these intelligences work, whether or not I happen to approve of how particular individuals use any particular intelligence.

In recent years, however, I have turned my energies to the uses to which human beings put their capacities. Working with my close colleagues Mihaly Csikszentmihalyi and William Damon and collaborators at several universities, I have been exploring the nature of "good work"—work that is at once excellent in quality and also socially responsible. We have been trying to understand how individuals who wish to carry out ethical and excellent work proceed at a time when things are changing very rapidly (thanks in part to technology), when market forces are very powerful, and when few if any forces can counter the dominance of the market (see Gardner, Csikszentmihalyi, & Damon, 2001; goodworkproject.org).

Earlier in this volume (chapter 2), I questioned the existence of a moral intelligence. I don't think that, in themselves, intelligences are moral or immoral. It is the *ends* to which intelligences are put that involve goals and values. I still believe this to be the case. But I contend that the challenge for society in the future is not simply to produce individuals who are intelligent, or more intelligent, however defined. Rather, it is to yoke our intellectual capacities to a sense of ethical responsibility—in short, to humanize intelligence. In whatever time I have left in my own professional life, that is the goal toward which my own work will be directed.

AUDIENCES FOR MI THEORY

When I committed myself in the early 1980s to write a 400-page, rather technical book (*Frames of Mind*), I thought that it would be of interest primarily to psychologists. Indeed, I thought that my audience would be largely developmental psychologists, who were my closest colleagues within psychology, and, to a lesser extent, neuropsychologists and cognitive psychologists, with whom I had recently been working. While there was some interest among colleagues, particularly those with whom I had personal relations, the book did not have much of an audience among psychologists, to whom it seemed somewhat exotic—and among psychometricians, as I noted earlier, the book aroused antipathy. Psychometricians, who were basically wedded to a singular or hierarchical model of the intellect, did not find convincing my assertion that human beings instead have several relatively autonomous intelligences. They did not like the excursion to personal forms of intelligence. And they were particularly unable to accept an approach based on the synthesis of various kinds of information from different disciplines. Quoting early researchers, they believed that "intelligence is what the tests test." Naturally, they looked to the psychometric evidence for support or refutation of my "speculations."

I should add, as an aside, that MI theory has not encountered hostility in the areas of brain science or computer science. Lacking a commitment to a "singular" view of intelligence, researchers in these traditions have found the idea of multiple intelligences intriguing if not convincing (Damasio, 2003; Posner, 2004). Indeed, as a highly differentiated and modularized view of the brain has gained in persuasiveness, MI theory has seemed a natural, if somewhat general, fit (Geary, 2005; Pinker, 1997; Tooby & Cosmides, 1990).

I had never assumed that the principal audience of MI theory would be educators, and its principal applications in classrooms, first in the United States and gradually in other parts of the world. This reaction, which has continued to this day, surprised me. I can point to certain trends, which could be idiosyncratic, although for me they are revealing (Gardner, 2004a).

Initially, three groups were drawn to the theory. Probably first were special educators—those who deal with children who are outside the mainstream in schools. Sometimes these educators worked with students who had specific learning abilities—those with selective problems in reading, in mathematics, or, less frequently, in understanding other persons. Daily, these educators observed firsthand the jagged intelligence profiles of their students, and they were challenged somehow to get these children through school. MI theory spoke to them loudly, clearly, convincingly.

On the other end of the special education spectrum were those involved in education of the gifted and talented. Here there was a mixed, almost bimodal reaction. On the one hand, those who had been calling for a broader definition of gifted and talented (Marland, 1972; Renzulli, 1988) found sustenance in the delineation of multiple talents and the recognition of certain nonscholastic abilities. Early efforts were made to develop assessments of some of the noncanonical intelligences (Kornhaber, 1997; Maker & Nielson, 1996). Yet, among those of a psychometric leaning, there was extreme unease with the theory. For much of the gifted establishment, the high IQ is sacrosanct—it is one's ticket to membership in Mensa and ever more exalted heights. Anything seen as a challenge to IQ was a threat to be eliminated. And so some of the earliest interest in MI theory was among individuals who wanted to expunge it.

A second group attracted early to the theory were teachers and administrators in independent (private) schools. I think that this attraction occurred for three reasons. First, educators in this group are more likely to track new research, to read the book review press, and to see themselves as members of the "chattering classes." (When I travel abroad, I am much more likely to be invited to international or independent schools than to government schools.) Second, relatively free of government control, these schools have the luxury of carrying out experiments, including ones based on MI theory. Third, youngsters sent to independent schools are more likely to need and desire individual attention—because they have either special gifts or special problems. The classes are smaller, and teachers are expected to attend to each child, whose parents are spending considerable sums. MI ideas are more readily understood and adopted when one is working with ten to fifteen members in a class than when one has a class of thirty, fifty, or even more pupils.

The third group attracted to the theory in its early years were those who work with young children—primary grades, kindergarten, preschool. For children at those levels, the heavy scholastic curriculum has not yet been imposed—or at least had not been imposed in the 1980s. Teachers of these young students are more developmentally oriented, they value play and exploration, and they have latitude in how they set up their classrooms spatially and temporally. Many already had richly stocked classrooms (the children's museum model) that featured learning or play centers. There was less of a stretch to embrace MI ideas, and more of a feeling that they were already carrying out education that was "MI" in spirit, even if the terms and the taxonomy were not familiar.

Although these three groups were the first to be drawn to MI theory, interest soon spread to wider circles. In each case, there was a fairly predictable order of interest and, to some extent, endorsement. While MI first was attractive to special educators, it soon became of interest to mainstream educators. While MI was first attractive to educators in independent schools, it became of interest to those in the public sector as well. And while MI was first attractive to those who work with young children, it gradually spread to older age groups as well.

A word on this "trickle-up" phenomenon. While I cannot provide exact figures, I can state the following trend with confidence. MI first was of interest to those working in the preschool and primary grades, then to those in middle school, then to those in high schools and community colleges that address diverse and underserved populations. By the 1990s, I was getting many inquiries about MI theory from secondary schools and colleges (Coreil, 2003; Diaz-Lefebvre et al., 1998; Weber, 2005). I noticed, however, that the inquiries tended to come from schools with a diverse, often multiracial population, one that exhibited various learning difficulties. These institutions were looking for any kind of help they could get with these challenging populations, and they saw MI theory as a possible aid. Also of note is that those involved in adult education, particularly with populations that had received little formal education, found MI a promising entry point and tool (Kallenbach & Viens, 2004).

By implication, then, I have identified the educational institutions that have shown the least interest in MI ideas. These are institutions that are highly selective—so they can choose the most scholastically gifted—and that follow a standard academic curriculum. They might well say, "If it ain't broke, don't fix it." Within these ranks I would certainly place my own university, Harvard, whose leadership was central in the development of IQ and SAT instruments and continues to value them today. Nonetheless, leaders of the admissions department at Harvard College often cite MI theory, and I do not believe they do so disingenuously. Harvard is interested in having an intellectually and culturally diverse student body, and so its admissions officers are on the lookout for potential students who stand out in the various intelligences—providing that there is evidence that they can handle the workload.

What of interest beyond educational institutions? MI theory has proved an easy sell to museums and other cultural institutions. Lacking a captive audience, these institutions are interested in providing activities and exhibitions that will attract a diverse public and encourage return visits. MI theory has been especially attractive to children's and other hands-on museums all over the world, many of which have mounted exhibitions on multiple intelligences or built their exhibitions around the different intelligences. But even in arts museums, MI ideas have had appeal because of the notion of different entry points to the same object (chapter 8). Materials suited to art museums have been developed by my colleague Jessica Davis (1996).

It is worth noting that MI ideas have in the past decade come to the attention of leaders and managers of businesses. Part of this interest stems from the widespread attention being paid to emotional intelligence, thanks to the pathbreaking writings of Daniel Goleman (1995, 1998). The interest also comes from the need to attract, maintain, and develop a diverse workforce, one that may not conform to the standard scholastic model of intellect. Other applications of MI theory, too, including the use of portfolios and the presentation of key ideas in multiple formats, have also proved attractive to businesspersons both in the United States and elsewhere.

Finally, a steady stream of books and articles about MI appear throughout the world. In most cases, I have little to do with these publications, although I do notice their accumulation on Internet search engines. An author gets a special rise when his ideas are featured "off the book page." MI theory has been featured in novels (by Richard Powers), television programs (*ER*), double crostic puzzles (*New York Times*), examinations of the intellect of horses (by Jane Smiley), and the popular board game *Cranium*, among other loci.

MI TOURS THE WORLD

Whatever its merits and demerits, MI theory has been generous to me. Responding to those who want to hear more about the theory from its originator, I have had the opportunity to visit many different states and to travel to many other nations. It has been fascinating to discover the ways in which the theory has been interpreted and the activities that it has catalyzed. In preparation for this book, I took notes for a year and a half—May 2004 to November 2005—on some of the intriguing things that I learned as I toured the geographical and the virtual worlds on the MI bandwagon.

Different Messages

Before visiting China in 2004, I had no idea how popular MI theory had become. In 2002 there was an MI conference in Beijing attended by over 2500 educators from nine provinces and seven countries, including Taiwan. There were seven plenary presentations by noted educators and 187 papers accepted for presentation. My colleague Zhilong Shen estimates that more than 100 books on MI have been published in Chinese.

In Shanghai I asked an English-speaking journalist if she could explain the great popularity of the theory in her country. "It is quite simple," she said. "In the United States, when people hear about multiple intelligences, they think about the special genius of their child—her unique configuration of intelligences, the potential that should be developed. In China, it is quite different. If there are eight separate intelligences, that is now eight things that all of our children need to become good in."

A Healthy Start

In Macau, I received a tour of the island from Mr. U. The next morning, he picked me up for my presentation at the Education Ministry. "Look what my wife picked up yesterday at the grocery store," he said. He showed me a multicolored flyer that depicted each of the intelligences on a separate leaf. The flyer, replete with illustrations, charts, and figures, was an advertisement for Frisogrow processed milk (see p. 246). The consumer was informed, "If you drink our milk, you will develop each of the different intelligences." Never before had it occurred to me that the MI in the theory might stand for MIlk!

Strange Bedfellows

Shortly after my visit to Macau, Mr. U. traveled to North Korea. In Pyongyang he visited the library and found only two books in English. One was the social critic Michael Moore's *Stupid White Men* (2004). The other was my 1983 book, *Frames of Mind: The Theory of Multiple Intelligences.*

The Project Zero Mosaic

At Project Zero, the research group I have been affiliated with for almost forty years, we have focused on education for understanding. Some of the project's work has involved the use of MI curricula and assessments in order to enhance student understanding. The combination of these thrusts has been featured in various American schools, such as the Ross School in East Hampton, Long Island, and Glendale Community College in Glendale, Arizona.

I was pleased to see similar efforts abroad. At the Montserrat School in Barcelona and at the MI International Foundation School in Philippines, I saw impressive integration of MI ideas under a rubric of education for understanding. And in the National College of Ireland in Dublin, President Joyce O'Connor has brought tertiary education to a previously underserved

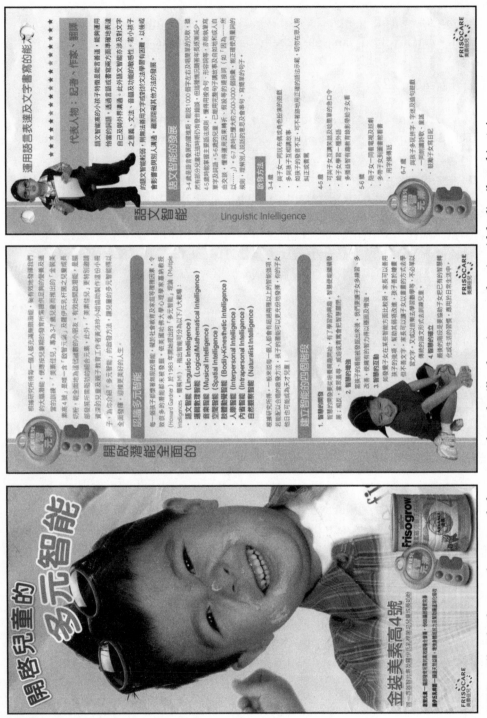

MI in milk: The front and two panels from a condensed milk advertisement that is widely distributed in Asia.

population, making use of ideas of understanding, multiple intelligences, and alternative assessment that were developed at Project Zero.

Multiple Intelligences and Good Work

After the development of MI theory and its various offshoots, my principal scholarly work has been the study of "good work"—work that is both excellent and ethical. For the most part, these two lines of investigation have been pursued independently of one another in my work. But on recent trips I encountered impressive combinations of these themes.

In Bangkok, Thailand, at the Concordian School, young students are taught three quite distinctive languages—Thai, Chinese, and English. It is a daunting challenge. Also featured at this school is an effort to develop the several intelligences and to inculcate virtues of responsibility, integrity, and trust. Conversations with Thai businessmen and with the revered Crown Princess of Thailand convinced me that the themes of internationalism, diversity, and ethics were a concern of the nation and that the idea of multiple intelligences might be catalytic in pursuing these themes.

In the Philippines, I spent a week with Mary Jo Abaquin, head of the MI International Foundation School. She mounted an impressive MI conference, bringing together educators from all over the Philippines as well as other countries in the Asia-Pacific region. At the conclusion of the conference, she presented awards to eight outstanding Philippine citizens. These persons stood out in a particular intelligence and had used their intelligences in ways that were ethical and humane—for example, a musician who worked with children in poverty and a naturalist who was trying to preserve the environment. The awardee in the interpersonal category was Corazon Aquino, the "People Power" president, who now runs an educational foundation. I was moved to see this pioneering effort to bring together the themes of multiple intelligences and good work.

Hot Topic

I had known for some years that educators in Denmark were interested in multiple intelligences. But I had not been aware of heated debates in the press about whether MI ideas were appropriate to introduce in classrooms. I was asked to weigh in on the side of MI. As I mentioned in chapter 4, the Schools Minister in the United Kingdom credited a rise in test scores to teachers' greater consciousness of the multiple intelligences of children. Again, this statement evoked considerable discussion among pundits. And in France, slow to respond to the idea of multiple intelligences, the prestigious newspaper *Le Monde* devoted a supplement to the question: "Why has multiple intelligences not had the influence in France that it has in other countries?"

Corporate World

As mentioned earlier, MI ideas are beginning to be used in business settings. In Colombia, I encountered Gerardo Gonzalez, CEO of Skandia International, a financial management company. Gonzalez gave a powerful cognitive analysis of corporate culture. He then drew on multiple intelligences theory to explain the ways in which one might change the theories, stories, and skills represented among the employees of a multinational corporation. According to him, it is necessary to present the desired change in culture in as many media and formats as possible, thus using the idea of "multiple representations" and "multiple entry points" that I expounded in chapter 8.

Recommendations, Regulations, and Legislation

Coming from a country where policymakers are loath to discuss multiple intelligences, I have been amazed to learn of jurisdictions in which the terminology of MI has been incorporated into white papers, recommendations by ministries, and even legislation. Although I have rarely seen the actual wording of the documents, I have heard from reliable sources that MI approaches are part of the policy landscape in such diverse lands as Australia, Bangladesh, Canada, China, Denmark, Ireland, and the Netherlands. A project undertaken by the European Union, called the Leonardo Project, has also featured MI ideas.

MI in All Its Glory

In August 2005 I had the pleasure of visiting Danfoss Universe, a brand-new facility near Sonderberg in southwestern Denmark. Danfoss Universe is a new kind of multipurpose venue that includes a traditional museum honoring the family that founded the facility, the Icelandic pavilion from the World Exhibition 2000, a conference center, a series of life-sized exhibits that allow hands-on learning in science, engineering, and technology, and ample park facilities for families to enjoy when the weather is nice.

For me, the main attraction of Danfoss Universe is the Explorama. This museum-sized facility houses approximately fifty ingenious original exhibits. Each has been explicitly designed so as to activate and foreground one or more specific human intelligences. For example, a linguistic exhibit features the learning of words in Japanese. Visitors imitate a word or phrase they hear and then see a visual representation of their vocalization; this representation is superimposed over the correct sound spectrum, that of a native speaker, so that visitors can assess the accuracy of their successive imitations. In another exhibit, visitors can create melodies on a theremin by moving their hands. Other exhibits tap bodily capacities (fine body movements, for example, and balancing oneself alone or with others), spatial abilities, and cooperative capacities. Among the most ingenious exhibits are Teambot, in which participants must work together to move an object held by a robot from one locus to another, and Mindball, in which two players wearing electrode-equipped headbands must attempt to lower their stress levels so that certain brain waves, converted by a computer, can be used to move a Ping-Pong ball into the other player's region.

The Explorama is the most authentic display of MI theory at work that I have ever seen. It is hard to imagine anyone—whether aged six or sixty—spending any time at the facility without gaining fresh insights into how one's own mind works and the ways in which the minds of others work differently. Visitors also have a wonderful opportunity to tap their intrapersonal intelligence. They can complete a set of questions that allow them to describe their profile of intelligences at the outset, before visiting the exhibits. Then, after spending time going through the facilities, they can respond again to the questions and see whether their own insights about themselves have been confirmed or called into question by their various performances.

Many people have attempted to devise tests of the multiple intelligences, and although their efforts have by no means been in vain, I feel that the Explorama's tapping of intelligences reaches a level of authenticity and excellence that has not been equaled. I wish that everyone interested in MI ideas could visit the Explorama. Since not everyone can make the trip, it would be great if Exploramas could be created elsewhere and if some of the exhibits could be made available interactively online—both options that may well come to pass.

A New Kind of Library

The New City School in St. Louis is one of the best of the schools that are based significantly on the idea of multiple intelligences, and it was one of the first to apply MI concepts (nearly two decades ago). In December 2005 I had the opportunity to revisit the school and to cut the ribbon for the first multiple intelligences library (to our knowledge) in the world. Initially the term MI library might sound like an oxymoron because libraries suggest a hegemony of books and hence of only one or two intelligences. Indeed, the MI library is generously stocked with books, both for children and for interested parents and adults. The books are organized with an eye toward the intelligences implied by their content. But what makes the library distinctive is its provision of a variety of learning environments in which children can exhibit and develop various intelligences—areas for drawing and three-dimensional construction; for creations in film and digital media; for theatrical performances; for musical explorations; for group work for children as well as comfortable areas in which adults can sit, relax, have a cup of coffee, and read alone or with their children. The library is even open on weekends, when others in the community can use it. During my visit, I met people from Norway and from Alaska who told me that, before long, the New City School library would not be the only MI library in the world.

They Got There First—Schools

For almost twenty-five years, I have been an enthusiastic supporter of the remarkable preschools of Reggio Emilia in Northern Italy (see chapter 5). Our respective groups at Reggio and Project Zero have exchanged ideas, materials, and visits for many years. In 1996, we undertook a large-scale collaboration with Reggio Children focusing particularly on issues of group learning and documentation of learning. This collaboration culminated in *Making Learning Visible: Children as Individual and Group Learners* (Guidici, Rinaldi, & Krechevsky, 2001). Reggio has used the evocative banner "The Hundred Languages of Children." While we share many of the same educational goals and enthusiasms, it is important to note that Reggio had developed most of its ideas and practices before becoming familiar with MI ideas. Project Zero's principal contribution has been to articulate, and to provide something of a theoretical rationale for, the indispensable example of the thirty-three schools in Reggio.

They Got There First—Ideas

In addition to these firsthand observations, I also benefit from correspondents in various lands. From Ireland, Brian McEnery introduced me to the idea of *duchas*—forty different modes of intelligence that were identified in early Celtic history. From India, Vasanthi Thiagarajan has told me about the ten heads of Ravan. Each of the first nine heads represents a different intelligence that can be yoked to my proposed intelligences. The tenth is the intelligence that is "beyond intelligence—the intelligence of nonexistence."

LINES OF FURTHER STUDY AND PRACTICE

Identification and Delineation of Intelligences

Once the idea of multiple intelligences had been articulated, it was as if the genie had been released from the bottle. Writers and practitioners from various domains have since proposed a whole smorgasbord of intelligences, including financial intelligence, moral intelligence, spiritual intelligence, emotional intelligence, and sexual intelligence, just to name a few. Not surprisingly, I am comfortable with an expanded notion of intelligence. My major strictures are that there need to be criteria for an intelligence (otherwise, anything goes) and that intelligences need to be described independently of how they should be used (otherwise, description is confounded with prescription).

From my vantage point, the most important inputs for this endeavor will be from the biological sciences. As we learn more about the development and functioning of the human brain, we will be able to identify those capacities that are hardwired into the nervous system as well as those that are relatively plastic—more flexible, more susceptible to experiences. We will also know how neurological structures and functioning differ from the norm in people who exhibit unusual performances and unusual profiles. Similarly, as we come to identify the roles of various genes and gene complexes, this information will serve as another constraint on how we describe human capacities. Genetic studies are likely to reveal whether specific intellectual strengths, such as musical or spatial intelligence, are under the control of specific genes or gene complexes. Studies of identical and fraternal twins reared together and apart will enhance our understanding of the extent to which different intellectual profiles are heritable and modifiable.

I am reasonably certain that twenty-five years from now, our thinking about the nature and boundaries of various intelligences will be highly differentiated and quite different from our conceptions today. Biological evolution proceeds in its own way, which defies both logic and the categories offered by common sense. But I am confident that the idea of multiple intelligences will survive. That is because, whatever evidence may accrue to support notions of "general intelligence," we still need to account for the vast differences across individuals and for the variegated profiles of strengths and weaknesses. Both these phenomena require an accounting in terms of multiple intelligences. Moreover, by that future date, we may well know whether it makes sense to speak of a separate existential intelligence, perhaps lodged deep in the temporal lobes.

So much for "wetware," as human brain functioning is sometimes called. Intelligences are computational mechanisms; work in the "dryware" computer realm is likely to enhance our understandings as well. While we cannot carry out certain kinds of experiments on human beings (a state of affairs for which we should be grateful), it is possible to model various intellectual capacities on paper and in computer simulations, and through such modeling it is possible to determine which tasks can be carried out with one kind of mechanism, which can be carried out with other mechanisms, and which might require a combination of mechanisms or even a new kind of mechanism. Such simulations will provide another invaluable lens on the organization of the mind, the extent to which it is best modeled through a variety of mental modules, and how best to describe these modules.

The Nurturance and Education of Intelligences

Of course, computational studies and the biological sciences may not be restricted to the identification and modeling of human intelligences. They may also enhance them in various ways. Computers may be used to teach materials in a multiplicity of ways. They can serve as prostheses, enhancing capacities that may be compromised in certain people. Thus, for example, computers can enhance bodily-kinesthetic capacities in those who are physically handicapped, or they can display and manipulate geometric images for those whose spatial capacities are impoverished. They can also allow people to simulate experiences that are too difficult or too expensive—or impossible—to enact in a classroom—such as an expedition to a remote time or a distance place.

My guess is that the best educational interventions will continue to come from ingenious educators using simple materials and their wits. Famed mathematics educator Robert Moses (2001) teaches algebra to seventh and eighth graders in Boston, drawing on their knowledge of the Boston public transportation system. Educator Annick Winokur has coined the term *sportsometry* to describe how she teaches mathematical and spatial reasoning through studying the bounces of a basketball (Garriga, 2004). Physics teacher Walter Smith, at Haverford, has set up a Web site (www.physicssongs.org) that features musical fragments that have proved effective in conveying concepts in physics to college students (Conkey, 2005).

The Power of Ideas

The original title for my first book on MI, *Frames of Mind*, was *The Idea of Multiple Intelligences*. I still like this title because "multiple intelligences" is basically an idea—a seemingly simple one that turns out to be unsettling, provocative, even radical. Even now, after twenty-five years, it is still difficult for me to embrace it totally and to reject the hegemonic idea of a single intelligence. At the start of the twenty-first century, the idea of a single, one-dimensional intelligence holds sway, at least in most of the Western world. Critics of MI would say that is because the unitary view is essentially correct; I would say it is because it is so difficult to dislodge a concept once it has been entrenched in language and thinking.

No one understood this point better than the great economist John Maynard Keynes. In a famous passage, he observed: "The ideas of economists and political philosophers, both when they are right and when they are wrong, are more powerful than is commonly understood. Indeed, the world is ruled by little else. Practical men, who believe themselves to be quite exempt from any intellectual influences, are usually the slaves of some defunct economist" (Keynes, 1935, p. 383). Even more pointedly, Keynes once remarked: "The real difficulty in changing any enterprise lies not in developing new ideas but in escaping from the old ones" (Keynes, 1935, p. viii).

In attempting to change the minds of persons, the scholar (or the activist) has available a number of levers (Gardner, 2004b). These range from the scholar's tools of reason and research, to the powerful person's ability to manipulate rewards and punishments, to the teacher's capacity to take advantage of real-world events and to appear resonant, likable, and trustworthy. Attempts to change minds, however, are unlikely to succeed in the long run unless the people behind them are aware of and able to counter the many resistances others may have to the idea in question. As Keynes notes, the old ideas are difficult to scuttle.

As a scholar seeking to popularize an idea, I have used a variety of levers but have relied largely on reason and research. On their own, these levers may throw doubt on the traditional view of intelligence, but they seldom suffice to reach a "tipping point" (Gladwell, 2000). I have found that people are likely to become converts to MI theory on the basis of more personal experiences: being able to think of themselves or someone they love in a new way, or seeing a new way of teaching, or learning to succeed where others have failed. Even then, however, the old idea or theory rarely disappears entirely. In the best circumstance, a new paradigm is more likely to be adopted by the next generation, which is less under the sway of the old idea and finds the new idea to be the more natural one—resulting in what historian of science Thomas Kuhn (1962) calls a paradigm shift.

I frequently see this struggle taking place between the old and the new views of intellect. One day I read in the newspaper that a convict in Virginia may be executed because his IQ has risen from 59 in 1998 to 74 in 2005 (Liptak, 2005). What a way to make a decision, I groan. Another day I read that an excellent secondary school teacher of diesel engineering in Ohio is being retained even though he has failed a written Educational Testing Service test on "principles of effective instructional strategies." In its wisdom, the state of Ohio has decided to declare a moratorium on the use of such tests for vocational educational teachers (Winerip, 2005). That is a step forward; I relax and shrug my shoulders. I hope that your experience with this book has moved you a few steps forward toward a more differentiated, more nuanced view of intelligence, or that it has at least generated a few spirited discussions within yourself or with others.

Appendix A

Acknowledgments

Funders

The work on the theory of multiple intelligences reported in this book was supported by the following organizations:

Atlantic Philanthropies
Carnegie Corporation
William T. Grant Foundation
Lilly Endowment
Markle Foundation
James S. McDonnell Foundation
Rockefeller Brothers Fund
Rockefeller Foundation
Spencer Foundation
Bernard Van Leer Foundation

Collaborators

My thanks go to the following for their assistance with various aspects of this book or the research reported in it:

Tina Blythe
Educational Testing Service

Drew Gitomer
Patricia Graham
Harvard Project Zero
Christian Hassold
Tom Hatch
Mindy Kornhaber
Mara Krechevsky
Jonathan Levy
Kenneth Marantz
Seana Moran
Lindsay Pettingill
Pittsburgh Public School System
Joseph Walters
Margaux Wexberg
Dennie Wolf
Reineke Zessoules

Appendix B

Chapter Credits

Chapter 1. In a Nutshell

The chapter was adapted from: Gardner, H. (1987, May). Developing the spectrum of human intelligences. *Harvard Educational Review, 57* (2), 187–193. Copyright © 1987 by the President and Fellows of Harvard College. All rights reserved. The article was based on an informal talk given on Harvard University's 350th anniversary, September 5, 1986.

Chapter 2. The View After Twenty-five Years

Parts of this chapter were adapted from: Walters, J., & Gardner, H. (1985). The development and education of intelligences. In F. Link (Ed.), *Essays on the intellect* (pp. 1–21). Washington, DC: Curriculum Development Associates. Copyright © 1985 by the Association for Supervision and Curriculum Development. All rights reserved.

Chapter 3. Beyond Intelligence: Other Valued Human Capacities

The chapter was adapted in part from: Gardner, H. (2000). The giftedness matrix: A developmental perspective. In R. Friedman & B. Shore (Eds.), *Talents unfolding: Cognition and development* (pp. 77–88). Washington, DC: American Psychological Association. Based on a paper presented at the Symposium on Giftedness, University of Kansas, Lawrence, KS, February 1992.

CHAPTER 5. FREQUENTLY ASKED
QUESTIONS ABOUT THEORY AND PRACTICE

Some of the questions and answers in this chapter were adapted from: Walters, J., & Gardner, H. (1986). The theory of multiple intelligences: Some issues and answers. In R. Sternberg & R. Wagner (Eds.), *Practical intelligences* (pp. 163–181). New York: Cambridge University Press.

CHAPTER 6. NURTURING
INTELLIGENCES IN EARLY CHILDHOOD

The chapter was adapted from: Krechevsky, M., & Gardner, H. (1990). The emergence and nurturance of multiple intelligences: The Project Spectrum approach. In M.J.A. Howe (Ed.), *Encouraging the development of exceptional skills and talents* (pp. 221–244). Leicester, England: British Psychological Society.

CHAPTER 7. PROJECTS DURING THE ELEMENTARY YEARS

Some of the material in this chapter was adapted from: Gardner, H. (1991). The *unschooled mind: How children learn, and how schools should teach* (pp. 214–219). New York: Basic Books.

CHAPTER 9. DISCIPLINED INQUIRY IN HIGH SCHOOL:
AN INTRODUCTION TO ARTS PROPEL

The chapter was adapted from: Gardner, H. (1996). The assessment of student learning in the arts. In D. Boughton, E. Eisner, & J. Ligtvoet (Eds.), *International perspectives on assessment and evaluation in art education*; and Gardner, H. (1989). Zero-based arts education: An introduction to Arts PROPEL. *Studies in Art Education, 30* (2), 71–83.

CHAPTER 10. ASSESSMENT IN CONTEXT:
THE ALTERNATIVE TO STANDARDIZED TESTING

The chapter was adapted from: Gardner, H. (1991). Assessment in context: The alternative to standardized testing. In B.R. Gifford & M.C. O'Connor (Eds.), *Changing assessments: Alternative views of aptitude, achievement, and instruction* (pp. 77–120). Boston: Kluwer.

CHAPTER 11. SOCIETAL CONTEXTS

The chapter was adapted in part from: Kornhaber, M., Krechevsky, M., & Gardner, H. (1990). Engaging Intelligence. *Educational Psychologist, 25* (3–4), 177–199.

Appendix C

Works Related to Multiple Intelligences

There are many hundreds of books, articles, and other media presentations on MI theory, and no one—myself included—is able to keep up with them. Here I list those of my own writings about MI that are not already listed in the References section of the book. I also include a small set of selected writings and materials by others. At www.howardgardner.com I keep a complete, up-to-date list of materials about MI theory that come to my attention.

Books by Howard Gardner
About Multiple Intelligences

Gardner, H. (1983). *Frames of mind: The theory of multiple intelligences.* New York: Basic Books. Tenth Anniversary Edition with new introduction. New York: Basic Books, 1993. Twentieth Anniversary Edition with new introduction. New York: Basic Books, 2004.

Gardner, H. (1993). *Multiple intelligences: The theory in practice.* New York: Basic Books.

Gardner, H. (1999). *Intelligence reframed: Multiple intelligences for the 21st century.* New York: Basic Books.

Gardner, H. (2006). *The development and education of the mind: The collected works of Howard Gardner.* London: Taylor and Francis.

Selected Works About
Multiple Intelligences Theory

Authored by Howard Gardner

Gardner, H. (1984). The development of competence in culturally-defined domains. In R. Shweder & R. Levine (Eds.), *Culture theory: Essays on mind, self, and emotion.* New York: Cambridge University Press.

Gardner, H. (1985). On discerning new ideas in psychology. *New Ideas in Psychology, 3,* 101–104.

Gardner, H. (1985). Towards a theory of dramatic intelligence. In J. Kase-Polisini (Ed.), *Creative drama in a developmental context.* Lanham, MD: University Press of America.

Gardner, H. (1987). The assessment of intelligences: A neuropsychological perspective. In M. Meier, A. Benton & L. Diller (Eds.), *Neuropsychological rehabilitation.* London: Churchill Publishers.

Gardner, H. (1987). The theory of multiple intelligences. *Annals of Dyslexia, 37,* 19–35.

Gardner, H. (1988). Beyond a modular view of mind. In W. Damon (Ed.), *Child development today and tomorrow* (pp. 222–239). San Francisco: Jossey-Bass. Also in W. Damon (Ed.) (1987), *New directions for child development,* Tenth Anniversary Edition.

Gardner, H. (1988). Challenges for museums: Howard Gardner's theory of multiple intelligences. *Hand to Hand, 2* (4), 1–7. Salt Lake City, UT: Children's Museum Network.

Gardner, H. (1988). Multiple intelligence in today's schools. *Human Intelligence Newsletter, 9* (2), 1–2.

Gardner, H. (1988). The theory of multiple intelligences: Educational implications. In *Language and the world of work in the 21st century.* Boston: Bureau of Transitional Bilingual Education, Massachusetts Department of Education.

Gardner, H. (1989). Intelligences. In K. Jervis and A. Tobler (Eds.), *Education for democracy: Proceedings from the Cambridge School conference on progressive education.* Weston, MA: The Cambridge School. Reprinted in *Putney Post,* Winter 1992, 16–20, 30.

Gardner, H. (1989). *To open minds: Chinese clues to the dilemma of contemporary education.* (Especially chapters 1–4). New York: Basic Books.

Gardner, H. (1990). Building on the range of human strengths. *Churchill Forum, 12* (1), 1, 2, 7.

Gardner, H. (1990). Intelligence in seven steps. In D. Dickinson (Ed.), *Creating the future.* Aston Clinic, England: Accelerated Learning Systems, Inc., pp. 68–75. Also published in *Intelligent connections, 1* (1), Fall 1991, pp. 1, 3, 7, 8; in *Harvard Graduate School of Education Alumni Bulletin, 36* (1), Fall 1991, 17–19. Reprinted in *Provoking Thoughts, 4* (2), 1992.

Gardner, H. (1991). Cognition: A Western perspective. In D. Goleman and R.A.F. Thurman (Eds.), *MindScience: An East-West dialogue* (pp. 75–87). Boston: Wisdom Publications. Based on a paper delivered at *Symposium on Mind Science: The Dialogue Between East and West,* conducted at the Massachusetts Institute of Technology, Cambridge, MA, March 1991.

Gardner, H. (1991). The nature of intelligence. In A. Lewin (Ed.), *How we think and learn* (pp. 41–46). Washington, DC: National Learning Center.

Gardner, H. (1992). From intelligence to intelligences and beyond. *Synapsia: The International Brain Club Journal, 3* (3), 5–8. Paper presented at the Young Presidents' Organization, Boston, 1991.

Gardner, H. (1992). A new edition of *Frames of mind.* In *Developing Human Intelligence. New Horizons for Learning, 13* (1), 10–11.

Gardner, H. (1993). "Choice Points" as multiple intelligences enter the school. *Intelligence Connections, 3* (1).

Gardner, H. (1993). Intelligence and intelligences: Universal principles and individual differences. [An essay on "Diagnosis of Mental Operations and Theory of the Intelligence."] Prepared for festschrift in honor of the 80th birthday of Professor Barbel Inhelder. *Archives de psychologie, 61* (238), 169–172.

Gardner, H. (1993). The "intelligence-giftedness" complex. In H. Rosselli and G. MacLauchlan (Eds.), *Blueprinting for the future.* Proceedings from the *Edyth Bush Symposium on Intelligence,* University of South Florida, Tampa.

Gardner, H. (1993). Les dimensions de l'intelligence spatiale. *MScope revue, 6,* 45–53.

Gardner, H. (1993). Music as Intelligence. *Kodaly Envoy, 20* (1), 14–21.

Gardner, H. (1993). Opening minds. *Demos,* (1), 1–5. Reprinted in: G. Mulgan (Ed.), *Life after politics: New thinking for the twenty-first century* (pp. 101–110). London: Fontana Press, 1997.

Gardner, H. (1993). The relationship between early giftedness and later achievement. *Ciba Conference,* No. 178, pp. 175–186. Chichester, England: John Wiley and Sons. Paper presented at *The Origins and Development of High Ability,* CIBA, London.

Gardner, H. (1993, Winter). The school and the work place of the future. *Synapsia: The International Brain Club Journal,* 22–26.

Gardner, H. (1993). The unschooled mind: Why even the best students in the best schools do not understand. *International Schools Journal, 26,* 29–33. Originally presented as the Alec Peterson Lecture to the International Baccalaureate Conference, Geneva, December 1992. See also *IB World Magazine,* 1993.

Gardner, H. (1994). Are intelligence tests intelligent? In R.H. Ettinger, R.L. Crooks, and J. Stein (Eds.), *Psychology: Science, behavior, and life,* 3rd ed. (pp. 214–221). Fort Worth, TX: Harcourt Brace College Publishers.

Gardner, H. (1994). Entry on multiple intelligences theory. In R. Sternberg (Ed.-in-Chief), *Encyclopedia of human intelligence,* vol. 2 (pp. 740–742). New York: Macmillan.

Gardner, H. (1994). On intelligence. In R.H. Ettinger, R.L. Crooks, and J. Stein (Eds.), *Psychology: Science, behavior, and life* (pp. 515–521). Fort Worth, TX: Harcourt Brace College Publishers.

Gardner, H. (1994). Multiple intelligences. *Quest.* Published by Kumon Institute of Education, Seoul, Korea.

Gardner, H. (1994). Multiple intelligences: A view from the arts. *Issues 1994,* 5–22. Based on a talk delivered to a conference of the Art Educators of New Jersey, October 1993.

Gardner, H. (1995). *ECT* interview of the month. *Early Childhood Today, 10* (1), 30–32.

Gardner, H. (1995). Limited visions, limited means: Two obstacles to meaningful educational reform. *Daedalus, 124* (4), 101–105.

Gardner, H. (1995, Dec 26). The meaning of multiple intelligence [sic]. *Post-Dispatch* (St. Louis, MO), p. 15B.

Gardner, H. (1995, Dec). "Multiple intelligences" as a catalyst. *English Journal, 84* (8), 16–18.

Gardner, H. (1995). Perennial antinomies and perpetual redrawings: Is there progress in the study of mind? In R. Solso and D. Massaro (Eds.), *Science of the mind: 200l and beyond* (pp. 65–78). New York: Oxford University Press.

Gardner, H. (1995, Sept). Why would anyone become an expert? [Critique of A. Ericsson and N. Charness, Expert performance: Its structure and acquisition]. *American Psychologist, 50* (9), 802–804.

Gardner, H. (1996). Probing more deeply into the theory of multiple intelligences. *NASSP Bulletin,* 1–7.

Gardner, H. (1996). Zur Entwicklung des Spektrums der menschlichen Intelligenzen. *Beitrage zur Lehrerbildung, 14* (2), 198–209.

Gardner, H. (1997). Developmental views of multiple intelligence [sic]. In G.O. Mazur (Ed.), *Twenty year commemoration to the life of A.R. Luria (1902–1977)* (pp. 61–79). New York: Semenenko Foundation.

Gardner, H. (1997). Fostering diversity through personalized education: implications of a new understanding of human intelligence. [Journal of UNESCO's International Bureau of Education], *Prospects, 27* (3), 347–363. Translated and Reprinted: French, *Perspectives, 27* (3), 369–387; Spanish, *Perspectivas, 27* (3), 371–389; Russian; Chinese; Arabic.

Gardner, H. (1997). Is musical intelligence special? In V. Brummett (Ed.), *Ithaca Conference '96: Music as intelligence: A sourcebook.* Ithaca, NY: Ithaca College. Based on a conference keynote, Ithaca College, September 1996.

Gardner, H. (1997). Multiple intelligences as a partner in school improvement. *Educational Leadership, 55* (1), 20–21.

Gardner, H. (1997, March 1). Our many intelligences: Kinds of minds. *The Mini Page.* A children's supplement to local newspapers, edited by Betty Debnam, © Universal Press Syndicate.

Gardner, H. (1998). Extraordinary cognitive achievements: A symbols systems approach. In W. Damon (Ed.-in-Chief), *Handbook of child psychology,* 5th ed., vol. 1, *Theoretical models of human development* (pp. 415–466). New York: Wiley.

Gardner, H. (1998, March 19). An intelligent way. (London) *Independent,* Education Supplement, pp. 4, 5 [A response to John White, *Do Howard Gardner's multiple intelligences add up?* London: Institute of Education University of London, 1998].

Gardner, H. (1998, Nov 9). Letter to the editor in reply to Collins "Seven kinds of smart" (Oct 19, 1998). *Time.*

Gardner, H. (1998). A multiplicity of intelligences. *Scientific American presents: Exploring intelligence* (a special issue of *Scientific American*), pp. 19–23.

Gardner, H. (1999). Are there additional intelligences? The case for naturalist, spiritual, and existential intelligences. In J. Kane (Ed.), *Education, information, and transformation* (pp. 111–131). Upper Saddle River, NJ: Prentice-Hall. Reprinted in *Gifted Education Press Quarterly, 11* (2), Spring 1997, pp. 2–5.

Gardner, H. (1999, Dec 5). Getting smart about intelligence. *Philadelphia Inquirer,* p. D7. Reprinted: Rethinking the concept of intelligence, *Boston Globe,* 1 Jan 2000, p. A23.

Gardner, H. (1999). Howard Gardner debates James Traub on multiple intelligences. *Cerebrum: The Dana Forum on Brain Science, 1* (2).

Gardner, H. (1999). Intelligence. Entry in the *Fontana/Norton dictionary of modern thought.*

Gardner, H. (1999). Multiple approaches to understanding. In C.M. Reigeluth (Ed.), *Instructional-design theories and models: A new paradigm of instructional theory.* Mahwah, NJ: Erlbaum Associates.

Gardner, H. (1999, Feb). Who owns intelligence? *Atlantic,* 67–76.

Gardner, H. (2000). The case against spiritual intelligence [Response to R. Emmons, The psychology of ultimate concern: Personality, spirituality, and intelligence, *International Journal for the Psychology of Religion, 10* (1), 27–34.

Gardner, H. (2000). Let's get past the bell curve. *Cerebrum, 2* (4), 7–9 [letter to the editor in response to L. Gottfredson, Pretending that intelligence doesn't matter, *Cerebrum,* Summer 2000].

Gardner, H. (2000). Using multiple intelligences to improve negotiation theory and practice. *Negotiation Journal, 16* (4), 321–324. Based on remarks made March 10, 2000, at Harvard University Law School.

Gardner, H. (2001). Creators: Multiple intelligences. In K. Pfenninger and V. Shubik (Eds.), *The origins of creativity* (pp. 117–143). New York: Oxford University Press. Based on a presentation to the Given Biomedical Conference, Aspen, CO, 1993.

Gardner, H. (2001). [Interview.] La conception standard de l'intelligence est fausse. In Jean-Claude Ruano-Barbalan (Ed.), *Sciences Humaines,* 2, 165–172.

Gardner, H. (2002). The three faces of intelligence. *Daedalus,* 139–142. Translated into German in *Gluck,* 391–99.

Gardner, H. (2003). Multiple intelligences after twenty years. Paper presented at the annual meeting of the American Educational Research Association, Chicago, April 21, 2003. Available at www.howardgardner.com.

Gardner, H. (2003). Three distinct meanings of intelligence. In R. Sternberg, J. Lautrey, and T. Lubart (Eds.), *Models of intelligence: International perspectives,* pp. 43–54. Washington, DC: American Psychological Association.

Gardner, H (2004). Letter to the editor Re: Intelligence. *Wilson Quarterly,* Fall issue.

Gardner, H. (2006, in press). A blessing of influences. In J. Schaler (Ed.), *Gardner under fire.* Chicago: Open Court.

Coauthored with Howard Gardner

Baker, L., Gardner, H., et al. (1993). Intelligence and its inheritance: A diversity of views. In T. Bouchard and P. Propping (Eds.), *Twins as a tool of behavioral genetics* (pp. 85–108). Chichester, England: Wiley.

Baum, S., Viens, J., & Slatin, B., in consultation with H. Gardner. (In preparation). *Pathways to multiple intelligences: A guide to implementation.*

Blythe, T., White, N., & Gardner, H. (1995). Teaching practical intelligence. *What research tells us* [series of booklets]. West Lafayette, IN: Kappa Delta Pi.

Cicerone, P.E., with Gardner, H. (2000, Oct). Tanti individui, tante intelligenze. Interview in *Le Scienze,* (386), 12–13.

Delacampagne, C., with Gardner, H. (2000, Dec). Howard Gardner: l'intelligence au pluriel. *La recherche,* (337), 109–111.

Gardner, H., & Checkley, K. (1997, Sept). [Interview] The first seven . . . and the eighth: A conversation with Howard Gardner. *Educational Leadership,* 55 (1), 8–13.

Gardner H., Hatch, T., & Torff, B. (1997). A third perspective: The symbol systems approach. In R. Sternberg and E. Grigerenko (Eds.), *Intelligence, heredity, and environment* (pp. 243–268). New York: Cambridge University Press.

Gardner, H., & Schmidt, R. (1992, Fall). [Interview with Howard Gardner]. *Learning 2001, 3* (3), 4–6.

Gardner, H., & Shores, E.F. (1995, Summer). [Interview] Howard Gardner on the eighth intelligence: Seeing the natural world. *Dimensions of Early Childhood*, 5–7.

Gardner, H., & Viens, J. (1990). Multiple intelligences and styles: Partners in effective education. *Clearinghouse Bulletin: Learning/Teaching Styles and Brain Behavior, 4* (2), 4–5. Seattle, Washington: Association for Supervision and Curriculum Development.

Gardner, H., & Walters, J. (1988). Managing intelligences (Tech. Rep. No. 33). Cambridge, MA: Harvard University Graduate School of Education, Project Zero.

Gardner, H., Walters, J., & Hatch, T. (1992). If teaching had looked beyond the classroom: The development and education of intelligences. *Innotech Journal, 16* (1), 18–36.

Goldman, J., & Gardner, H. (1988). Multiple paths to educational effectiveness. In D.K. Lipsky and A. Gartner (Eds.), *Beyond separate education: Quality education for all students* (pp. 121–140). Baltimore: Brookes.

Granott, N., & Gardner, H. (1994). When minds meet: Interactions, coincidence, and development in domains of ability. In R.J. Sternberg and R.K. Wagner (Eds.), *Mind in context: Interactionist perspectives on human intelligence* (pp. 171–201). New York: Cambridge University Press.

Hatch, T., & Gardner, H. (1990). If Binet had looked beyond the classroom: The assessment of multiple intelligences. *International Journal of Educational Research* (pp. 415–429). Reprinted (abridged): *Innotech Journal, 16* (1), 1992, 18–36. Reprinted in: *NAMTA Journal, 21* (2), 1996, 5–28; and B. Torff (Ed.), *Multiple intelligences and assessment,* Arlington Heights, IL: IRI Skylight, 1997.

Kornhaber, M., & Gardner, H. (In press). Multiple intelligences: Developments in implementation and theory. In R.J. Sternberg and M. Constas (Eds.), *Translating education theory and research into practice.*

Kornhaber, M., & Gardner, H. (1993). Varieties of excellence and conditions for their achievement. Paper prepared for Commission on Varieties of Excellence in the Schools, New York State. New York: National Center for Restructuring Education, Schools, and Teaching.

Kornhaber, M., & Gardner, H. (1995). Solving for g and beyond. *Triumph of discovery: A chronicle of great adventures in science* (pp. 121–123). New York: Henry Holt and Scientific American.

Krechevsky, M., & Gardner, H. (1990). Multiple intelligences, multiple chances. In D. Inbar (Ed.), *Second chance in education: An interdisciplinary and international perspective* (pp. 69–88). London: Falmer Press.

Krechevsky, M., & Gardner, H. (1994). Multiple intelligences in multiple contexts. In D.K. Detterman (Ed.), *Current topics in human intelligence*, vol. 4, *Theories of intelligence* (pp. 285–305). Norwood, NJ: Ablex.

Krechevsky, M., Hoerr, T., & Gardner, H. (1995). Complementary energies: Implementing MI theory from the laboratory and from the field. In J. Oakes and K.H. Quartz (Eds.), *Creating new educational communities* (pp. 166–186). Ninety-fourth Yearbook of the National Society for the Study of Education (Part I). Chicago: University of Chicago Press.

Ramos-Ford, V., Feldman, D.H., & Gardner, H. (1988, Spring). A new look at intelligence through Project Spectrum. *New Horizons in Learning*, pp. 6, 7, 15.

Ramos-Ford, V., & Gardner, H. (1991). Giftedness from a multiple intelligences perspective. In N. Colangelo and G. Davis (Eds.), *The handbook of gifted education* (pp. 55–64). Boston: Allyn and Bacon.

Solomon, B., Powell, K., & Gardner, H. (1999). Multiple intelligences and creativity. In M. Runco and S. Pritzker (Eds.-in-Chief), *Encyclopedia of creativity*. San Diego: Academic Press.

Torff, B., & Gardner, H. (1999). The vertical mind: The case for multiple intelligences. In M. Anderson (Ed.), *The development of intelligence* (pp. 139–159). London: University College London Press.

Veenema, S., & Gardner, H. (1996, Nov/Dec). Multimedia and multiple intelligences. *American Prospect*, pp. 69–75. Based on a presentation at the Massachusetts Institute of Technology, Cambridge, MA, June 4, 1996.

Viens, J., Chen, J-Q., & Gardner, H. (1997). Theories of intelligence and critiques. In J.L. Paul, et al. (Eds.), *Foundations of Special Education* (pp. 122–141). Pacific Grove, CA: Brooks-Cole.

von Károlyi, C., Ramos-Ford, V., & Gardner, H. (2003). Multiple intelligences: A perspective on giftedness. In N. Colangelo and G. Davis (Eds.), *Handbook of gifted education*, 3rd ed. (pp. 100–112). Boston: Allyn and Bacon.

Walters, J., Krechevsky, M., & Gardner, H. (1985). Development of musical, mathematical, and scientific talents in normal and gifted children (Tech. Rep. No. 31). Cambridge, MA: Harvard University Graduate School of Education, Project Zero.

Wexler-Sherman, C., Gardner, H., & Feldman, D. (1988). A pluralistic view of early assessment: The Project Spectrum approach. *Theory into Practice, 27*, 77–83.

White, N., Blythe, T., & Gardner, H. (1992). Multiple intelligence theory: Creating the thoughtful classroom. In A. Costa, J. Bellanca, and R. Fogarty (Eds.), *If mind matters: A foreword to the future, 2* (pp. 127–134). Palatine, IL: Skylight Publishers.

Williams, W., Blythe, T., White, N., Li, Jin, Gardner, H., & Sternberg, R. (2002). Practical intelligence for school: Developing metacognitive sources of achievement in adolescence. *Developmental Review, 22* (2), 162–210.

Selected Works by Others
About Multiple Intelligences Theory

A. Books and Monographs

Armstrong, T. (2003). *The multiple intelligences of reading and writing: Making the words come alive.* Alexandria, VA: Association for Supervision and Curriculum Development.

Armstrong, T. (2003). *You're smarter than you think: A kids guide to multiple intelligences.* Minneapolis: Free Spirit.

Arnold, E. (2001). *MI strategies for kids: Brilliant brain selects spelling strategies.* Tucson, AZ: Zephyr Press.

Arnold, E. (2001). *MI strategies for kids: Magnificent mind magnifies meaning when reading.* Tucson, AZ: Zephyr Press.

Boggeman, S., Hoerr, T.R., & Wallich, C. (1996). *Succeeding through multiple intelligences.* St. Louis: New City School.

Borba, M. (2002). *Building moral intelligence: The seven essential virtues that teach kids to do the right thing.* Tucson, AZ: Zephyr Press.

Brunner, I., & Rottensteiner, E. (2002). *Eine Entdeckungsreise ins Reich der Multiplen Intelligenzen: Auf die schillernd bunte Welt der Begabungen.* Baltmannsweiler, Germany: Schneider Verlag Hohengehren.

Chamberlain, V. (1996) *Starting out on MI way: A guide to multiple intelligences in the primary school.* Bolton, England: Centre for the Promotion of Holistic Education.

Champion, Pei Pei (2002). *Champion BoPoMo & Hanyu Pinyin: A new multi-intelligence and multi-media approach in teaching and learning Chinese.* Taiwan: Cheng Chung Book Co.

DeAmicis, B. (2001). *Multiple intelligences made easy: Strategies for your curriculum.* Tucson, AZ: Zephyr Press.

Ellison, L. (2001). *The personal intelligences.* Thousand Oaks, CA: Corwin.

EUC Sjaelland Denmark. (2004). *AMPVOC: Assessing multiple intelligence performance in vocational students.* (8 work packages). EU Leonardo da Vinci Project. (www.eucsj.dk)

Filograsso, N. (2002). *Fuga dal centro: Appunti per una pedagogia della persona.* Urbino: QuattroVenti.

FinVoc Project Team. (2003). *MI resource book for teachers.* FinVoc pilot project on multiple intelligences. EU Leonardo da Vinci Project.

Fogarty, R., and Bellanca, J. (Eds.) (1995). *Multiple intelligences: A collection.* Pallantine, IL: IRI/Skylight.

Forest, L. (2001). *Crafting creative community: Combining cooperative learning, multiple intelligences and wisdom.* San Clemente, CA: Kagan Publishing.

Gaffney, K. (2004). *Chrysalis: Professional development for artists in education.* New York: Black Bear Books.

Glasgow, J. (2001). *Using young adult literature: Thematic activities based on Gardner's multiple intelligences.* Norwood, MA: Christopher-Gordon Publishers.

Glock, J., et al. (1999). *Discovering the naturalist intelligence.* Tucson, AZ: Zephyr Press.

Griss, S. (1998). *Minds in motion: A kinesthetic approach to teaching elementary curriculum.* Portsmouth, NH: Heinemann.

Jack, B. (1996). *Moving on MI way: A guide to multiple intelligences in the secondary school.* Bolton, England: Centre for the Promotion of Holistic Education.

Kagan, L. (2000). *Multiple intelligences: Structures and activities.* San Clemente, CA: Kagan Publishing.

Kagan, S. (2000). *Multiple intelligences: Evaluating the theory, validating the wisdom.*

Kagan, S., & Kagan, M. (2002). *Multiple intelligences: The complete MI book.* San Clemente, CA: Kagan Publishing.

Lawall, G. (Ed.). (2000). *Teachers guide, Ecce Romani 1: A Latin reading program.* Upper Saddle River, NJ: Prentice-Hall.

Lazear, D. (2003). *Eight ways of teaching: The artistry of teaching with multiple intelligences,* 4th ed. Tucson, AZ: Zephyr Press.

Lazear, D. (2003). *Higher-order thinking the multiple intelligences way.* Tucson, AZ: Zephyr Press.

Lazear, D. (2003). *Outsmart yourself: Sixteen proven strategies for becoming smarter than you think you are.* Tucson, AZ: Zephyr Press.

Lazear, D., & Costa, A. (2001). *Pathways of learning: Teaching students and parents about multiple intelligences,* 2nd ed. Tucson, AZ: Zephyr Press.

Loh, W.I., & Jacobs, G. (2003). *Nurturing the naturalist intelligence.* San Clemente, CA: Kagan Publishing.

Santoianni, F. (1996). *Didattica configuarzionale: Modelli multipli a coordinate modulari.* Naples, Italy: Edizioni Scientifiche Italiane.

Serrano, A.M. (2003). *Inteligencias multiples y estimulacion temprana.* Mexico: Editorial Trillas.

Smyth, P. (2004). *"Charlotte's Web" write ideas.* United Kingdom: Bromley Education Services.

Stankard, B. (2003). *How each child learns: Using multiple intelligence in faith formation.* Mystic, CT: Twenty-Third Publications.

Stefanakis, E. (2002). *Multiple intelligences and portfolios: A window into the learner's mind.* Portsmouth, NH: Heinemann.

Svedberg, L., & Zaar, M. (1998). *Boken om pedagogerna.* Stockholm: Liber.

Teele, Sue (2004). *Overcoming barricades to reading: A multiple intelligences approach.* Thousand Oaks, CA: Corwin Press.

Torff, B. (Ed.). (1997). *Multiple intelligences and assessment: A collection of articles.* Arlington Heights, IL: IRI/Skylight Training & Publishing, Incorpora.

B. Theses, Dissertations, and Papers

AERA Conference (2003). Sixteen papers on multiple intelligences presented at the Annual Meeting of the American Educational Research Association, Chicago, April 21–25.

Davies, R. (2005). MI in the teaching and learning of history. University of Hull, England.

International Conference on Pushing Forward the National Education and Improving Students' Quality. (2002). Seven keynote speeches and 187 papers on multiple intelligences: Research on the development and assessment of multiple intelligence. Beijing, August 16–18.

Ena, A. (2001). H. Gardner e la pedagogia modulare. *Tesi di laurea in pedagogia,* Universita Degli Studi di Bari (Italy).

Haley, M. (2003). Learner-centered instruction and the theory of multiple intelligences with second language learners. Powerpoint presentation.

Jones, J. (2003). A Multi-cultural comparison of the factor structure of the MIDAS for adults/college students. Paper presented at the Annual Meeting of the American Educational Research Association, Chicago, April 21, 2003.

Kallenbach, S., & Viens, J. (Eds.) (2001). Multiple intelligences in practice. Teacher research reports for the Adult Multiple Intelligences Study. NCSALL Occasional Paper. Cambridge, MA: National Center for the Study of Adult Learning and Literacy, Harvard Graduate School of Education.

Kallenbach, S., & Viens, J. (2002). Open to interpretation: Multiple intelligences theory in adult literacy education. (NCSALL Report No. 21). Cambridge, MA: National Center for the Study of Adult Learning and Literacy, Harvard Graduate School of Education.

Keirl, S. (2002). Hedgehogs, foxes, crows, and other "intelligent" beings: Explorations of the relationship between multiple intelligence theory and design and technology. Conference paper delivered to Learning in Technology: Challenges for the 21st Century, Gold Coast, Australia, December 5–7, 2002.

Kornhaber, M. (2003). What educators report are the benefits of MI to student learning. Paper presented at the Annual Meeting of the American Educational Research Association, Chicago, April 21–25, 2003.

McCarthy, K.E. (2004). A study of Howard Gardner's theories of multiple intelligences and their implications in the collegiate oboe studio. Unpublished dissertation, Indiana University, Indiana.

Menchaca, M. (2004). Optimizing distributed learning delivery models: An asset class approach to distance learning. Paper delivered at ED-MEDIA, Switzerland.

Meng, W. (2003, Nov). Multiple intelligences and teaching according to students' traits. Presented at National Natural Science Funding Forum, Beijing.

Neville, A. (2000). Native American students' self-perceptions regarding Gardner's multiple intelligences. University of South Dakota.

Noble, T. (2003). Integrating the revised Bloom's taxonomy with multiple intelligences: A planning tool for curriculum differentiation. Paper presented at the Annual Meeting of the American Educational Research Association, Chicago, April 21, 2003.

Posner, M. (2003). Neural systems and individual differences: A commentary on *Frames of mind: The theory of multiple intelligences*. Paper presented at the Annual Meeting of the American Educational Research Association, Chicago, April 21, 2003.

Savas, P. (2003). Multiple intelligences and second language acquisition: Connections. Unpublished paper; contact author at perihans@ufl.edu.

Salsberry, T., & Miller, S. (1999). Female superintendents: Perceptions of their use of multiple intelligences. Presented at the American Educational Research Association's annual meeting in Montreal, Quebec, April 22, 1999.

Viens, J., & Kallenbach S. (2001). Multiple intelligences resources for the adult basic education practitioner: An annotated bibliography. NCSALL Occasional Paper. Cambridge, MA: National Center for the Study of Adult Learning and Literacy, Harvard Graduate School of Education.

Wang, W.K. (2004). Implementing multiple intelligence theory in Taiwan. Unpublished paper; contact author at wkwang@mail.cyut.edu.tw.

Wang, W.K. (2002). Multiple intelligences approaches to assessment. *A Tribune for Elementary Education, 148,* 94–104.

Wang, W.K. (2002). The curriculum design for teaching with multiple intelligence. *Curriculum and Instruction Quarterly, 5*(1), 1–20.

Wang, W.K. (2001). Multiple intelligence for early education. *Taiwan Education Review, 606,* 10–20.

Wang, W.K. (2001). Child's multiple intelligence and 6–15 articulated curriculum. *Early Education Information, 126,* 8–14.

Wang, W.K. (2001) Understand child's multiple intelligence. *Early Education Information, 125,* 14–15.

Wang, W.K. (2000). The multiple intelligence school. *Practice Teachers Quarterly, 5* (4), 88–91.

Wexler, D. (2004). Understanding multiple intelligences. Unpublished paper. Northridge: California State University, Northridge.

Selected Works About Howard Gardner and/or Multiple Intelligences Theory

Allis, S. (1999, July). The master of *un*artificial intelligence. *Boston Globe,* D1, 5.

Armstrong, T. (1993). *Seven kinds of smarts: Identifying and developing your multiple intelligences.* New York: Penguin Books.

Baum, S., Viens, J., & Slatin, B. (2005). *Multiple intelligences in the elementary classroom: Pathways to thoughtful practice.* New York: Teachers College Press.

Bolanos, P.J. (1994, Jan). From theory to practice: Indianapolis Key School applies Howard Gardner's multiple intelligences theory to the classroom. *School Administrator, 51* (1), 30–31.

Bruner, J.S. (1983). State of the child. Review of *Frames of mind. New York Review of Books,* October 27, 1983.

Campbell, L., Campbell, B., & Dickinson, D. (2003). *Teaching and learning through multiple intelligences,* 3rd ed. Boston: Allyn and Bacon.

Coreil, C. (Ed.). (2003). *Multiple intelligences, Howard Gardner, and new methods in college teaching.* Papers from the fifth annual Urban Conference: Pedagogical Innovations in Higher Education. Jersey City: New Jersey City University.

Feldman, D. (2003). The creation of multiple intelligences theory: A study in high-level thinking. In R. K. Sawyer et al., *Creativity and development* (pp. 139–185). New York: Oxford University Press.

Fogarty, R., & Bellanca, J. (Eds.). (1995). *Multiple intelligences: A collection.* Pallantine, IL: IRI/Skylight.

Healy, Y. (1995, Jan). Playing mind games. *Irish Times.*

Hoerr, T. (1996, Winter). Education: One size does not fit all. *Private School Administrator.*

Hyland, A. (2000). *Multiple intelligences: Curriculum and assessment project.* Cork: University of Cork.

Koff, S. (2003). Special issue: The theory of multiple intelligences. *Journal of Dance Education* 3, 1, 2003.

Kornhaber, M. (2001). Howard Gardner. In J. Palmer (Ed.), *Fifty modern thinkers on education: From Piaget to the present* (pp. 272–279). New York: Routledge.

Kornhaber, M., Fierros, E., & Veenema, S. (2004). *Multiple intelligences: Best ideas from research and practice.* Boston: Pearson Education.

Kornhaber, M. (2004, Aug). Psychometric superiority? Check the facts— Again. Op-ed. *EdNext.*

Lazear, D. (1991) Seven ways of knowing: Teaching to the multiple intelligences. Palatine, IL: Skylight Publishing.

Martin, J. (2004). *Profiting from multiple intelligences in the workplace.* Aldershot, England: Gower Press.

Olson, L. (1988, Jan 27). Children flourish here: Eight teachers and a theory changed a school world. *Education Week, 7* (18), 1, 18–19.

Puchta, H., & Rinvolucri, M. (2005). *Multiple intelligences in EFL: Exercises for secondary and adult students.* Hiebling Languages.

Shen, Z. (2004). *Howard Gardner, arts, and multiple intelligences.* Beijing.

Torff, B. (Ed.). (1997). *Multiple intelligences and assessment: A collection of articles.* Arlington Heights, IL: IRI/Skylight Training & Publishing, Incorpora.

Viadero, D. (2003). Staying power. *Education Week,* June 4, 24–27.

Viens, J., & Kallenbach, S. (2004). *Multiple intelligences and adult literacy: A sourcebook for practitioners.* New York: Teachers College Press.

Weber, E. (2005). *MI strategies in the classroom and beyond: Using roundtable learning.* Boston: Allyn & Bacon.

Winner, E. (2004). Howard Gardner: A biography. In R. Lerner & C. Fisher (Eds.), *Applied developmental science encyclopedia.*

Weinreich-Haste, H. (1985). The varieties of intelligence: An interview with Howard Gardner. *New Ideas in Psychology* 3/4, 47–65.

OTHER MI MATERIALS

I. Videos

Gardner, H. (Writer), & DiNozzi, R. (Producer/Director). (1996). *MI: Intelligence, Understanding, and the Mind* [Motion picture]. Los Angeles: Into the Classroom Media.

Gardner, H. (Writer), & DiNozzi, R. (Producer/Director). *Creativity and Leadership: Making the Mind Extraordinary.* (1998) R. DiNozzi, Producer. Los Angeles: Into the Classroom Media.

II. Web Sites

MIapp Project: http://www.miapp.net
Project Zero: http://www.pz.harvard.edu
WIDE World: http://www.wideworld.pz.harvard.edu

Appendix D

References

Albert, K., & Runco, M. (1986). The achievement of eminence: A model based on a longitudinal study of exceptionally gifted boys and their families. In R. Sternberg & J. Davidson (Eds.), *Conceptions of giftedness* (pp. 332–357). New York: Cambridge University Press.

Amabile, T. (1983). *The social psychology of creativity.* New York: Springer-Verlag.

Anderson, M. (1987). Inspection time and the development of intelligence. Paper delivered to British Psychological Society Conference, Sussex University, England.

Arnheim, R. (1969). *Visual thinking.* Berkeley: University of California Press.

Arts, Education, and the Americans. (1977). *Coming to our senses.* New York: McGraw-Hill.

Ascher, C. (1988). Improving the school-home connection for poor and minority urban students. *Urban Review, 20,* 10923.

Bailyn, B. (1960). *Education in the forming of American society.* Chapel Hill: University of North Carolina Press.

Bamberger, J. (1982a). Growing up prodigies: The midlife crisis. In D. Feldman (Ed.), *Developmental approaches to giftedness and creativity: New directions for child development,* vol. 17, pp. 61–78). San Francisco: Jossey-Bass.

Bamberger, J. (1982b). Revisiting children's drawings of simple rhythms: A function reflection-in-action. In S. Strauss (Ed.), *U-shaped behavioral growth.* New York: Academic Press.

Barron, F. (1969). *Creative person and creative process.* New York: Holt, Rinehart and Winston.

Bennis, W., & Biederman, P.W. (1997). *Organizing genius: The secrets of creative collaboration.* Reading, MA: Addison-Wesley.

Bereiter, C. (1985). The changing face of educational disadvantagement. *Phi Delta Kappan, 66,* 538–541.

Berger, R. (1991). Building a school culture of high standards: A teacher's perspective. In V. Perrone (Ed.), *Expanding student assessment* (pp. 32–39). Alexandria, VA: Association for Supervision and Curriculum Development.

Bijou, S., & Baer, D. (1965). *Child development.* New York: Appleton-Century-Crofts.

Binet, A., & Simon, T. (1905). Methodes nouvelles pour le diagnostique du niveaux intellectuel des anormaux [New methods for the diagnosis of the intellectual level of the abnormal]. *L'annee psychologique, 11,* 236–245.

Brainerd, C. (1978). The stage question in cognitive-developmental theory. *Behavioral and Brain Sciences,* 2, 1213–1273.

Bransford, J.D., Franks, J.J., Vye, N.J., & Sherwood, R.D. (1989). New approaches to instruction: Because wisdom can't be told. In S. Vosniadou & A. Ortony (Eds.), *Similarity and analogical reasoning* (pp. 470–497). New York: Cambridge University Press.

Brembeck, C. (1978). Formal education, non-formal education, and expanded conceptions of development. Occasional paper No. 1. East Lansing, MI: Non-formal Education Information Center, Institute for International Studies in Education, Michigan State University.

Brookover, W.B. (1985). Can we make schools effective for minority students? *Journal of Negro Education, 54,* 257–268.

Brown, J.S., Collins, A., & Duguid, P. (1989). Situated cognition and the culture of learning. *Educational Researcher, 18* (1), 32–42.

Brown, N. (1987 Aug). Pivotal points in artistic growth. Presentation at the 1987 Arts PROPEL summer workshop, Pittsburgh, PA.

Brown, R., & Herrnstein, R. (1975). *Psychology.* Boston: Little, Brown.

Bruner, J.S. (1990) *Acts of meaning.* Cambridge: Harvard University Press.

Buros, O.K. (Ed.). (1938). *The 1938 mental measurements yearbook.* Highland Park, NJ: Gryphon Press.

Burton, J., Lederman, A., & London, P. (Eds.). (1988). *Beyond DBAE: The case for multiple visions of art education.* Dartmouth, MA: University Council on Art Education.

Callahan, R. (1962). *Education and the cult of efficiency.* Chicago: University of Chicago Press.

Carroll, J.B. (1993). *Human cognitive abilities: A survey of factor analytic techniques.* New York: Cambridge University Press.

Carson, A.D. (1998). The relation of self-reported abilities to aptitude test scores: A replication and extension. *Journal of Vocational Behavior, 53,* 353–371.

Cascio, W.F. (1995). Whither industrial and organizational psychology in a changing world of work? *American Psychologist, 50,* 928–939.

Case, R. (1985). *Intellectual development: Birth to adolescence.* New York: Academic Press.

Ceci, S.J. (1990). *On intelligence . . . more or less: A bio-ecological theory of intellectual development.* Englewood Cliffs, NJ: Prentice-Hall.

Chen, J.-Q., & Gardner, H. (2005). Assessment based on multiple intelligences theory. In D. Flanagan & P. Harrison (Eds.), *Contemporary intellectual assessment: Theories, tests, and issues,* 2nd ed. New York: Guilford Press.

Chideya, F. (1991, Dec 2). Surely for the spirit, but also for the mind. *Newsweek,* p. 61.

Chubb, J.E. (1988). Why the current wave of school reform will fail. *Public Interest, 90,* 29–49.

Cochran, M. (1987). The parental empowerment process: Building on family strengths. *Equity and Choice, 4* (1), 9–23.

Cohen, B.N. (2003). Applying existential theory and intervention to career decision-making. *Journal of Career Development, 29* (3), 195–210.

Collins, A., & Brown, J.S. (1988, April). Cognitive apprenticeship and social interaction. Paper presented at the American Educational Research Association, New Orleans.

Collins, A., Brown, J.S., & Newman, S.E. (1989). Cognitive apprenticeship: Teaching the craft of reading, writing, and mathematics. In L. Resnick (Ed.), *Cognition and instruction: Issues and agendas.* Hillsdale, NJ: Lawrence Erlbaum.

Comer, J. (1980). *School power.* New York: Free Press.

Comer, J. (1984). Home-school relationships as they affect the academic success of children. *Education and Urban Society, 16,* 323–337.

Comer, J. (1988a, Aug). The social factor. *New York Times,* "Education Life," 27–31.

Comer, J. (1988b). Educating poor minority children. *Scientific American, 259* (5), 42–48.

Conkey, C. (2005, March 17). It's all relative: Songs to make physics easier. *Wall Street Journal,* p. B1.

Connell, M.W., Sheridan, K., & Gardner, H. (2003). On abilities and domains. In R.J. Sternberg & E. Grigorenko (Eds.), *Perspectives on the psychology of abilities, competencies, and expertise* (pp. 126–155). New York: Cambridge University Press.

Conner, J., & Plasman, J. (2003). Gaining the advantages of team intelligence. *HR, Human Resources Planning, 26* (3), 8.

Coreil, C. (Ed.). (2003). *Multiple intelligences, Howard Gardner, and new methods in college teaching.* Papers from the fifth annual Urban Conference:

Pedagogical Innovations in Higher Education. Jersey City: New Jersey City University.

Coren, S. (1994). *The intelligence of dogs: Canine consciousness and capabilities.* New York: Free Press.

Coy, P. (2004, March 22). The future of work: Flexible, creative, and good with people? You should do fine in tomorrow's job market. *Business Week,* 50–52.

Cronbach, L. (1984). *Essentials of psychological testing.* New York: Harper and Row.

Cronbach, L., & Snow, R. (1977). *Aptitudes and instructional methods.* New York: Irvington.

Cross, K.P., & Angelo, T. (1988). *Classroom assessment techniques: A handbook for faculty.* Ann Arbor, MI: National Center for Research to Improve Postsecondary Teaching and Learning (NCRIPTL).

Csikszentmihalyi, M. (1988a). Society, culture, and person: A systems view of creativity. In R.J. Sternberg (Ed.), *The nature of creativity* (pp. 325–339). New York: Cambridge University Press.

Csikszentmihalyi, M. (1988b). Motivation and creativity: Towards a synthesis of structural and energistic approaches to cognition. *New Ideas in Psychology, 6* (2), 159–176.

Csikszentmihalyi, M. (1990a). Literacy and intrinsic motivation. *Daedalus, 119* (2), 115–140.

Csikszentmihalyi, M. (1990b). *Flow.* New York: HarperCollins.

Csikszentmihalyi, M. (1996). *Creativity.* New York: HarperCollins.

Csikszentmihalyi, M., & Robinson, R. (1986). Culture, time, and the development of talent. In R. Sternberg (Ed.), *Conceptions of giftedness* (pp. 264–284). New York: Cambridge University Press.

Csikszentmihalyi, M., Rathunde, K., & Whalen, S. (1993). *Talented teenagers: The roots of success and failure.* New York: Cambridge University Press.

Dagley, J.C., & Salter, S.K. (2004). Practice and research in career counseling and development—2003. *Career Development Quarterly, 53* (2), 157–998.

Damasio, A. (2003). Panelist on "Does evidence from the neurosciences support the theory of multiple intelligences?" Annual Meeting of the American Educational Research Association, Chicago, April 21, 2003.

Damon, W. (1990). Reconciling the literacies of generations. *Daedalus, 119* (2), 33–53.

Darwin, C. (1859). *On the origin of species.* London: John Murray.

Davis, J. (1996). *The MUSE book.* Cambridge, MA: Harvard University Graduate School of Education, Project Zero.

Davis, J. (2005). *Framing education as art.* New York: Teachers College Press.

Dawis, R.V. (1996). Vocational psychology, vocational adjustment, and the workplace. *Psychology, Public Policy, and Law, 2* (2), 229–248.

Dewey, J. (1938). *Experience and education.* New York: Collier.

Dewey, J. (1959). *Art as experience.* New York: Capricorn.

Diaz-Lefebvre, R., et al. (1998, Jan). What if they learn differently: Applying multiple intelligences theory in the community college. *Leadership Abstracts, 11* (1). Available from the League for Innovation in the Community College, 26522 La Alameida, Ste. 370, Mission Viejo, CA 92691.

Dobbs, S. (Ed.). (1988). *Research readings for discipline-based art education: A journey beyond creating.* Reston, VA: National Art Education Association.

Edmonds, R. (Ed.). *A discussion of the literature and issues related to effective schooling.* Cambridge, MA: Harvard University, unpublished manuscript.

Eisner, E. (1987). *The role of discipline-based art education in America's schools.* Los Angeles: Getty Center for Education in the Arts.

Ellis, A.P.J., Hollenbeck, J.R., Ilgen, D.R., Porter, C.O.L.H., West, B.J., & Moon, H. (2003). Team learning: Collectively connecting the dots. *Journal of Applied Psychology, 88* (5), 821–835.

Ewens, T. (1988). Flawed understandings: On Getty, Eisner, and DBAE. In J. Burton, A. Lederman, & P. London (Eds.), *Beyond DBAE: The case for multiple visions of art education* (pp. 5–25). North Dartmouth, MA: University Council on Art Education.

Eysenck, H.J. (1967). Intelligence assessment: A theoretical and experimental approach. *British Journal of Educational Psychology, 37*, 81–98.

Eysenck, H.J. (1979). *The nature and measurement of intelligence.* New York: Springer-Verlag.

Feldman, D.H. (1980). *Beyond universals in cognitive development.* Norwood, NJ: Ablex.

Feldman, D.H. (with Goldsmith, L.). (1986). *Nature's gambit.* New York: Basic Books.

Feldman, D.H., & Gardner, H. (1989). *Project Spectrum: July 1987–June 1989* (Final Annual Report to the Spencer Foundation).

Feyerhern, A.E., & Rice, C.L. (2002). Emotional intelligence and team performance: The good, the bad and the ugly. *International Journal of Organization Analysis, 10* (4), 343–363.

Fischer, K.W. (1980). A theory of cognitive development. *Psychological Review, 87*, 477–531.

Fisher, K., & Fisher, M.D. (1998). *The distributed mind: Achieving high performance through the collective intelligence of knowledge work teams.* New York: AMACOM.

Fodor, J. (1983). *Modularity of mind.* Cambridge, MA: MIT Bradford Press.

Fordham, S., & Ogbu, J. (1986). Black students' school success: Coping with the "burden of acting white." *Urban Review, 18,* 176–206.

Fredericksen, J.R., & Collins, A. (1989). A systems theory of educational testing. *Educational Researcher, 18* (9), 27–32.

Gallwey, T. (1976). *Inner tennis.* New York: Random House.

Gardner, H. (1973). *The arts and human development.* New York: Wiley.

Gardner, H. (1975). *The shattered mind.* New York: Vintage.

Gardner, H. (1980). *Artful scribbles.* New York: Basic Books.

Gardner, H. (1982). *Art, mind, and brain.* New York: Basic Books.

Gardner, H. (1983a). Artistic intelligences. In S. Dobbs (Ed.), Art and the mind [special issue]. *Art Education, 36* (2), 47–49.

Gardner, H. (1983b). *Frames of mind: The theory of multiple intelligences.* New York: Basic Books.

Gardner, H. (1985). *The mind's new science.* New York: Basic Books.

Gardner, H. (1986a). Notes on cognitive development: Recent trends, future prospects. In S. Friedman, K. Klivington, & R. Peterson (Eds.), *The brain, cognition, and education.* New York: Academic Press.

Gardner, H. (1986b). The development of symbolic literacy. In M. Wrolstad & D. Fisher (Eds.), *Toward a greater understanding of literacy.* New York: Praeger.

Gardner, H. (1988a). Creative lives and creative works: A synthetic scientific approach. In R.J. Steinberg (Ed.), *The nature of creativity* (pp. 298–321). New York: Cambridge University Press.

Gardner, H. (1988b). Creativity: An interdisciplinary perspective. *Creativity Research Journal, 1,* 8–26.

Gardner, H. (1989a). Balancing specialized and comprehensive knowledge: The growing educational challenge. In T.J. Sergiovanni & J.H. Moore (Eds.), *Schooling for tomorrow: Directing reforms to issues that count* (pp. 148–165). Boston: Allyn & Bacon.

Gardner, H. (1989b). *To open minds: Chinese clues to the dilemma of contemporary education.* New York: Basic Books.

Gardner, H. (1989c). The school of the future. In J. Brockman (Ed.), *Ways of knowing: The reality club #3.* Englewood Cliffs, NJ: Prentice-Hall.

Gardner, H. (1989d). Zero-based arts education: An introduction to Arts PRO-PEL. *Studies in Art Education, 30* (2), 71–83.

Gardner, H. (1990a). *Arts education and human development.* Los Angeles: Getty Center for Education in the Arts.

Gardner, H. (1990b). The assessment of student learning in the arts. Paper presented at the conference on assessment in arts education, Holland, December 1990.

Gardner, H. (1991a). Assessment in context: The alternative to standardized testing. In B.R. Gifford & M.C. O'Connor (Eds.), *Changing assessments: Alternative views of aptitude, achievement, and instruction* (pp. 77–120). Boston:
   Kluwer.

Gardner, H. (1991b). Intelligence in seven phases. Paper delivered at the Centen-
   nial of the Harvard Graduate School of Education, September 1991.

Gardner, H. (1991c). *The unschooled mind: How children learn, and how schools
   should teach.* New York: Basic Books.

Gardner, H. (1993). *Creating minds: An anatomy of creativity seen through the
   lives of Freud, Einstein, Picasso, Stravinsky, Eliot, Graham, and Gandhi.* New
   York: Basic Books.

Gardner, H. (1995a). *Leading minds.* New York: Basic Books.

Gardner, H. (1995b, Nov). Reflections on multiple intelligences: Myths and messages. *Phi Delta Kappan, 77* (3), 200–209.

Gardner, H. (1997). *Extraordinary minds.* New York: Basic Books.

Gardner, H. (1999a). *Intelligence reframed: Multiple intelligences for the 21st century.* New York: Basic Books.

Gardner, H. (1999b). *The disciplined mind.* New York: Simon and Schuster.

Gardner, H. (2000). Project Zero: Nelson Goodman's legacy in arts education.
   Journal of Aesthetics and Art Criticism, 58 (3), 245–249.

Gardner, H. (2004a). Audiences for the theory of multiple intelligences. *Teachers
   College Record, 106* (111), 212–219.

Gardner, H. (2004b). *Changing minds.* Boston: Harvard Business School Press.

Gardner, H., Csikszentmihalyi, M., & Damon, W. (2001). *Good work: When excellence and ethics meet.* New York: Basic Books.

Gardner, H., Feldman, D., & Krechevsky, M. (Eds.) (1998). *Project Spectrum:
   Frameworks for early childhood education.* New York: Teachers College Press.

Gardner, H., & Hatch, T. (1989). Multiple intelligences go to school. *Educational
   Researcher, 18,* 4–10.

Gardner, H., Howard, V., & Perkins, D. (1974). Symbol systems: A philosophical,
   psychological, and educational investigation. In D. Olson (Ed.), *Media and
   symbols.* Chicago: University of Chicago Press.

Gardner, H., Kornhaber, M., & Wake, W. (1996). *Intelligence: Multiple perspectives.* Fort Worth, TX: Harcourt, Brace.

Gardner, H., & Perkins, D. (Eds.). (1988). Art, mind, and education. *Journal of
   Aesthetic Education* [special issue on Project Zero], *22* (1).

Gardner, H., & Winner, E. (1982). First intimations of artistry. In S. Strauss
   (Ed.), *U-shaped behavioral growth.* New York: Wiley.

Gardner, H., & Wolf, C. (1988). The fruits of asynchrony: Creativity from a psychological point of view. *Adolescent Psychiatry, 15,* 106–123.

Garriga, M. (2004, March 20). Shaping skills. *New Haven Registry*, p. B1.

Geary, D.C. (2005). *The origin of mind: Evolution of brain, cognition, and general intelligence.* Washington, DC: American Psychological Association.

Gelman, R. (1978). Cognitive development. *Annual Review of Psychology, 29,* 297–332.

Getty Center for Education in the Arts. (1986). *Beyond creating: The place for art in American schools.* Los Angeles: J. Paul Getty Trust.

Getzels, J.W., & Csikszentmihalyi, M. (1976). *The creative vision: A longitudinal study of problem finding in art.* New York: John Wiley and Sons.

Gilligan, C. (1982). *In a different voice: Psychological theory and women's development.* Cambridge, MA: Harvard University Press.

Gladwell, M. (2000). *The tipping point: How little things can make a big difference.* Boston: Little, Brown.

Gladwin, T. (1970). *East is a big bird: Navigation and logic on a Puluway atoll.* Cambridge, MA: Harvard University Press.

Goleman, D. (1995). *Emotional intelligence.* New York: Bantam Books.

Goleman, D. (1998). *Working with emotional intelligence.* New York: Bantam Books.

Goodman, N. (1968). *Languages of art.* Indianapolis: Bobbs-Merrill.

Goodman, N., Perkins, D., & Gardner, H. (1972). *Summary report, Harvard Project Zero.* Available as Technical Report from Harvard Project Zero. Cambridge, MA: Harvard Graduate School of Education.

Gottfredson, L.S. (1986). Occupational aptitude patterns map: Development and implications for a theory of job aptitude requirements. *Journal of Vocational Behavior, 29,* 254–291.

Gould, S.J. (1981). *The mismeasure of man.* New York: Norton.

Gould, S.J. (1989). *Wonderful life: The Burgess shale and the nature of history.* New York: Norton.

Gruber, H. (1981). *Darwin on man,* 2nd ed. Chicago: University of Chicago Press.

Gruber, H. (1985). Giftedness and moral responsibility: Creative thinking and human survival. In F. Horowitz & M. O'Brien (Eds.), *The gifted and talented: developmental perspectives.* Washington, DC: American Psychological Association.

Guidici, C., Rinaldi, C., & Krechevsky, M. (Eds.). (2001). *Making learning visible: Children as individual and group learners.* Cambridge, MA: Harvard Graduate School of Education, Project Zero.

Guilford, J.P. (1950). Creativity. *American Psychologist, 5,* 444–454.

Guilford, J.P. (1967). *The nature of human intelligence.* New York: McGraw-Hill.

Halberstam, D. (1972). *The best and the brightest.* Greenwich, CT: Fawcett Publications.

Heath, S.B. (1983). *Ways with words.* New York: Cambridge University Press.

Haley, M.H. (2004). Learner-centered instruction and the theory of multiple intelligences with second language learners. *Teachers College Record, 106* (1), 163–180.

Henderson, A. (1987). *The evidence continues to grow: Parent involvement improves student achievement.* Columbia, MD: National Committee for Citizens in Education.

Herrnstein, R., & Murray, C. (1994). *The bell curve: Intelligence and class structure in American life.* New York: Free Press.

Heubert, J. (1982). *Minimum competency testing and racial discrimination: A legal analysis, policy summary, and program review for education lawyers.* Cambridge, MA: Harvard Graduate School of Education, unpublished manuscript.

Hoerr, T.R. (2000). *Becoming a multiple intelligences school.* Alexandria, VA: Association for Supervision and Curriculum Development.

Hoffmann, B. (1962). *The tyranny of testing.* New York: Crowd-Collier Press.

Hofstadter, R. (1963). *Anti-intellectualism in American life.* New York: Knopf.

Holland, J. (1997). *Making vocational choices: A theory of vocational personalities and work environments,* 3rd ed. Englewood Cliffs, NJ: Prentice-Hall.

Houdé, O. (2004). *La psychologie de l'enfant.* Paris: Presses Universitaires de France.

Houdé, O., & Tzourio-Mazoyer, N. (2003). Neural foundations of logical and mathematical cognition. *Nature Reviews Neuroscience, 4* (6), 507–515.

Hunter, J.E. (1986). Cognitive ability, cognitive aptitudes, job knowledge, and job performance. *Journal of Vocational Behavior, 29,* 340–362.

Jackson, C. (1996). Managing and developing a boundaryless career: Lessons from dance and drama. *European Journal of Work and Organizational Psychology, 5* (4), 617–628.

Jackson, P. (1987). Mainstreaming art: An essay on discipline based arts education. *Educational Researcher, 16,* 39–43.

Jacques, E. (1989). *Requisite organization.* Arlington, VA: Cason Hall.

Jensen, A.R. (1980). *Bias in mental testing.* New York: Free Press.

Jensen, A.R. (1987). Individual differences in the Hick paradigm. In P. Vernon (Ed.), *Speed of information processing and intelligence.* Norwood, NJ: Ablex.

Johnson-Laird, P.N. (1983). *Mental models.* Cambridge, MA: Harvard University Press.

John-Steiner, V. (2000). *Creative collaboration.* New York: Oxford University Press.

Kagan, J., & Kogan, N. (1970). Individual variation in cognitive processing. In P. Mussen (Ed.), *Handbook of child psychology.* New York: Wiley.

Kallenbach, S., & Viens, J. (2004). Open to interpretation: MI theory in adult literacy education. *Teachers College Record, 106* (1), 58–66.

Kammeyer-Mueller, J.D., & Wanberg, C.R. (2003). Unwrapping the organizational entry process: Disentangling multiple antecedents and their pathways to adjustment. *Journal of Applied Psychology, 88* (5), 779–794.

Kaplan, E. (1983). Process and achievement revisited. In S. Wapner & B. Kaplan (Eds.), *Toward a holistic developmental psychology.* Hillsdale, NJ: Lawrence Erlbaum.

Kaplan, J.A., & Gardner, H. (1989). Artistry after unilateral brain disease. In F. Boller & J. Graffman (Eds.), *Handbook of neuropsychology,* vol. 2. New York: Elsevier Science Publishers.

Keating, D. (1984). The emperor's new clothes: The "new look" in intelligence research. In R. Sternberg (Ed.), *Advances in the psychology of human intelligence,* vol. 2 (pp. 1–45). Hillsdale, NJ: Lawrence Erlbaum.

Keller, E. (1983). *A feeling for the organism.* San Francisco: Freeman.

Kelso, G.I. (1977). The relation of school grade to ages and stages in vocational development. *Journal of Vocational Behavior, 10* (3), 287–301.

Keynes, J.M. (1935). *The general theory of employment, interest, and money.* New York: Harcourt, Brace.

Klitgaard, R. (1985). *Choosing elites.* New York: Basic Books.

Kobayashi, T. (1976). *Society, schools, and progress in Japan.* Oxford, England: Pergamon.

Kolodinsky, R.W., Hochwarter, W.A., & Ferris, G.R. (2004). Nonlinearity in the relationship between political skill and work outcomes: Convergent evidence from three studies. *Journal of Vocational Behavior, 65,* 294–308.

Kornhaber, M. (1997). *Seeking strengths: Equitable identification for gifted education and the theory of multiple intelligences.* Doctoral dissertation, Harvard Graduate School of Education.

Kornhaber, M. (2004). How many intelligences? *Education Next, 4* (4), 6.

Kornhaber, M.L., Fierros, E.G., & Veenema, S.A. (2004). *Multiple intelligences: Best ideas from research and practice.* Boston: Pearson/Allyn and Bacon.

Kotter, J.P. (1990). *A force for change: How leadership differs from management.* New York: Free Press.

Krechevsky, M., & Seidel, S. (1998). Minds at work: Applying multiple intelligences in the classroom. In R.J. Sternberg & W.M. Williams (Eds.), *Intelligence, instruction, and assessment: Theory into practice* (pp. 17–42). Mahwah, NJ: Lawrence Erlbaum Associates.

Kuhn, T. (1962). *The structure of scientific revolutions*. Chicago: University of Chicago Press.

Laboratory of Comparative Human Cognition. (1982). Culture and intelligence. In R. Sternberg (Ed.), *Handbook of human intelligence* (pp. 642–719). New York: Cambridge University Press.

Lash, J. (1980). *Helen and teacher: The story of Helen Keller and Anne Sullivan Macy*. New York: Delacorte.

Lave, J. (1977). Tailor-made experiments and evaluating the intellectual consequences of apprenticeship training. *Quarterly Newsletter of the Institute for Comparative Human Development, 1*, 1–3.

Lave, J. (1980). What's special about experiments as contexts for thinking? *Quarterly Newsletter of the Laboratory of Comparative Human Cognition, 2*, 86–91.

Leler, H. (1983). Parent education and involvement in relation to the schools and to parents of school-aged children. In R. Haskins & D. Adams (Eds.), *Parent education and public policy* (pp. 141–180). Norwood, NJ: Ablex.

Levine, M. (2002). *A mind at a time*. New York: Simon and Schuster.

LeVine, R.A., & White, M.I. (1986). *Human conditions: The cultural basis of educational development*. New York: Routledge & Kegan Paul.

Lewin-Benham, A. (2006). *Possible schools*. New York: Teachers College Press.

Levy, F., & Murnane, R.J. (2004). *The new division of labor: How computers are creating the next job market*. Princeton, NJ: Princeton University Press.

Lewis, M. (Ed.) (1976). *Origins of intelligence*. New York: Plenum Press.

Lipman, M., Sharp, A.M., & Oscanyan, F. (1990). *Philosophy in the classroom*. Philadelphia: Temple University Press.

Liptak, A. (2005, Feb 6). Inmate's rising IQ score could mean his death. *New York Times*, p. 11.

Lowenfeld, V. (1947). *Creative and mental growth*. New York: Macmillan.

MacKinnon, D. (1961). Creativity in architects. In D.W. MacKinnon (Ed.), *The creative person* (pp. 291–320). Berkeley, CA: Institute for Personality Assessment Research.

Maker, C., & Nielson, A. (1994 Fall). *Teaching/learning models of education of the gifted*. Austin, TX: Pro-Ed.

Malkus, U., Feldman, D., & Gardner, H. (1988). Dimensions of mind in early childhood. In A.D. Pelligrini (Ed.), *The psychological bases of early childhood* (pp. 25–38). Chichester, England: Wiley.

Marland, S.P., Jr. (1972). Our gifted and talented children: A priceless national resource. *Intellect, 101*, 6–9.

Martin, J. (2001). *Profiting from multiple intelligences in the workplace*. Hampshire, England: Gower Publishing.

Mayer, J.D., & Salovey, P. (1997). What is emotional intelligence? In P. Salovey & D.J. Sluyter (Eds.), *Emotional development and emotional intelligence: Educational implications* (pp. 3–31). New York: Basic Books.

Menuhin, Y. (1977). *Unfinished journey.* New York: Knopf.

Messick, S. (1988). Validity. In R. Linn (Ed.), *Educational measurement,* 3rd ed. New York: Macmillan.

Moore, M. (2004). *Stupid white men: And other sorry excuses for the state of the nation!* New York: Regan Books.

Moran, S., & Gardner, H. (2006). Extraordinary achievements: A developmental and systems analysis. In W. Damon (Series Ed.), *The handbook of child psychology,* 6th ed., vol. 2, D. Kuhn & R. Siegler (Eds.), *Cognition, perception and language.* New York: Wiley.

Moran, S., & Gardner, H. (2007, in preparation). Do we need a "central intelligence agency"? In L. Meltzer (Ed.), *Understanding executive function: Implications and opportunities for the classroom.* New York: Guilford Press.

Morgeson, F.P., Delaney-Klinger, K., Mayfield, M.S., Ferrara, P., & Campion, M.A. (2004). Self-presentation processes in job analysis: A field experiment investigating inflation in abilities, tasks, and competencies. *Journal of Applied Psychology, 89* (4), 674–686.

Moses, R. (2001). *Radical equations: Math literacy and civil rights.* Boston: Beacon Press.

Neill, D.M., & Medina, N.J. (1989). Standardized testing: Harmful to educational health. *Phi Delta Kappan, 70,* 688–697.

Neisser, U. (1983). Components of intelligence or steps in routine procedures? *Cognition, 15,* 189–197.

Newell, A., & Simon, K.A. (1972). *Human problem-solving.* Englewood Cliffs, NJ: Prentice-Hall.

Oakes, J. (1986a). Keeping track, part I: The policy and practice of curriculum inequality. *Phi Delta Kappan, 68,* 12–17.

Oakes, J. (1986b). Keeping track, part 2: Curriculum inequality and school reform. *Phi Delta Kappan, 68,* 148–154.

Ogbu, J. (1978). *Minority education and caste: The American system in cross-cultural perspective.* New York: Academic Press.

Olson, D. (1996). Towards a psychology of literacy: On the relations between speech and writing. *Cognition, 60* (1), 83–104.

Olson, L. (1988, Jan 27). Children flourish here: Eight teachers and a theory changed a school world. *Education Week, 7* (18), 1, 18–19.

Peirce, C.S. (1940). *Philosophical writings of Peirce* (J. Buchler, Ed.). London: Routledge and Kegan Paul.

Perkins, D.N. (1981). *The mind's best work.* Cambridge, MA: Harvard University Press.

Perkins, D.N., & Leondar, B. (Eds.). (1977). *The arts and cognition.* Baltimore: Johns Hopkins University Press.

Piaget, J. (1950). *The psychology of intelligence.* San Diego: Harcourt Brace Jovanovich.

Piaget, J. (1983). Piaget's theory. In P. Mussen (Ed.), *Handbook of child psychology,* vol. 1. New York: Wiley.

Pinker, S. (1997). *How the mind works.* New York: Norton.

Polanyi, M. (1958). *Personal knowledge.* Chicago: University of Chicago Press.

Posner, M.I. (2004). Neural systems and individual differences.*Teachers College Record, 106* (1), 24–30.

Powell, A.G., Farrar, E., & Cohen, D.K. (1985). *The shopping mall high school: Winners and losers in the educational marketplace.* Boston: Houghton Mifflin.

Prati, L.M., Douglas, C., Ferris, G.R., Ammeter, A.O., & Buckley, M.R. (2003). Emotional intelligence, leadership effectiveness, and team outcomes. *International Journal of Organizational Analysis, 11* (1), 21–41.

Prediger, D.J. (1999). Basic structure of work-relevant abilities. *Journal of Counseling Psychology, 46* (2), 173–184.

Ramos-Ford, V., Feldman, D.H., & Gardner, H. (1988). A new look at intelligence through Project Spectrum. *New Horizons for Learning, 8* (3), 6–7, 15.

Ravitch, D., & Finn, C. (1987). *What do our seventeen-year-olds know?* New York: Harper and Row.

Renninger, A.K. (1988). Do individual interests make a difference? In *Essays by the Spencer Fellows 1987–1988.* Cambridge, MA: National Academy of Education.

Renzulli, J.S. (1988). A decade of dialogue on the three-ring conception of giftedness. *Roeper Review, 11* (1), 18–25.

Resnick, L. (1987). The 1987 presidential address: Learning in school and out. *Educational Researcher, 16* (9), 13–20.

Resnick, L., & Neches, R. (1984). Factors affecting individual differences in learning ability. In R. Sternberg (Ed.), *Advances in the psychology of human intelligence,* vol. 2 (pp. 275–323). Hillsdale, NJ: Lawrence Erlbaum.

Rogoff, B. (1982). Integrating context and cognitive development. In M. Lamb & A. Brown (Eds.), *Advances in developmental psychology,* vol. 2. Hillsdale, NJ: Lawrence Erlbaum.

Ruth, B. (1948). *The Babe Ruth story as told to Bob Considine.* New York: American Books-Stratford Press.

Salomon, G. (1979). *Interaction of media, cognition, and learning.* San Francisco: Jossey-Bass.

Sarason, S. (1983). *Schooling in America: Scapegoat or salvation.* New York: Free Press.

Sattler, J.M. (1988). *Assessment of children,* 3rd ed. San Diego: Sattler.

Scarr, S. (1981). Testing for children. *American Psychologist, 36,* 1159–1166.

Schaler, J. (Ed.). (2006, in press). *Gardner under fire.* Chicago: Open Court.

Schon, D. (1984). *The reflective practitioner.* New York: Basic Books.

Scribner, S. (1986). Thinking in action: Some characteristics of practical thought. In R. Sternberg & R.K. Wagner (Eds.), *Practical intelligence: Nature and origins of competence in the everyday world.* New York: Cambridge University Press.

Seidel, S., & Walters, J. (1991). *Five dimensions of portfolio assessment.* Cambridge, MA: Harvard Graduate School of Education, Project Zero.

Seidel, S., Walters, J., Kirby, E., Olff, N. Powell, K., Scripp, L., & Veenema, S. (1997). *Portfolio practices: Thinking through assessment of children's work.* Washington, DC: National Education Association.

Selfe, L. (1977). *Nadia: A case of extraordinary drawing ability in an autistic child.* New York: Academic Press.

Senge, P.M. (1992). *The fifth discipline: The art and practice of the learning organization.* New York: Random House.

Shimizu, H. (1988). *Hito no tsunagari ["Interpersonal continuity"] as a Japanese children's cultural context for learning and achievement motivation: A literature review.* Cambridge, MA: Harvard Graduate School of Education, unpublished manuscript.

Sizer, T. (1984). *Horace's compromise.* Boston: Houghton Mifflin.

Smiley, J. (2004). *A year at the races: Reflections on horses, humans, love, money, and luck.* New York: Knopf.

Snow, C.E., & Ferguson, C.A. (1977). *Talking to children: Language input and acquisition.* Cambridge, England: Cambridge University Press.

Soldo, J. (1982). Jovial juvenilia: T.S. Eliot's first magazine: *Biography, 5,* 25–37.

Spearman, C. (1904). "General intelligence," objectively determined and measured. *American Journal of Psychology, 15* (2), 201–293.

Spencer, L.M., Jr., & Spencer, S.M. (1993). *Competence at work: Models for superior performance.* New York: John Wiley and Sons.

Squire, L. (1986). Mechanisms of memory. *Science, 232,* 1612–1619.

Sternberg, R. (1977). *Intelligence, information processing, and analogical reasoning.* Hillsdale, NJ: Lawrence Erlbaum.

Sternberg, R. (1985). *Beyond IQ.* New York: Cambridge University Press.

Sternberg, R. (1988a). A three-facet model of creativity. In R.J. Sternberg (Ed.), *The nature of creativity* (pp. 125–147). New York: Cambridge University Press.

Sternberg, R.J. (1988b). *The triarchic mind.* New York: Viking.

Sternberg, R.J. (1996). *Successful intelligence: How practical and creative intelligence determine success in life.* New York: Simon & Schuster.

Strauss, S. (1982). *U-shaped behavioral growth.* New York: Academic Press.

Thomson G. (1939). *The factorial analysis of human ability.* London: University of London Press.

Thurstone, L. (1938). *Primary mental abilities.* Chicago: University of Chicago Press.

Tooby, J., & Cosmides, L. (1990). On the universality of human nature and the uniqueness of the individual: The role of genetics and adaptation. *Journal of Personality, 58* (1), 17–67.

Uzgiris, I., & Hunt, J.M. (1966). *An instrument for assessing infant intellectual development.* Urbana: University of Illinois Press.

Vernon, P.E. (1971). *The structure of human abilities.* London: Methuen.

Vygotsky, L.S. (1978). *Mind in society: The development of higher psychological processes.* Cambridge, MA: Harvard University Press.

Wallach, M. (1971). *The intelligence/creativity distinction.* Morristown, NJ: General Learning Press.

Wallach, M. (1985). Creativity testing and giftedness. In F. Horowitz & M. O'Brien (Eds.), *The gifted and talented: Developmental perspectives.* Washington, DC: American Psychological Association.

Walters, J., & Gardner, H. (1986). The crystallizing experience: Discovering an intellectual gift. In R. Sternberg & J. Davidson (Eds.), *Conceptions of giftedness* (pp. 306–331). New York: Cambridge University Press.

Weber, E. (2005). *MI strategies in the classroom and beyond: Using roundtable learning.* Boston: Allyn & Bacon.

Weller, L.D. (1999). Application of the multiple intelligences theory in quality organizations. *Team Performance Management, 5* (4), 136–142.

White, M. (1987). *The Japanese educational challenge: A commitment to children.* New York: Free Press.

Wilson, K.S. (1988). The Palenque Design: Children's discovery learning experiences in an interactive multimedia environment. Doctoral dissertation, Harvard Graduate School of Education.

Winerip, M. (2005, April 20). Test reprieve keeps top teacher on job. *New York Times*, p. A23.

Winn, M. (1990, April 29). New views of human intelligence. *New York Times, The Good Health Magazine.*

Winner, E. (1982). *Invented worlds.* Cambridge, MA: Harvard University Press.

Winner, E. (Series Ed.). (1991–1993). *Arts PROPEL handbooks.* Cambridge, MA: Educational Testing Service and Project Zero.

Winner, E., Blank, P., Massey, C., & Gardner, H. (1983). Children's sensitivity to aesthetic properties of line drawings. In D.R. Rogers & J.A. Sloboda (Eds.), *The acquisition of symbolic skills.* London: Plenum Press.

Winner, E., & Hetland, L. (2000). The arts and academic achievement: Evaluating the evidence for a causal link. *Journal of Aesthetic Education, 34* (3–4), 3–10.

Winner, E., Rosenblatt, E., Windmueller, G., Davidson, L., & Gardner, H. (1986). Children's perceptions of "aesthetic" properties of the arts: Domain specific or pan artistic? *British Journal of Developmental Psychology, 4,* 149–160.

Wolf, D. (1988a). Opening up assessment. *Educational Leadership, 45* (4), 24–29.

Wolf, D. (1988b). Artistic learning: What and where is it? *Journal of Aesthetic Education, 22* (1), 144–155.

Wolf, D. (1989). Artistic learning as conversation. In D. Hargreaves (Ed.), *Children and the arts.* Philadelphia: Open University Press.

Wolf, D., Davidson, L., Davis, M., Walters, J., Hodges, M., & Scripp, L. (1988). Beyond A, B, and C: A broader and deeper view of literacy. In A. Pelligrini (Ed.), *Psychological bases of early education.* Chichester, England: Wiley.

Wolf, D., & Gardner, H. (1980). Beyond playing or polishing: The development of artistry. In J. Hausman (Ed.), *The arts and the schools.* New York: McGraw-Hill.

Wolf, D., & Gardner, H. (1981). On the structure of early symbolization. In R. Schiefelbusch & D. Bricker (Eds.), *Early language: Acquisition and intervention.* Baltimore: University Park Press.

Wolf, D., & Gardner, H. (Eds.). (1988). *The making of meanings.* Unpublished manuscript. Available as Harvard Project Zero Technical Report. Cambridge, MA: Harvard Graduate School of Education, Project Zero.

Woolf, V. (1976). *Moments of being.* Sussex, England: University Press.

Zessoules, R., Wolf, D.P., & Gardner, H. (1988). A better balance: Arts PROPEL as an alternative to discipline-based arts education. In J. Burton, A. Lederman, & P. London (Eds.), *Beyond DBAE: The case for multiple visions of art education* (pp. 117–129). Dartmouth, MA: University Council on Art Education.

Zigler, E., & Weiss, H. (1985). Family support systems: An ecological approach to child development. In R. Rapoport (Ed.), *Children, youth, and families* (pp. 166–205). Cambridge, England: Cambridge University Press.

Subject Index

NAMES INDEX